BONNEY'S GUIDE
to
JACKSON'S HOLE
&
GRAND TETON
NATIONAL PARK

Bonney's Guide
to
Jackson's Hole
&
Grand Teton
National Park

BY
LORRAINE G. BONNEY

HOMESTEAD PUBLISHING
Moose, Wyoming

Dedicated to Orrin H. Bonney
who started it all.

Library of Congress Catalog Card Number: 94-76321
ISBN 0-943972-32-9
Printed in the United States of America on acid free, recycled paper.

1 3 5 7 9 10 8 6 4 2

Published by
HOMESTEAD PUBLISHING
Box 193 • Moose, Wyoming 83012

Acknowledgments

The list is too long, but at least let me thank Carl Schreier for seeing the possibilities, his editorial crew who unconfused a lot of stuff with their plethora of commas—I think. To the dedicated gang at the Teton County Historical Center, especially Rita Varley, Teton County Clerk's accommodating Dottie Hodges, keeper (now retired) of old maps. And others that I've pestered for information or exploratory trips, like the always knowledgeable Bob Rudd, Kent Fiske, Donald and Gladys Kent, Beverly Wood, Eric Skove, Rene Shields, Copley Smoak, John Bruce Adams and Adrienne Brown. My devotion to the works of that unsurpassed geological-archaeological triangle, the Love family—Dr. Dave, Jane, and Professor Charlie—is only surpassed by the equanimity with which I use their works and words.

Let me note here that this second major go-round with Bonney's Guide has brought forcefully to my attention the stunning changes in the valley due to "progress." Since no one reads acknowledgments, I guess it's safe to tip the old hat to Cactus Ed, whose thoughtful advice was "Run those rivers, climb those mountains, encounter the griz, and piss on the developers' graves."

Lorraine Bonney
Kelly, Wyoming
spring 1995

Contents

ACKNOWLEDGMENTS 5
HOWDY, STRANGER 11
THE EARTH'S STORY 13
MAN IN JACKSON'S HOLE 17
VACATIONING IN JACKSON'S HOLE 20
    Weather and What To Wear 29
GENERAL INFORMATION 29
    Administration 29
    Services and Accommodations 31
    How to use this book 31
HOBACK (Southeast) ENTRANCE — TRIP 1 32
SOUTH PARK LOOP — TRIP 1a 45
SNAKE RIVER (Southwest) ENTRANCE — TRIP 2 53
TETON PASS (West) ENTRANCE — TRIP 3 61
SPRING GULCH ROAD — TRIP 3a 75
TOGWOTEE PASS (East) ENTRANCE — TRIP 4 80
    Spread Creek Road 89
TURPIN MEADOWS ROAD — TRIP 4a 94
YELLOWSTONE (North) HIGHWAY — TRIP 5 100
    Colter Bay 113
    Jackson Lake Lodge 119
GRASSY LAKE RECLAMATION ROAD — TRIP 5a ... 121
THE PARK LOOP - TRIP 6 (a,b,c,d, and e) 126
TETON PARK ROAD — TRIP 6a 126
    Signal Mountain Road 131
    Moran Turnout (Mts. Moran, Woodring, Thor, Bivouac) 133
JENNY LAKE ROAD — TRIP 6b 136
    Cathedral Group Turnout (Mt. Owen) 136
    String and Leigh Lakes 137
    Trails — String, Leigh and Holly Lakes 138
    Jenny Lake 141
    Peaks West of Jenny Lake (Teewinot, Storm Point, Ice Point,
        Symmetry Spire, Cube Point, Mt. St. John, Rockchuck) 142
    Jenny Lake Trail 145
    Hidden Falls and Cascade Canyon 146
    Lake Solitude 147

Teton Crest Trail 148
TETON PARK ROAD — TRIP 6c 149
Lupine Meadows, Glacier Trail 152
Glacier Gulch Turnout (Nez Perce, South Teton, Middle Teton, Grand Teton, Disappointment Peak) 155
Deaths on Grand Teton 159
Lakes Trail 165
Windy Point Turnout (Buck Mountain) 167
Moose Village and Park Headquarters 167
National Park Story 169
MOOSE JUNCTION NORTH TO MORAN JUNCTION — TRIP 6d 176
Deadman's Bar 179
Cunningham Cabin 181
MORAN JUNCTION WEST TO JACKSON LAKE LODGE JUNCTION — TRIP 6e 186
Teton Wilderness Area 187
MOOSE JUNCTION TO JACKSON — TRIP 7 193
National Elk Refuge — The Elk Story 197
VISITING JACKSON — TRIP 8 205
Early Jackson 209
Winter Sports 214
GRANITE CREEK ROAD — TRIP 9 217
WILSON-FALL CREEK ROAD — TRIP 10 219
MOOSE-WILSON ROAD — TRIP 11 222
FLAT CREEK ROAD — TRIP 12 227
Outlaws 230
The Countess's Place 237
ANTELOPE FLATS ROAD, MORMON ROW, AND KELLY ROAD — TRIP 13 240
Kelly Flood 250
GROS VENTRE ROAD — TRIP 14 255
Gros Ventre Slide 258
BIBLIOGRAPHY 271
PHOTOGRAPHIC CREDITS 273
INDEX 275

MAPS
1-JACKSON'S HOLE 10
2-COLTER BAY 114
3-JACKSON LAKE LODGE 117
4-STRING AND LEIGH LAKES TRAILS 139
5-JENNY LAKE TRAILS 147
6-JENNY LAKE AREA 152
7-TAGGART-BRADLEY 165

Bonney's Guide
to
Jackson's Hole
&
Grand Teton
National Park

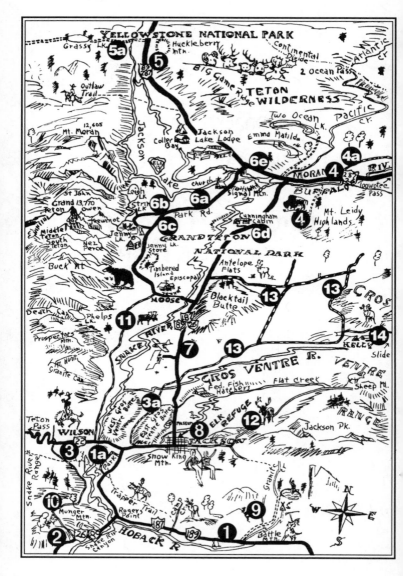

Howdy, Stranger

They call it Jackson's Hole...

Welcome to this isolated valley, rimmed high by some of the finest summits of the Rockies, echoing with the colorful history of the Old West. Since prehistoric days, the rugged scenery and the promise of wild game lured the generations into the valley, the first of which watched the last great ice sheet shrink back into the canyons, leaving its signature of mountain lakes before receding.

Its gripping past tells of small family bands of Early People that trekked over its passes, camped on its rivers and lake shores; of youthful aborigines questing for visions and inspirations in high-sited altars; of young men of the reckless fur-trade era who gambled lives for fortunes; of tireless scientists and geologists discovering the complexities of the valley; of sturdy homesteaders defying the valley's isolation, rocky floor, and bitter winters to make homes. Today's adventurers are little different, still finding themselves spellbound by the dramatic landscape of Jackson's Hole. They hunt its hills, fish its streams, study its treasures, and challenge its spires.

So, where is this paradise? Jackson's Hole stretches south from Yellowstone National Park 50 miles or more; the 12-mile-wide valley is basined by the Continental Divide and Gros Ventre Range on the east and the spectacular Tetons on the west. It has been called "Jackson's Hole" since fur trader Bill Sublette named it for his partner Davey Jackson, who, it is said, spent the winter of 1929 along the shore of Jackson Lake. A "hole" to the trappers was a mountain-encircled valley named for the trapper who most frequented it, like Ogden's Hole in Utah, Pierre's Hole in Idaho, and Brown's Hole in Colorado.

As generations wound down from its high entrances—Hoback Rim, and Togwotee, Union, and Teton passes—and through its pinebelted slopes to the sage-green valley floor, they were confronted with the same overpowering scene: jagged Teton peaks rising 5,000... 6,000... 7,000 feet up. And they recognized the mighty backdrop to this secluded valley for what it was, truly heroic country.

Those first visitors reveled in the Tetons' magnificence, naming the peaks as they saw fit. To the Indians, they were the "Hoary-Headed Fathers" or "Many Pinnacles;" to the first wandering white men, they became the "Pilot Knobs;" to government surveyor F.V. Hayden, they looked like shark's teeth. Nobody saw the craggy peaks as female breasts. As N. P. Langford—member of the first party to climb the Grand in 1872—put it diplomatically years later: "Tis distance that lends enchantment to... these mountains, for when nearly approached, those beautiful curvilinear forms that obtained for them this delicate appellation become harsh and rugged and angular." So what happened?

The name Pilot Knobs was still in use in 1824, when Alexander Ross of the Hudson's Bay Company and his earthy French Canadian crew passed and named three cratered buttes on the Idaho plains (near Craters of the Moon) the Trois Tetons because of their silhouetted likeness to female breasts. Said Ross: "I went to examine the Trois Tetons... three little hills...."

The next year, his compadre, trapper Peter Skene Ogden, directed by Ross, headed for the "region of the Upper Snake River," which describes very well the location of both the "three little hills" and the Pilot Knobs. Ogden saw the former and named them the "Trois Butes." Eight days later, he saw the more prominent "Trois Tettons," which he described as "very high." Thus the name, soon anglicized, became the Three Tetons, the South, Middle and Grand. They make far more acceptable breasts as seen from the west than they do from the east side. Today, we have the Teton Range topped by its highest summit, the Grand Teton, for which Grand Teton National Park is named.

For centuries, the bitter winters drove man and beast alike

from this valley. Then, in the late 19th century, a hardier genera-
tion came along, determined to homestead the land. They tried to
transform the boulder-strewn valley into ranch and agricultural
country but the fight was tough. When the chance came, many
sold out.

The marks made by those intrepid settlers on the land have
grown dimmer as the national park has taken over. Although sagebrush has replaced hayfields and log houses have disappeared
beneath wrecking bars, their cabin-spun stories, honed by
pokerfaced raconteurs, will survive—if we help. Like the Indian
and trapper, they are part of our American heritage, as is controversy that thrives here, for there are as many differing ideas as
there are men, and both rise and fall with the times.

Of the eight ancient trails leading into Jackson's Hole, five continue to be followed by today's highways; three can only be traveled trapper-style, on horseback. We will follow both highways and
trails, seeing the country through the eyes of different generations.
We hope their stories will entertain and inform you, and give a
deeper understanding of this fascinating valley.

Welcome to Jackson's Hole!

THE EARTH'S STORY

Poised like a great stone wave about to break over Jackson
Hole, the Tetons are the ultimate picture postcard of breathtaking
mountain scenery. With no foothills intervening, you can look
straight up to the 13,770-foot snowcapped summit of the Grand
Teton, a mile and a half above the valley floor.

Neither coy nor shy, the startling beauty of the range is flaunted
brazenly; they are "les Tetons." What isn't revealed, however, is the
demanding nature of the creature, the shifting moods, the deceiving charm that overcomes sensibilities, and always... the constant
challenge. Like all beauties, the range doesn't come cheap to those
who brave its rocky slopes and cliffs; climbing-related deaths in
the Tetons are second only to those recorded in Yosemite.

The Tetons and Jackson Hole share one of the most complete,
complex, and fascinating histories in North America. Of the four
great geologic eras—Precambrian, Paleozoic, Mesozoic, Cenozoic—
that contributed to the tempering and shaping of this dramatic

landscape, the oldest and longest, the Precambrian, lasted some 4.5 billion years. It took up seven-eighths of geologic time, 90 percent of the Earth's history. During that time, most of the action in the Jackson Hole area occurred some 10 to 20 miles below the Earth's surface, where Precambrian layers of gneiss and schist were being sheared and folded. Molten rock from the Earth's interior was forced along fractures in the older rocks, in multiple injections, to form pegmatite—pink and light gray granite, seen today as crosshatchings and taffy-like squiggles of granite and gneiss. The final Precambrian injections created the black diabase dikes obvious on the Middle Teton and Mt. Moran. When the Precambrian Era closed, any surface features had been eroded to a nearly featureless plain.

Eons passed; a 500-million-year interval of shallow seas swept intermittently across the future site of Jackson Hole, depositing miles-thick layers of sandstone, shale, and limestone. As the seas came and left, the climate slowly changed and the region stabilized into luxuriant Everglades-type jungles. Dinosaurs reigned. More seas returned. At the end of the Mesozoic Era, some 65 million years ago, the flat, monotonous landscape of floodplains and coastal swamps gave little hint of the coming storm—the Laramide Revolution, which ushered in the birth of the Rocky Mountains. The Laramide was one of the most exciting, earth-shaking chapters in the history of North America. It literally would tear the landscape apart.

In what later would be Jackson's Hole, the revolution began with restless quivers that arched into the broad, low, northwest-trending ancestral hump of the Teton-Gros Ventre mountains. Mountains rising to the northwest forced gushing rivers to push quartzite boulders into the Hole area, spreading an awesome 600 cubic miles of gold-bearing gravel—the Harebell Formation. This formation best tells the story of the last population explosion of reptiles, such as the horned *Triceratops*.

As the Mesozoic ended, future Wyoming mountain ranges began to stir; the ancestral Teton-Gros Ventre arch continued to grow. Seas drained. Dinosaurs faded.

The Cenozoic—the most recent and shortest of the big eras and the final half inch of the imaginary yardstick—opened with the Tertiary Period. This was a time of mammals, mountains, lakes, and volcanoes. The overthrust mountains rumbled in from the southwest, uprooted from their Idaho/Utah locations to slide, overlap and pile into southwestern Wyoming. They buried younger rock, and "collided" with mountains still firmly rooted in their Precambrian cores—the ancestral Tetons at Teton Pass and the ancestral Gros Ventres at Cache Creek, near the town of Jackson. The Gros Ventres and Wyoming's easterly mountains heaved into existence, and continued to build up as the random geometries of the Laramide Revolution climaxed in the violent birth of the Rocky Mountain chain. In the Teton area, the Buck Mountain reverse fault boosted up the deeply buried Teton Precambrian core 2,000 feet before stopping. But the Tetons as we know them still lurked below the surface.

The cataclysmic age of mountain building settled down about 50 million years ago, and was followed by intense volcanic activity from the Yellowstone-Absaroka area, which layered Wyoming with untold quantities of lava, rocks and flying ash. These materials filled basins and buried mountains, creating a dull land of hills. Some 99 percent of the Earth's history had passed... and still there were no Tetons. The Precambrian rock still was buried deep.

Then, during the last 10 million years—an eye blink in geologic time—a series of jerks and violent earthquakes shook the Teton area. The land stretched and ruptured, and a 50-mile-long crack split the Earth. West of the big split, a north-south trending normal fault, the Teton block lurched higher, exposing its jagged eastern flank—the emerging Teton Range. East of the fault, the valley sank deeply into the ground to create Jackson Hole. As the range tipped up in sporadic jolts, it exposed the ancient crystalline rocks. It also carried the stratified sediments of half a billion years on its back. But the elements fiercely attacked and eroded those sediments, removing all the history from the highest peaks.

Meanwhile, the valley floor was sinking dramatically as magma far below the Earth's surface was pulled north to replenish the erupting volcanoes in the Yellowstone-Absaroka area. This same material later would return to Jackson Hole in a fiery cloud to bury the north end of the Tetons. The sinking valley floor broke into blocks and, like "ice cubes in a bucket of water," some of them poked up as the buttes we see today.

The first freshwater lake—shallow, 40-mile-long Teewinot

Lake—filled the valley. When the lake vanished, it left 5,000 feet of limestone that resemble snowbanks in summer. Mammals proliferated; earthquakes, valley faulting and more lakes came and went. As geologic time crept on, extensive river systems built up and stream erosion stripped 15,000 feet of sediment and Precambrian rock from the still-rising mountain block. The streams cut V-shaped canyons, whittled down the raw Teton block, and filled the Hole with debris, which great rivers carried away.

At this juncture, the Tetons were still blocks of stone. Then, about 2 million years ago, the climate cooled dramatically and ushered in the Ice Age. Tremendous rivers of ice 3,000 feet thick began to flow out of the Absaroka, Wind River, and Teton mountain ranges. These awesome rivers of ice filled the valley, bulldozing and scraping away humongous quantities of rock and gouging out even larger canyons. The Ice Age had started the tremendous job of sculpting the Teton blocks of stone into spires; its scratches still can be seen above the modern Teton timberline.

Rock that resisted erosion by nature's earth-moving ice machines formed the peaks that we see today. When the ice-river melted, it left a barren valley of boulders. As the Ice Age weakened, the climate fluctuated, causing glaciers to advance and retreat repeatedly through the continuously rising mountains. The last three episodes, however, had the greatest impact on the Tetons, as we see them today. Like sculptors chipping and chiseling away at a block of marble, each glacial episode carved and refined the towering crags in its own distinguishing way, and each advanced a shorter distance down the slope than its predecessors.

The effects of the last major glacial event, the Pinedale, are most evident today. Its glaciers retreated up the major canyons, its ice cut the final cirques and sharpened peaks and aretes. The Pinedale glaciers also spilled onto the valley floor where they melted and formed moraines around the canyon mouths and left glittering piedmont lakes.

To complete this idyllic mosaic of snow, rock and ice, meadows and sagebrush quickly covered the barren, rocky land, and forests of lodgepole pine invaded the lower elevations, softening the scoured landscape.

The forces of nature, striving for perfection by shaping and honing the land constantly, thus created the ultimate—a cameo in a matchless setting, a cluster of peaks dominated by one matchless work of art—the Grand Teton!

The masterpiece was ready for visitors.

A GUIDE TO COMMON TETON ROCKS

Layered Gneisses: Oldest Precambrian rock in the Tetons composed chiefly of quartz, feldspar, biotite (black mica), and hornblende (often in rodlike crystals). Different proportions of these minerals account for the banded look. Layers of mainly quartz and feldspar are light gray or white; darker gray layers contain more biotite and hornblende; e.g. lower Death Canyon and Paintbrush trails. "Bright-eyed" gneiss has a magnetite spot; the white halo lacks biotite; e.g. lower Death Canyon trail; south and north Teton Range.

Schist: Found in gneisses, it is a flaky rock with much mica. The somber gray/brown gneisses and schists often have contrasting light/white granite dike intrusions; e.g.similar to gneiss.

Granite: This crystalline igneous rock, younger than gneiss and fine-grained, is composed principally of gray quartz and white feldspar. This gives it a white or light gray look; e.g. the Grand Teton.

Pegmatite: Very coarse-grained igneous rock, usually occurring in veins; like granite in mineral composition; e.g. Death Canyon.

Man in Jackson's Hole

From the Gros Ventre Range, the eyes of Paleolithic man must have watched as the Pinedale glaciers shrank back into the Teton Range and the ice retreated into shadowed crevices, where they dwindled and died.

With the ice gone, these high-country people—from about 9,000 years ago to 1,600 A.D.—spent summers camped in the huge meadows at the north end of the then-natural Jackson Lake. For 6,000 years, they used, just short of actual cultivation, the Hole's plant ecosystem. The Early People revisited base camps, exploiting the valley's seasonal resources by fishing, gathering plants, and hunting—the only way of life ever completely in tune with the ecosystem of Jackson's Hole.

By 1803, when France had sold the region between the Rocky Mountains and the Appalachians to the United States, Lewis and Clark were setting out to explore the vast Indian territory. They never reached Jackson's Hole but there is evidence that one of their party—John Colter—snowshoed through during his famous solo 500-mile trek in 1807-08. His partly undetermined route took him through the Cody area and on into Yellowstone National Park and Montana. His route through Jackson Hole remains a puzzle and the subject of much debate. But because of his information about the area, fur brigades began heading west.

When Easterner John Jacob Astor started his Pacific Fur Co. in 1810, he kicked off the fur-trapping era with his ambitious plan to establish a chain of posts from the Great Lakes to the Columbia. He intended to beat out the British companies for the lucrative trade. Astor sent two expeditions to the West Coast—one by boat around Cape Horn and the other by land, under Wilson Price Hunt, via Jackson's Hole. The latter Astorian party opened the way for that picturesque fellow, the independent trapper, who worked the streams in this virgin area until the whims of fashion crushed the life from the fur trade some 20 years later.

Jackson's Hole became the favorite trapping grounds of the enigmatic loner, David Edward "Davey" Jackson, who, with part-ners Jedediah Smith and Bill Sublette, made a fortune from the fur trade. While Sublette supplied goods from St. Louis, Jackson, the field man, directed the trapping operations. Jackson's fears that another pregnancy would kill his wife kept him in the wilderness, where he became "a rather noted beaver trapper." Jackson disap-peared from history's pages when he died from typhoid fever on Christmas Eve, 1837.

When fashion dictated silk rather than beaver hats, the fur trade dwindled, and mountain men like Jim Bridger had to find other callings. They applied their immense knowledge of the coun-try to guiding government expeditions. Several of these expedi-tions made their way through Jackson's Hole for two decades, be-ginning in 1860. They mapped the area and unblushingly named peaks after themselves; they made the world aware of the Teton and Yellowstone areas. The earlier tall tales of the mountain men had been scarcely believed, but maps and pictures now presented a different story.

The Hayden Surveys represent one of the greatest mass stud-ies accomplished in the West. Dr. Ferdinand V. Hayden first led his U.S. Geological and Geographic Survey of the Territories into the valley in 1872. Hayden, a former physician and teacher-turned-geologist, who packtrained across the West in his weather-frayed frock coat, had a restless curiosity for which the Indians called him "Man Who Picks Up Stones Running." His revolutionary ideas included hiring experts to help. For instance, he hired an Omaha photographer, William H. Jackson, to record the look of the land as they passed through. With wet negatives made on the spot by floating chemicals onto glass, Jackson deftly made the first photographs of the Tetons, hard to duplicate with today's equipment.

The early exploration of Jackson's Hole cannot be passed by without mention of Lt. Gustavus C. Doane, whose name will appear throughout this book. Because of a long-frustrated ambition to explore the Arctic, Doane pulled some strings and received military orders to organize a small expedition to winter explore the Snake River by boat, beginning with its headwaters in the Yellowstone area and ending at the mouth of the Columbia River. The party's battle to survive the winter of 1876 will make for an exciting story when we cross their route.

As early as 1863, prospectors had invaded the area, seeking the mother lode of the microscopic gold that they found in the valley's streams. If they had struck pay dirt, the Jackson's Hole story and scenery would be very different. While the miners were not seeking solitude, horse thieves found its isolation handy. And wealthy hunters discovered that the valley was an ideal game paradise. As hunters, miners and rustlers began frequenting the valley, some stayed, built cabins, and settled as early as 1884.

More permanent settlement came with the Mormons who struggled their wagons over the passes into the Hole, homesteaded, and helped establish the first towns. The last great change would be the coming of Grand Teton National Park, but we'll let the guide book tell that story.

Come along with us now and hear the stories of the valley known as Jackson's Hole, stories sometimes lovable, humorous, ambitious and savage.

Modern usage has dropped the "'s" from Jackson's Hole but we will retain the older name because of its century-long association with the region by trappers, homesteaders, and its first white residents.

Vacationing in Jackson's Hole

Boating

Cruises across Jenny or Jackson lake will whisk you with re-freshing coolness over sparkling water to the base of the mountains, where you can hike through the range's thick forests and explore its waterfalls, deep canyons, and ancient rocks.

Canoeing and kayaking offer exciting ways to explore the smaller lakes. Hand-propelled craft are allowed on Jenny, Jackson, Phelps, Emma Matilda, Two Ocean, Taggart, Bradley, Bearpaw, Leigh and String lakes. Motor boats are limited to Jenny Lake (maximum of 7.5 horsepower), Phelps and Jackson lakes; sailboating, water skiing, windsurfing, and jet skiing are allowed on Jackson Lake only.

Boat permits are available from the park visitor centers for a fee. You can rent boats and canoes at Jenny Lake and Moose, and at the Jackson Lake marinas at Leeks, Colter Bay and Signal Mountain Lodge.

A float trip down the Snake River to Moose offers an ideal way to see animals—the earlier in the day, the better—and the colorful Teton panorama reflected in the changing pace of rapid waters. Commercial companies operate half-day, full-day, and multi-day river and lake floats.

Photography

To the park visitor, the snow-dusted towers of the Tetons are photogenic lures. Turnouts along the roads provide for picture-taking vistas, as well as plaques that identify the visible peaks. For the more active photographer, trails will open unlimited vistas.

For ideas about where to go and how to frame your own pictures, attend the evening lectures by park naturalists; their excellent pictures, taken with time and study, will get you going in the right direction. Jackson has several photo shops that sell camera supplies, make small repairs, and process film. Equipment and film are sold at park stores and lodges as well.

Anyone wielding a camera should be aware that the clear mountain atmosphere makes peaks seem deceivingly close. The road nearest the Grand actually lies four miles away horizontally and an unbelievable mile and a third below the summit. Overexposure is the most common error in Teton photos, so take the necessary steps and treat the peaks as bright subjects to get the proper light value.

On the other hand, underexposure is the most common error when shooting wildlife, especially at dawn and dusk (See *Wildlife* section for more details). Forest light is less intense than it appears to the eye. Animals, which are mostly dark, usually are seen in shade, motionless for the moment, naturally camouflaged, and difficult to detail. For best results, allow more light than indicated by your photometer. The new, faster color films and a telephoto lens will pay off when hunting wildlife with your camera.

Remember, these animals are wild. Photographing animals from inside a parked car disturbs them least and, in the case of the larger mammals, is safer.

If you are more interested in photographing wildflowers, carry a portrait lens for close-ups and a wide-angle lens for those gorgeous fields of wildflowers.

Fishing

Despite the millions of visitors it gets each year, Jackson's Hole still offers good fishing in its lakes and streams. The Snake River drainage remains one of the few areas in the West that boasts a native cutthroat trout population capable of maintaining itself through natural reproduction. Whitefish, brown, and mackinaw, or lake trout, also challenge anglers.

Until the spring runoff clears, about July 1, lakes offer better fishing opportunities than streams. Be advised, however, against wearing waders near or in swift water. Beaver-pond fishing usually is good.

The best plan is to follow the locals, starting at high-altitude lakes, then moving on to the smaller tributaries, and saving the rivers for July. By August, expect excellent fishing along Flat Creek inside the National Elk Refuge, in the Gros Ventre, Hoback and Buffalo Fork rivers, and in the side channels of the Snake River. The main channel of the Snake often stays high until mid-August, when fishing improves.

And you can't go wrong using the favorite tackle of the old-timers. For trout fishing, try brown or gray hackles, black gnats, royal coachman, or black ant; for lake fishing, try trolling in the evening with a spinner; and for fishing with hooks try a No. 8 or 10, and a 10-pound line.

Fishing regulations vary from year to year and from location to location, so check with the Wyoming Game and Fish Department office in Jackson or a fishing shop before casting. A Wyoming fishing license is required for fishing inside and outside of the park. Jackson Lake generally is open for fishing year-round, except during the spawning season in October. While Jenny, Leigh, Phelps and Two Ocean lakes are open to fishing year-round, the Snake can only be fished April 1 through October.

Fishing information, equipment and maps are available at tackle stores in Jackson, Moose, and Colter Bay; boats are available for rent at Jackson Lake, Colter Bay, Jenny Lake, and Signal Mountain Lodge. Fishing guides are for hire in the Jackson area and in the park at Moose, Signal Mountain Lodge, Colter Bay, Moran and Jackson Lake Lodge. Check the telephone book for current listings.

Guest ranches throughout the park have horsepack guides on staff to take you into the backcountry to explore the less-fished streams and lakes.

Hunting

Big-game hunting in Jackson's Hole has attracted visitors since prehistoric days, when early nomads came through the valley to hunt migrating pronghorn antelope, bison, and bighorns. According to the early journals of white men, European noblemen, trappers, and prospectors reported successful hunts during the 1800s. But what they hunted then differs from what today's hunters stalk. For instance, elk and moose are relative newcomers, and have replaced the once massive herds of pronghorn antelope.

Each fall, some 80 outfitters set up camps throughout the Bridger-Teton National Forest, and provide meals, shelter, guides, and pack and saddle horses for hunters. These services are extremely popular, so hunters should make early arrangements if they would like to hire an outfitter.

General big-game licenses apply to elk, deer and bear, but moose and sheep are hunted by special permit through drawings conducted by the Wyoming Game and Fish Department (WG&F). Non-residents can hunt only with a licensed resident or guide in wilderness areas. The list of annual hunting dates and areas usually is available by May 15. For a list of Teton County outfitters or information about hunting in the park, on the National Elk Refuge, or within the national forest, write to the Wyoming Game & Fish Department in Cheyenne, or WG&F District Office, P.O. Box 67, Jackson, WY 83001.

Hiking

If you like to hike, the 245 miles of trails will give you ample means to explore the Teton high country, its mountain lakes and valley ridges. Here, you will find four climatic zones—transition, Canadian, Hudsonian, and Arctic alpine—and the accompanying vegetation, from alpine to grasses, compressed accordion-like into a mile of elevation. Usually, you would have to travel the equivalent of 2,000 to 3,000 miles to see the same changes in landscape, from deciduous and coniferous forests to Arctic tundra. In Jackson's Hole, you get firsthand knowledge of the geology, animal and vegetation changes while following the "Bloom Belt" up the mountain sides. Long after favorite flowers have faded on the valley floor, their dwarf cousins are blooming in the high cirques.

The best way to get acquainted with the hiking options in Jackson's Hole is to begin with a naturalist-guided party, or try any of the do-it-yourselfers in the Jenny Lake area, such as the Bradley-Taggart lakes trail. The Bridger-Teton National Forest maintains easy trails into the less-known, more-isolated Gros Ventre and Teton wilderness areas, the Wyoming and Snake River ranges, and the Mount Leidy Highlands. Whichever trails you choose—the well-marked park trails or the lightly signed forest trails—will take you into another world of icy streams and lakes, and of wildlife, geology, solitude and scenery.

Mountain Biking

For great views, good exercise and a chance to get close to nature, try some fat-tire touring on the valley's backcountry roads and trails. By hitting the dirt tracks, you can explore Grand Teton National Park and the nearby Bridger-Teton National Forest more intimately. Teton Park Road (Trips 6a & 6c) and Jenny Lake Road (Trip 6b) have wide shoulders and superb views of the Tetons. In the Jackson area, beginners can start out with easy rides on Cache

The Three Tetons (top)—the Grand, Middle and South Tetons—named from the West. The foreground is Table Mountain, photographed by W.H. Jackson in 1872.

Boating (above) on Jenny Lake.

Gneiss (above, right)—taffy-like squiggles of pegmatite, muscavite and quartz.

Climbing School with Glenn Exum (right).

Golden-mantled ground squirrel (below).

Creek (Trip 12, Mile 0.6), the National Elk Refuge road (Trip 12, Mile 1.0), the South Park Loop (Trip 1a), the Antelope Flats-Kelly loop (Trip 13), and the 16-mile RKO Road in the park (Trip 6a, Mile 4.3), which is a jeep trail with several short, steep climbs, if taken from north to south. Moderate favorites include the Cache Creek-Game Creek circle (Trip 12, Mile 1.0) up to the saddle east of Snow King Mountain and down to U.S. 89-191 and Jackson, the Old Pass Road (see Trip 3, Mile 12.1), and the ride down Leeks Canyon after taking the ski lift to the top of Snow King Mountain. Advanced toughies include Black Canyon (Trip 3, Mile 12.0), and Phillips Ridge and Canyon (Trip 3, Mile 13.6). Several bike-touring companies and a local club offer guided rides, a good way for beginners to start.

Horseback Riding and Pack Trips

Sure-footed mountain horses can also help you explore the backcountry. All riders, no matter their proficiency, will find a riding animal of choice at Jackson Lake Lodge, Colter Bay, or the dude ranches, where horses, guides, sleeping equipment and food are provided for pack trips into the wildernesses for unforgettable hunting, fishing or scenery gazing.

Snowmobiling

A new adventure has been added to the park's winter attractions—the Continental Divide Snowmobile Trail. Grand Teton Park's link in this enterprising effort allows snowmobilers to buzz between Atlantic City (South Pass) and Mammoth Hot Springs in north Yellowstone via Jackson Hole.

The trail utilizes U.S. 287 through Jackson Hole, as follows: Dubois to Moran over Togwotee Pass (Trip 4); Moran to Jackson Lake Junction (Trip 6e), and the Yellowstone Highway from Jackson Lake Junction to Yellowstone South Entrance (Trip 5).

Other major and connecting snowmobile trails in Jackson Hole are Teton Park Road (Trip 6a, including Signal Mountain Road, and part of 6c); Jenny Lake Road (Trip 6b), and Grassy Lake Road—Flagg Ranch to Ashton, Trip 5a.

A park entry fee and the usual fee for a snowmobile sticker are some of the costs. The Continental Divide Trail opened in the winter of 1994-95 on an experimental basis to iron out the rough spots, and fees were waived for those traveling on the new territory. Where snowmobilers must share the roadway with vehicles, flashing lights will warn all motorists of the mixed traffic. Also, trail use will be carefully monitored because of environmental, wildlife and safety concerns.

Highway Exploring

To enjoy Jackson Hole to its fullest, drive its roads in a leisurely manner, nose into its delightful nooks and crannies, absorb its history, and thrill yourself with its beauty.

With over 300 miles of roads awaiting you, the first choice should be the vital Park Loop, 45 miles of road that reveal the heart of Grand Teton National Park. The Loop is comprised of the Park Road, Jenny Lake Road, and the Jackson Hole Highway (U.S. 26-89-191).

All told, the five entrance roads provide 150 miles of scenery-filled, history-steeped, and geology-packed touring. But there also are 143 miles of winding backcountry roads with surprises around every curve.

Wildlife

For a close look at wildlife in its natural habitat, use your car, boat or feet to explore the Snake River oxbow and the willow bottoms east of Jackson Lake (See *Photography* section for details). While driving along the highway, car jams usually alert you to moose, deer, buffalo, coyotes, pronghorn antelope, bear, and elk; enjoy, but don't block the road. Timbered Island, near Jenny Lake, has a small permanent herd and plenty of elk bugling in the fall. The animals must not, however, be harassed. Saucy small animals, such as chattering chipmunks and ground squirrels, butterball marmots, and whistling conies (pikas), will tease you along the trails. But remember that park regulations prohibit feeding these critters; whatever you might offer them is not their natural food.

Birds are an all-summer attraction because of the valley's fascinating and varied resident bird population, ranging from tiny hummingbirds to trumpeter swans. Heading the waterfowl list for interesting sightings are the trumpeters, pelicans and herons. Common birds-of-prey sightings are bald eagles, osprey and hawks, but it is possible to see the rare peregrine or prairie falcons as well.

In any case, pick up a prestamped *Birds of Jackson Hole Checklist*—with its list of more than 300 species—at park visitor centers, Forest Service and National Elk Refuge headquarters, or the Wyoming Game and Fish office, to report any unusual sightings by marking the checklist and dropping it into a mailbox. Good records are important because birds also serve as indicators of biodiversity. When the bird population diminishes, something is drastically wrong.

Extravagant flower displays bless June and July with fields of scarlet gilia, blue lupine, and balsamroot. August produces vivid displays of fireweed, wild hollyhock, and Indian paintbrush. By August and September, tiny clusters of alpine flowers in rock-garden landscapes greet the highcountry hiker.

Mountain Climbing

The intricately folded and faulted rocks of the Tetons, eroded into spectacular spires, are a challenge to climbers the world over. The Grand Teton alone attracts thousands who long to write their names in the summit register.

So, how do you begin climbing? Many enroll in a mountaineering school. If you choose this route, you can expect to begin learning the mysteries of climbing techniques, language, ropes, knots, and rappelling, as well as a rudimentary knowledge of mountain hardware, like carabiners, by the second day. Soon, you will be spidering your way up the rough walls of practice rocks. And you'll never forget the finale of your lesson—a dramatic 20-foot rappel (descent by rope) down an overhanging cliff. The two-day lesson is a must in order to climb the Grand with the schools.

From the climbing lesson, you can graduate with the help of the mountaineering schools to the two-day ascent of the Grand. Unless you are very fit and experienced, the Grand, Owen and Moran usually require two days. You can climb other minor Teton peaks in one long day. A number of climbs are suited to knowledgeable beginners—meaning they have no *technical* difficulties but do require route finding skills—or for acclimatizing. These climbs include Storm Point, Rockchuck, Woodring, and Disappointment. Currently, a non-fee (this may change) backcountry permit is required for overnight trips in the park.

The number of climbing accidents has increased in recent

years, and the highly trained park rescue team, organized in 1952, stands by for any emergency. But care and planning should be the watchwords for Teton climbers. Only experienced mountaineers equipped with ice axes and other appropriate tools, including good boots, should cross steep snow slopes.

Another factor to consider when climbing in the Tetons is the weather. Be prepared for sudden changes; climbers cannot see storms blowing in from the west. As snow and weather conditions vary considerably from day to day, information about summer conditions is available at the Jenny Lake Ranger Station and park headquarters (739-3300). Avalanche-hazard forecasts are available during winter months from park headquarters (739-3300), and the U.S. Forest Service (733-2664). With the potential for storms catching climbers and hikers by surprise, carry extra layers of clothing to prevent hypothermia, the prime cause of human fatality in mountain country. And remember, solo climbing is done at your own risk.

Both Exum Mountain Guides & School of American Mountaineering and Jackson Hole Mountain Guides & Climbing School offer guides, daily climbing schools, and climbs into the Tetons and other ranges. (See the Yellow Pages under Mountain Climbing Instruction) If you want to bunk near the major trailhead, the Climbers' Ranch, south of Jenny Lake, is operated by the American Alpine Club and has dormitories, a cooking area and showers. For information about these accommodations, call 733-7271, from June 15 through Sept. 10.

For **climbing registration**, check with the Jenny Lake Ranger Station concerning current requirements. Through 1994, regulations required check-in/check-out for all climbs, and for off-trail travel above 7,000 feet. Since 1994, however, the NPS has replaced registration for day climbs with a "voluntary-registration" system. The key message is: "Let a responsible person know exactly where you are going and when you expect to return." If you have no one with whom to leave that information, the voluntary-registration system is available at the Jenny Lake Ranger Station during the summer season. Again, backcountry permits are required for overnight trips.

WEATHER AND WHAT TO WEAR

Weather

The Tetons probably have more favorable weather than any other mountain vacation area in the West. Because the range is isolated like an atmospheric island, most storms split and swing north or south of the range. The weather can and does change quickly, however, and sudden afternoon thunder showers, hail, or snow can hit at any time of the year. Also, mosquitoes can be bad in June.

Clothing

In this high mountain country, layering for warmth and comfort works best when incorporating a base layer, an insulating layer, and an outer layer of rainwear. The cotton shorts and T-shirt you wear on a sunny morning can prove insufficient when you reach 10,000 feet or when a surprise afternoon thunder shower drops the temperature dramatically. Then your trousers, sweater (not cotton), and wind jacket will be worth their weight. Breathable cotton works fine on hot sunny days, but wool pile and synthetics that wick away the moisture from your body are a better bet. Combine that with a set of 100-percent waterproof rain gear and you're set.

The key is to dress functionally for whatever activity you are planning, be it hiking, climbing, or horseback riding. Because most trails are rocky, lightweight cleated boots are good for short trips, while heavier boots are better for longer hauls. If you plan to climb, rock shoes—which you can rent in Jackson and at Moose—are recommended.

GENERAL INFORMATION

Administration

When visiting any community, it helps to understand which political bodies govern what in the area. Jackson's Hole lies entirely within Teton County. Of the 1,838,720 acres, just 4 percent, or about 75,000 acres, are privately owned. State and local governments own about 7,000 acres, or 0.3 percent, while the federal government holds about 94.5 percent, or 1,738,382 acres. Of the lands under federal control, the U.S. Forest Service administers 1,367,649 acres, the National Park Service 309,994 acres, the Bureau of Reclamation 26,255 acres, the U.S. Fish & Wildlife Service 24,700 acres, and the Bureau of Land Management 9,784 acres (all figures are approximate).

The part of the Bridger-Teton National Forest that is in Teton County lies mostly east of Grand Teton National Park and north to the Yellowstone boundary. The Bridger-Teton, the largest national forest in the lower 48 states, forms the arm and leg of a magnificent body of wilderness in northwestern Wyoming, known as the Greater Yellowstone Ecosystem. The forest supervisor, with an office at 340 N. Cache in Jackson, manages forest uses—grazing, timber cutting, mining, wildlife and recreation—to derive the greatest possible economic and some social benefits of the land. For specific information about forest land in Jackson's Hole, contact the Jackson and Blackrock ranger districts.

While Grand Teton National Park does not administer the lion's share of the public lands, its superintendent deals with a growing number of visitors each season. The park's protective force includes rangers, who operate entrance stations, patrol roads, campgrounds and trailer areas, enforce mountaineering, boating, backcountry, and other regulations, answer questions, and guide and direct visitors. In addition, the educational force of park naturalists operate visitor centers, conduct nature walks and campfire programs about Park Service management of wildlife, habitat, and geology of the area.

Although the U.S. Bureau of Reclamation controls the dam and water levels at Jackson Lake, the park administers the lake's recreational aspects. The U.S. Fish & Wildlife Service operates two facilities in Jackson's Hole: At the National Fish Hatchery, 3.8 miles north of Jackson, the USFWS specializes in production of native cutthroat and lake trout for stocking Idaho and Wyoming waters; and on the National Elk Refuge northeast of Jackson, the federal government winter feeds the Jackson Hole elk herd after it migrates down from high summer ranges. Each of the wildlife facilities offers tours during the appropriate seasons.

The Wyoming Game & Fish Department, which has a district office at 360 N. Cache in Jackson, establishes big-game hunting seasons (see *Hunting* section), sells hunting and fishing licenses, controls and manages game and fish outside park boundaries, and cooperates with the park hunt.

Services and Accommodations

For all services—including religious, medical, emergency, accommodations (motels, lodges, guest ranches), transportation and car-rental information, contact the Jackson Hole Area Chamber of Commerce, P.O. Box E, Jackson WY 83001; (307) 733-3316. The Chamber remains open summer evenings to help visitors find rooms.

For services and information about Grand Teton National Park, contact the superintendent at Moose, WY 83012; (307) 739-3300.

Write to Grand Teton Lodge Co., P.O. Box 240, Moran, WY 83013 concerning reservations and accommodations within the park. This company operates cabins at Colter Bay and Jenny Lake Lodge and cottages at Jackson Lake Lodge.

For all information and maps related to the Bridger-Teton National Forest, contact the supervisor at P.O. Box 1888, 340 N. Cache, Jackson WY 83001; (307) 739-5500.

Write to Wyoming Tourism, I-25 at College Ave. , Cheyenne, WY 82002, or call 307-777-7777 for its directory of Wyoming motels, hotels, dude ranches, campsites and resorts.

How to Use this Book:

At each stop, two figures—the interval and accumulative mileages—are given. The first figure, interval mileage, gives the distance between two stops—the indicated stop and the previous stop. The second figure, accumulative mileage, indicates the total distance since the beginning of that trip.

Trip 1
HOBACK (SOUTHEAST) ENTRANCE
Via Rock Springs and Hoback Canyon to Jackson
(49 miles)

In 1811, the first white men warily inched their pack train over the dangerously exposed Indian trail that overhung the rushing river 200 feet below. Since then, Hoback Canyon has been a major entrance into Jackson's Hole. The first to come down the Hoback, however, were the migrating animals. For centuries, in the spring and fall, antelope by the thousands, buffalo and deer, poured down the Hoback, one of their main routes, between summer range in Jackson Hole and snow-free winter grasslands farther south. Some of the deeply beaten trails survive to this day. Prehistoric tribesmen and Indians followed these same paths; then the trappers.

As one of the oldest trapper trails in the West, it took 111 years before a usable road replaced the precarious trail and opened up this scenic and colorful canyon to safer travel. Ever since the road was built in 1922, however, the Hoback Canyon highway's maintenance has been a nightmare.

After Andrew Henry abandoned his fort west of the Tetons in 1811, three of his men decided to head back East. On their way, John Hoback, Jacob Reznor and Edward Robinson tried beaver trapping in Jackson's Hole. Then the frozen, starving trio continued eastward until they met up with Wilson Price Hunt's westbound Astorian party. They agreed to guide Hunt's group to

Oregon. And so, this motley caravan of five fur-trapping partners, several Kentucky hunters with their long rifles, and 40 French rivermen, earthbound and afoot, wrangled 112 packhorses down through the Hoback Canyon on Sept. 24, losing one horse at the ledges when it fell 200 feet. Two days later, while camped on the banks of the Snake River, Hunt named the river they had just descended for Hoback. Three years later, this same trio—Hoback, Reznor and Robinson—and others were massacred by Indians on Idaho's Boise River.

Adversity never seemed to deter the fur trappers. Jackson's Hole was beaver rich and, until 1843, Hoback Canyon remained the principal route for the likes of Jim Bridger, Bill Sublette and Davey Jackson. During that period, the heaviest traffic the canyon witnessed was during the climactic year of 1832, when most of the trade goods destined for the Rendezvous at Pierre's Hole (Teton Basin, Idaho) were brought this way. Because of intense rivalry, the location of the Rendezvous was always a matter of secrecy. That year, however, Bridger's rivals bird-dogged him to learn the way.

From **Rock Springs** (el. 6,271), it is 180 miles north via Pinedale and U.S. 191 to Jackson; you will cross the old Oregon Trail at Farson. The mileage for this trip begins at Hoback Rim, 19 miles west of Daniel Junction and 50 miles from Jackson Town.

0.0 0.0   **Hoback Rim** (el. 7,921) signals the topographic divide between the Colorado-Green River drainage basin and the basin formed by the Hoback, Snake, and Columbia rivers. From the Rim, you won't need a "Vista Point Ahead" sign to know you're looking at something special. Imagine how John Hoback must have felt as he shouted with delight and recognition at his first sight of the river—later named for him—knowing he was seeing the headwaters of the Columbia River.

From this point the scenery becomes increasingly exciting as the panorama of the **Wyoming Range** unfolds. Lying within the Bridger-Teton National Forest, the range stretches 55 miles south to culminate at Wyoming Peak (el. 11,378), hidden behind the range's northern mountains—(N-S) Ramshorn, Clause, Hoback, and Deadman peaks.

9.5 9.5   **Hoback River Crossing** marks the first of numerous river crossings. The early trappers called Hoback Basin Jackson's

Little Hole. A running branding iron, a traditional tool of the horsethief trade, was found near here, and now can been seen in the Jackson Hole Museum. Most access to the river is barred by private property.

0.1 9.6   Turnoff (S) for **Upper Hoback Road**. For 14 miles, this road follows the river into the Wyoming Range and gives access to Hoback Peak and some fair fishing.

3.7 13.3   **Bondurant** (el. 6,668). Named for an early settler, this small village, with its post office and school, is a center for dude ranchers and outfitters who pack into the Gros Ventre (N) and Wyoming (S) ranges. This small pastoral summer-home and ranching community usually is quiet, but hit it on the last Sunday in June and join the Bondurant Barbecue throngs feasting on a delicious barbecue roasted overnight in great pits, the old-fashioned way.

1.4 14.7   **Gros Ventre Range and Gros Ventre Wilderness Area.** This sedimentary mountain range (N), with its rolling, timbered foothills, dominates the view from the Hoback Guard Station (S). The Gros Ventres' block-like, weathered crags beckon sportsmen to some of the finer hunting grounds in North America. At the same time, its deeply scored and timbered gorges provide exciting territory for hikers to explore, and concealment for roaming herds of elk, mule deer, bear and bighorn sheep, whose trails crisscross the highest ridges.

Paleolithic people hunted the Gros Ventres when Pinedale glaciers still filled Jackson's Hole. Geologically, these mountains are the stratified bottoms of ancient inland seas that were uplifted, and then carved and scoured by glaciers. Erosion finished the job, and today we see grayish limestones and dolomites mixed with sandstone "red beds" in a blend of colorful tints. Its highest peak is Doubletop Peak (el. 11,682).

The heart of this foreland range, some 287,000 acres, has been contained in the Gros Ventre Wilderness since Oct. 30, 1984. Its boundaries include the skyline peaks.

1.5 16.2   **Dell Creek Road** turnoff (N). This access road leads to several trailheads in the wilderness area.

2.0 18.2   **Historical Markers**. The stone markers near the buildings (S) locate the old trapper route.

This spot also commemorates the **first Protestant sermon** in Wyoming, given by Rev. Samuel Parker on Sunday, Aug. 23, 1835, to his congregation of Indians and Jim Bridger's trappers. The dogmatic Parker records the event: "I did not feel any disposition to upbraid them for their sins, but endeavored to show them, that they are unfit for heaven." The Indians listened willingly. As trapper Joe Meek tells the story: "The men were as politely attentive as it was in their reckless natures to be, until, in the midst of the discourse, a band of buffalo appeared in the valley, when the congregation incontinently broke up... and every man made haste after his horse, gun, and rope, leaving Mr. Parker to discourse to vacant ground....About twenty fine buffaloes were killed, and the choice pieces brought to camp, cooked and eaten, amidst the merriment... of the hunters. On this noisy rejoicing, Mr. Parker looked with a sober aspect.... He rebuked the Sabbath-breakers quite severely." Meek notes, however, that the Reverend ate "heartily of the tender-loin afterwards."

0.2 18.4   **Mouth of Hoback Canyon**. The river leaves the broad basin, entering a deeply cut canyon of towering cliffs, scenic twists and geologic upheavals.

1.2 19.6   **Cliff Creek Road** Turnoff (S). This road penetrates the heart of the Wyoming Range. The seven-mile drive to the Cliff Creek trailhead takes you to a six-mile hike that ends at a dramatic box canyon, out of which the airy Cliff Creek Falls pours through a slot to fall 50 feet. Cliff Creek Pass and isolated valleys lie beyond.

1.9 21.5   **Battle Mountain** (el. 7,010), directly ahead, is composed of colorful red Nugget sandstone. The old Indian trail ascended the open grassy slopes to the pass right (NE) of this mountain, then descended to Granite Creek and back to the Hoback.

Battle Mountain marks the scene of a skirmish between a posse and the Bannock Indians. It occurred near the pass and caused the "Indian scare of 1895." The 1868 Treaty of Fort Bridger gave the Bannocks and Shoshones the right to hunt on unoccupied public land at any time. The Indians were accustomed to coming to Jackson's Hole for their meat supply, but "hunting seasons" were unknown to the tribe, a fact resented by the early settlers.

The summer of 1895 witnessed a series of posse-Indian confrontations because a new game law of that year closed big-game hunting for 10 months and required a $20 license for non-resident hunters. This incensed the settlers of Jackson's Hole because the

Indians could still hunt when and where they pleased. The settlers appealed to Gov. Richards, who insisted that the state's game and fish law be enforced. Several posses searched out the Indians in the valley, and some arrests were made. The climax of the summer's encounters came when a posse of 26 valley residents, under Constable Bill Manning, surprised, disarmed, and arrested a Bannock hunting party of 9 braves, 13 women and five children in Hoback Basin for allegedly breaking Wyoming game laws. With the women and children following and each Indian brave between two deputies, the column started back to Jackson for trial. While the party stopped in timber west of the pass, a trigger-happy deputy fired his gun. Thinking they were going to be killed, the women began wailing, and the braves made a break. In the melee that followed, Se-we-agat, an old Indian, was needlessly killed, Nemuts, a 20-year-old boy, was wounded, and a child was left behind. The rest escaped.

The folks of Jackson's Hole waited, fearing the Bannocks would hit the warpath. National newspapers picked up the story, publishing it with scary headlines: "All residents of Jackson Hole massacred," "Marauding Bannocks," and "200 Utes and 400 Lemhi Reported Joining Bannocks." Five black companies of the U.S. 8th Infantry were dispatched to the Hole. Settlers built forts on the ranches of Ervin Wilson, Robert Miller, and Pierce Cunningham, and collected there. Nothing happened, and the "battle" was over.

As a "test" case, the Bannock chief, Race Horse, was arrested. In the end, the U.S. Supreme Court ruled that wild game was the property of Wyoming and, therefore, state law held jurisdiction. The ramifications of the decision carried beyond a mere abrogation of treaty rights of Indians trying to feed half-starving families. It established a legal basis for state hunting laws. And the missing child? He was rescued and cared for by Mrs. Martin Nelson for a year, then returned to his mother; he later fought in World War I.

0.3 21.8 **Kozy Campground**. The old Indian ford is just below. From this vantage, Battle Mountain exposes the Jackson-Prospect thrust fault, a significant boundary between geological structures. Battle Mountain is the leading edge of southwestern Wyoming's overthrust ranges—the Wyoming, Hoback, Snake River and Salt River ranges, "rootless" ranges that were thrust eastward out of Idaho and/or Utah. East of Battle Mountain are the "rooted" basement rock uplifts of the Gros Ventre and Wind River ranges, which halted the northeast movement of the overthrusts. As the Hoback Canyon slices through a complicated array of overthrust faults and folds that raised the sedimentaries to form the Hoback Range, the question arises: How did this river cut a canyon 1,000 feet or more deep *across* the Hoback Range? By superposition? Perhaps when Hoback Basin was filled high with debris, the first glacier meltwaters energized the ancestral Hoback on its "high-level superimposed course" westward, at which time the river laid its course for slicing through the range.

1.2 23.0 **Granite Creek Junction.** The Hoback River bridge is just below the junction of Hoback River and Granite Creek. Both streams provide great kayaking during high water. When they clear in the spring, the first to do so, their accessibility makes them tailor-made for fishing the deep natural pools; try large No. 10 humpies, muddlers, elk hair caddis and Royal Wulffs.

Turnoff (N, Trip 9) to **Granite Hot Springs,** with its lovely campground, falls and swimming pool.

The settlers of Jackson's Hole told of great pronghorn antelope herds that migrated annually from the Green River and down the Hoback to Granite Creek. Here, the herd split: One group went up Granite, over the Gros Ventre Divide and down Cache Creek; the other followed the Hoback.

0.5 23.5 **The Hoback Shield.** This towering face on the north side of the highway has become a local fun spot for climbers to test and develop rock-climbing abilities—with a top rope, of course. Some 18 routes have ratings from 5.6 to 5.12b.

0.8 24.3 **Bull of the Woods** (S). Snow on these steep faces annually thunders down the gulch before leaping the frozen Hoback to run up the highway side. When it sags back to the ice, it appears as two avalanches meeting headlong on the river. Snowslides aren't the only danger on this stretch of river. With its pileup of big slide boulders, this curve in the river can challenge the unwary boater.

0.5 24.8 **Red Ledges** of Nugget sandstone. These Ledges were the reason that fur trappers disliked Hoback Canyon. Part of the old trail still can be seen heading toward the cliffs, where it crossed on exposed ledges 200 feet above the river. Many trappers lost pack stock at this site.

In 1832, Warren Ferris, a clerk for the American Fur Company, wrote: "[W]e all dismounted, and led our animals over the most dangerous places, but… three of them lost their footing, and were precipitated… into the river below. Two were… slightly injured, having fallen on their loads… but the other was instantly killed." That same year, Wyeth lost a horse on the westbound trip, and another when he returned. Isaac Rose told how their mule, Remus, packing two 100-pound bales of precious tobacco, rolled 300 feet into the swollen Hoback waters and was not seen again. Others, such as Robert Stuart (1812), Rev. Samuel Parker (1835), and Osborne Russell (1837), described the dangerous spot as well.

1.9 26.7 Picnic site. The bridge that linked the highway with a campground across the river was washed out by high water in the 1980s.

2.4 29.1 **Scenic overlook** and boat access. Near the river's edge are highly sulfurous springs that emerge along the Hoback fault where it crosses the Hoback. Shown on Rev. Parker's 1835 map, the cold, milky-colored springs—with an average temperature of 48 degrees Fahrenheit—once poured 5,000 gallons per minute into the Hoback. Early settlers called them "Whoopoop Spring," a name now laundered to "Stinking Springs." Pioneer forest ranger Al Austin found an unidentified body here, believed to have frozen. During winter, bighorn sheep hang out in the area.

1.2 30.3 **Bryan Flat Guard Station** and **Camp Davis** turnoff. The University of Michigan has operated the Camp Davis geology field school, the oldest of its kind, since it was established by Professor J. B. Davis in 1874. Forest ranger Al Austin built the first cabin on Bryan Flat and, during winters, expertly covered the territory on old pine skis with leather toe straps and wooden cleats for the heel (J.H. Museum). The road continues to Chevron's Grayback Willow-Adams Creek 1993 drilling site, which turned out to be a dry hole.

0.9 31.2 **Camp Creek**. At this point, the old trapper trail left the Hoback and went north, following the east side of Camp Creek half a mile. From there, it climbed the hill and descended Little Horse Creek a bit before crossing several ridges to the Snake River at Game Creek. Traces of that old trail can be found by following the dirt road (N) behind the store.

Many artifacts have been harvested from this site. Al Austin found an old rifle, only to mislay it; someone else found it (J.H. Museum). Jim Imeson found a hunting knife with the letters "G" and "R" separated by a crown that hung over a word of which only the first three letters—F-U-R—were legible. It likely was a Green River knife manufactured by J. Russell & Co. for the fur trade. A well-known trapper battle cry—"Give it to 'em up to the Green River"—demonstrates the popularity of this brand. Undoubtedly, these trusty butcher knives were used for many things. As late as 1957, people were finding artifacts in the area. Seven-year-old Edward B. Morse came upon a fully loaded flintlock, crusted with the cement of river bed sands, which he found farther downstream.

0.8 32.0 **White ledges**. The ledges above the thick conglomerate cliff to the north are limestones, formed in fresh water. Ancient bone fragments have been found in the gray claystone below the limestone, and a Pliocene horse's tooth turned up in the sandstone and shale above that layer.

2.8 34.8 **Hoback Junction**. U.S. 191-189 joins U.S. 26-89 and the Hoback joins the **Snake River**; boats can be taken out below the smaller Hoback bridge, above the confluence. A good re-energizer spot, the booming community offers everything from ice cream to trips on the Snake.

Several decades ago, a Mr. Rogers built an energy-saving home, the back wall of which cut into the corner hill. Geologists have wondered how the back wall of the house has fared because the hillside directly above is slumping badly. Owners answer, "OK!"

The Astorians describe the area. Hunt's westbound journal notes: "[W]e emerged from the mountains on the 27th [Sept. 1811] and halted at the confluence of a small river… with the one… the Americans have named Mad River, because of its swiftness…. On its banks, and a little above the confluence are situated the three peaks [the Tetons] which we had seen on the 15th…. We searched on the 28th for trees suitable for building canoes…. [O]n the 29th, we moved our camp lower down because the trees there were more suitable." Hunt's party planned to canoe the Snake, but when he sent three men down the Mad River to explore, they came back Oct. 2 and reported that it was unnavigable. Abandoning that plan, the party left Oct. 4 for Teton Pass.

DeLacy's party of prospectors also camped here in 1863, having come up the Snake. They were the first to pan the rivers of Jackson's Hole, but found only "color."

From Hoback Junction north, the highway has been a triumph in highway engineering, maintenance, and job security. For severing and destabilizing old landslides, seen as road bumps, constant maintenance is required.

0.7 35.5 **Snake River.** Below this stretch of highway, the river has been squeezed into a single channel by the Hoback foothill (el. 7,496) to the east and Munger Mountain (el. 8,383) to the west. It's hard today to believe that ice once flowed over most of this mountain. It was named for Munger, who panned gold on the river bars above. The trail used by the Hayden Surveys on Oct. 3, 1872, and by early-day renegades can be seen on the west side of the river.

Famous for its native and planted cutthroat trout, the Snake offers good to excellent fishing when it clears after the spring run-off. Fall fishing on rock and rubble bottoms is best.

0.6 36.1 **Horse Creek** (E). The road follows Horse Creek east. In one mile, it is joined by Little Horse Creek, where the trappers, Foy and More, probably were killed in the wake of the Battle of Pierre's Hole (Teton Basin, Idaho), and buried here, although the site is uncertain.

After the Pierre's Hole fight between Indians and trappers in 1832, the Gros Ventre warriors retreated over Teton Pass, through Jackson's Hole and up the Hoback, heading for the Green River drainage; their rear guard consisted of 30 braves. Five days after the battle, Captain Alfred K. Stephens left Pierre's Hole with six men, following the Indians' trail. They forded the icy Snake below the mouth of Mosquito Creek, rode down the east bank of the Snake, knee-deep in grass that was swarming with mosquitoes, and crossed the meadows of South Park (W). The Indian rear guard watched their movements. The trappers headed for the hills east of South Park—the highway crosses their route near Game Creek—and diagonalled southeast across the hills. When they descended to the forks of Horse Creek, they were ambushed. Foy and More were killed, and Stephens was wounded seriously.

Stephens and the other survivors fled to Pierre's Hole. Although W.A. Ferris takes credit for burying the bodies, Captain Bonneville says he buried them a month later. A year later,

Nathaniel Wyeth wrote in a letter: "Saw no Indians but saw the bones of Mr. More killed by the Blackfeet last year and buried them." In 1904, Al Austin found a white man's skull on Horse Creek near the trail crossing; for many years, the skull was exhibited at Roy Van Vleck's hardware. A soapstone cooking dish also was found in the area (J.H. Museum).

Horse Creek has been the site of other confrontations. When A.A. Anderson, first supervisor of the Yellowstone Timber Reserve, got word that 60,000 sheep had been turned loose in the Teton Division and were being guarded by herders, Anderson deputized 65 armed men at "Horse-creek." They found 1,500 sheep and several herders and escorted them east out of the reserve.

0.1 36.2 **Hoodoo Rocks and Swinging Bridge**. For a change of pace, turn east on Henry Road (old U.S. 191) and drive along the base of the foothills for a closer view of the stark Hoodoo rocks to the east. These monuments to wind and water erosion provide a good point for spotting prairie falcons. A mile beyond the Porcupine Creek Greenhouse, the road rejoins the main highway (W) across the Snake's steel bridge. (Old U.S. 191 continues north to a dead end.)

Above the bridge on the west bank, the cement pylon of the cable Swinging Bridge is visible. Built in 1937 for $3,900, the Swinging Bridge was featured in *Reader's Digest.* It swung dizzily over the Snake River until 1961, scaring everyone except Grandma Grisamer and a few other South Park residents who crossed the bridge by necessity.

3.7 39.9 **South Park Bridge**. This busy major river access point is at the mouth of Flat Creek, to the east. Both Flat Creek and the Snake were moved here by earthquakes that tipped the valley floor eastward in recent geologic times. Between Hoback Junction and Jackson, the highway has paralleled the Hoback normal fault, which lies to the east. Also east of the bridge, you'll notice the man-made Squaw Creek landslide, which has since buried the old highway. Activated by highway construction, the slumping hillside kept pushing the old highway into the river for years. Finally, after hundreds of thousands of dollars worth of repairs, the highway department gave up the battle and rerouted the road to the west side of the Snake.

0.1 40.0 Parking (W) at the gate. The levees make good biking, hiking, and bird-watching paths; it's also a pelican hang-out.

0.6 40.6 **Game Creek**. The old trapper trail from Teton Pass crossed the Snake riverbottom before heading east up Game Creek and over the hills to reach the Hoback at Camp Creek. Robert Stuart's journal entry of Oct. 8, 1812 identified this cutoff.

0.6 41.2 Elk winter feeding grounds. A turnoff (W) leads to the feedgrounds and a picnic stop. It also gives us a chance to talk about the geography of South Park from this vantage of great pastoral beauty.

To the west sits the **Snake River Range**, one of the overthrust belt ranges. From Teton Pass, on the northwest horizon, it extends south for 22 miles until it is cut off by Snake River Canyon. Its highest point is Powder Peak (el. 9,862). Early travelers crossed the range at the north end via Mosquito Creek Pass. To the east are the Hoback Range and, at its base, the Hoback normal fault, paralleling U.S. 191.

0.1 41.3 **Horsethief Canyon** (E). John Wilson found a cache of strange branding irons in this canyon; one bore the markings, "7HL," a brand unknown in the Hole. Thus the canyon's name.

1.3 42.6 **South Park Loop Road** (W). This turnoff west leads past Jackson's Hole's first ranches and schoolhouse (see Trip 1a). From this point, South Park spreads north and west. With its luxurious meadows, graceful cottonwoods, ribboned Snake River, and surrounding mountains, South Park retains much of the charm of hay and ranching country that once characterized the entire valley. An extension of Jackson's Hole, the two valleys are separated by the Gros Ventre Buttes, four miles to the north. From the beginning, easier winters, finer hay and earlier springs lured white people to settle along Flat Creek (W).

0.5 43.1 The old **Cheney Post Office**. A quarter mile west, South Park's second post office sat on Selar Cheney's land, on the east bank of Flat Creek. The Cheneys were among the first stalwart souls to settle Jackson's Hole.

Forced from their drought-plagued desert valley in Utah, the five-family clan of Sylvester Wilson started its covered wagons north to Idaho in May, 1889. St. Anthony had no hay for their starving livestock, but Nick Wilson told them of a "hole" over the mountains where hay was plentiful. With two girls along to cook, the men rode over Teton Pass into Jackson's Hole, where they put up all the hay they needed with a borrowed mower and rake. They returned that fall with the families of Sylvester, his son, Ervin, his son-in-law, Selar Cheney, his brother, Nick Wilson, and others. Their epic 11-day struggle to drag the first wagons over roadless Teton Pass opened the way for homestead settlement in Jackson's Hole. They wintered with John Carnes, his wife, and bachelors John Holland, John Cherry and Will Crawford.

0.7 43.8   **Sylvester Wilson homestead**, west of Flat Creek (see Trip 1a, mile 0.4).

1.6 45.4   **Stephen Leek Ranch**. The white, two-story house to the west has been enlarged since Leek settled here in 1889. A writer, photographer, and state legislator, Leek's glass-plate photos of starving and dead elk were used for articles and lecture tours. He would photograph the elk from haystacks. Or, camouflaged in white against the snow and with white camera in hand, he would creep close to the slow-moving herd and shout "Hey!" Every beautiful animal, lifting its head or hoof alertly, would pose momentarily for the picture. Leek's photos publicized the dilemma of the elk and focused national attention on Jackson's Hole. Leek also introduced laws to protect the elk and subsequently the National Elk Refuge was established.

But Leek's interests were not limited to elk and photography. He operated one of the first dude ranches, introduced irrigation to the valley, and brought the first binder here in 1893. He also obtained the first water-powered sawmill, which the Whetstone Mining Co. brought from Idaho over Teton Pass in 1893. In March 1919, he and Fred Lovejoy showed the first moving-picture show at the old community Clubhouse. A grateful editor presented him with the first victrola in the Hole.

Earlier visitors left their traces on Leek's homestead. An old dugout canoe, presumably left by Hunt's party, was found in a beaver pond; Western Indians used bull-skin boats, and a dugout would have been of little use to early trappers.

The higher-than-usual fences around the haystacks in South Park originally were built to keep migrating elk from eating the settlers' hay during lean winters.

0.2 45.6   **Leek Canyon** (E). If you look north quickly, you'll get a momentary view of the snowy summit of the Grand Teton between West and East Gros Ventre buttes.

0.4 46.0 **Flat Creek**. From this vantage, Teton Pass lies to the west and Mount Glory is just to its north; the southeast face, Glory Bowl, is famous for its roadblocking avalanches and spring corn skiing.

0.5 46.5 **South Park Loop Road** (W) (Trip 1a).

0.6 47.1 **The "Y"**—now considered an "X" with the addition of another road—marks the junction of U.S. 191-189 and WY 22, which leads through Antelope Pass to Wilson (Trip 3).

A plaque at the "Y" commemorates the five Mormon families, which, under the leadership of Elijah N. "Uncle" Nick Wilson, came over Teton Pass in 1889. The second Jackson Post Office also was located at this spot and, in 1900, was operated by Mary A. Anderson; she also ran the Anderson Hotel, the valley's first such establishment. In 1901, the hotel and post office were moved closer to the Town Square, then enlarged and covered with brick. Antelope Pass also saw the valley's first brick kiln, operated by Jim Parker and Mullins; the enterprising pair made the brick used to build Pap DeLoney's store, the town's first bank building, as well as the LDS church.

1.7 48.8 Jackson Town Square.

Trip 1a
SOUTH PARK LOOP
(6.5 miles)

This trip will take you by Jackson Hole's first ranches and schoolhouse, the original hayland spreads, and rifle pits that were prepared in anticipation of an Indian raid in 1895. To begin the South Park Loop, turn west off of Trip 1, Mile 42.6, at the South Park sign, six miles south of the Town Square or eight miles north of Hoback Junction.

0.0 0.0 **South Park Loop Road**. The old fur-trapper trail diagonalled northwest across South Park, heading generally for the northwest corner of South Park, Boyles Hill and the Snake River ford. South Park Loop Road loosely parallels the route taken by those 19th century adventurers.

0.2 0.2 Melody Hereford Ranches, both south and north.

0.1 0.3 The Selar Cheney homestead (N, see Trip 1, Mile 43.1). Cheney's homestead north of the road now is part of Paul Von Gontard's Melody Ranch. One of the pioneers who pushed over Teton Pass with his family in 1889, Cheney settled here the next year. In 1891, his son, Howard Cheney, became the second white child born in the valley. After Francis Estes operated South Park's first post office from 1899-1901, Selar Cheney opened the Cheney post office about one-half mile north.

0.1 0.4 **Flat Creek Bridge**. The original Mormon homesteads were taken up along this section of Flat Creek because of the hay found here. The Sylvester Wilson homestead (N) still looks about like it did when he worked the open stretch of land lying west of Flat Creek. In 1889, Sylvester—brother of "Uncle" Nick Wilson—made three trips over Teton Pass. The purpose of the first trip was to put up hay for the winter; the second was to bring 80 head of horses into the valley. Then, on Oct. 28, six covered wagons left St. Anthony, Idaho, with Sylvester Wilson leading his family of 10, and the families of Selar Cheney, Ervin Wilson, and "Uncle" Nick Wilson and his daughter, about 20 people total, over Teton Pass. The first Latter Day Saint (Mormon) services here were held on Easter in 1890, with Sylvester Wilson presiding as elder. The first formal schooling in Jackson's Hole was in the Wilson home; parents chipped in to pay the teacher, Henry Johnson. With the school and church came the first cemetery as well; in the winter of 1891, two of Sylvester's children, Ellen and Joseph, died of diphtheria and were the first buried in the South Park Cemetery, on the hill to the west (see Mile 2.7). Sylvester also organized the church's first branch here in 1893, and he was instrumental in getting the first county school district in the valley. He also brought in the first hand-operated sawmill and riding plow. He was a musician; his wife, Mary, was a midwife. They had 12 children.

1.1 1.5 The former U Lazy U Ranch. This ranch (S) belonged to Jim Imeson, an early forest ranger. His wife, Susannah, was the daughter of early settler Ervin Wilson. This road, on the bench above the Snake River floodplain, gives an overview of the Shooting Iron ranches, named for the local geologic formation.

0.3 1.8 The old **John Wilson homestead** (E). The road curves north past the site of John Wilson's homestead, where children had their second session of schooling for six months. The parents took up a collection to pay Mr. Gardner, who taught in a one-room log cabin during the winter of 1895.

0.9 2.7 **South Park Cemetery Road** (W). This road climbs the hill 0.1 miles to a junction. Take a right past the one-way sign to the cemetery, with its magnificent 360-degree view. Lush hayfields still surround the hill; the Snake River and the Snake River Range are west; the Tetons are northwest; and the Hoback Range is east. When Sylvester Wilson's two children, 10-year-old Ellen and 12-year-old Joey, died, Sylvester brought them to the top of the hill to be buried, knowing it was high and dry. Sylvester and his wife, Mary, also rest here, near the lone pine tree that was

The Gros Ventre Range (top). Shoal Peak–center, Flying Buttress–right behind Deer Ridge–right.

Al Austin (above, right), the "Cowboy Poet," at Bryan Flat Ranger Station, c. 1910. In the fall of 1940, at age 72, he hiked up Arizona Creek—one of his favorite haunts—and died with his boots on.

The Old Swinging Bridge (above, right).

S. N. Leek photographing the Elk (left).

The first School (bottom).

planted by a school class years later. Most of the South Park home-steaders are buried here—including the Cheney, Robertson and Imeson families—and the Nick Wilson family graves also are here.

The narrow cottonwood-lined road passes the long-irrigated fields and hay fences reminiscent of early days—until progress erupts at the Rafter J subdivision. Mosquito Creek is almost west, and if the trappers were heading for that pass, they'd be cutting west to the Snake River ford four miles south of Wilson.

1.5 4.2 **Jackson Hole's first schoolhouse**. East and across a buck-and-rail fence on private property sits the remains of the valley's first permanent schoolhouse, looking pretty sad without a roof and windows. It was built in 1896, on land donated by Ervin Wilson. The logs were hauled from Wilson Canyon (E), and then peeled and notched before being lifted into place by unpaid pio-neers who wanted their children educated. Fathers built the benches and desks, and Susie Clark of Idaho Falls was the first teacher—hired with public funds. In spelling bees, children com-peted alongside their parents. At first, the school term lasted only three months but later grew to four, and finally to six months, di-vided between the spring and fall.

In addition to serving as a school, the building became the community center. Because travel was possible only in daylight, the socials and dances, typical of the frontier, lasted all night. News was exchanged at these gatherings, which became the grist for an issue of "The Jackson's Hole Kicker." The Hole's first elections also were held here. This log building continued to be used until 1907.

Ervin Wilson acquired the ranch's original 320 acres from the government. Half of the acreage was considered a "homestead" after he built a cabin and cultivated 40 acres; the remaining 160 acres was called "desert land," which he "proved up" by putting half of it into irrigation.

Life on these early homesteads was never easy. It's worth con-templating the experiences of Mary Jane Wilson Lucas (1871-1945), whose first husband was Ervin Wilson. What she describes is typical of the daily hardship faced by settlers in the valley:

"I was 18 years old; my baby Jim was 6 weeks. Our first night in Jackson's Hole [November 1889], we camped on the Gros Ven-tre River by a big campfire and sang all evening. Next morning Ervin went to look for a house as winter was setting in—we couldn't camp with a young baby. John Cherry let us have his best room.

"It was a hard winter and we lost our two cows. Our only food was elk meat and water gravy, and the baby lived on elk soup until he was 9 months old. In June, we bought a cow with a heifer calf and next winter enjoyed milk and butter.

"In the fall of 1890 we moved into our little one-room cabin with tamped dirt floor. After 15 months Ervin and Hy Adams whip-sawed by hand enough planks for the floor. Winter darkness came early. For light we used elk tallow in a dish, with a rag dipped in for a wick. We made good use of the game—meat, moccasins, shirts, gloves, and soap made from the grease and wood ashes. I carded wool, made yarn, knit it into socks for my husband, and used it for making quilts.

"On March 17, 1891, Effie Jane was born, the first white baby born in Jackson's Hole. There was no doctor; it would have taken weeks of travel on horseback to get one. Susannah and Sylvester Joy were born in the same one room where we lived 4 years. There were no stores. Once a year we went to Rexburg or Idaho Falls for supplies, the trip taking 10 days.

"Many antelope came in during May, stringing along the hill-sides like sheep, thousands of them, always within rifle shot of the cabin. Indians came early each spring and stayed until the snow. But they were peaceable—only hunting. Occasionally when I was alone with only my baby for company they came to the house for supplies—coffee, sugar, and flour. I was always frightened and gladly gave them what they asked to get rid of them. They paid me with buckskin. As the country built up, the antelope left as the Indians did."

0.5 4.7 Turn east down this short lane. At 0.1 miles is the gate of the Wilford W. and Adeline Neilson property, the former Ervin Wilson homestead. Behind the old barn and other buildings sits the grayish shell that housed the doughty *Jackson's Hole Courier*, the valley's only paper for many years. It was moved to the Neilson Ranch from its original Jackson site, north of the Jackson State Bank.

Neilson was appointed prosecuting attorney for the new County of Teton in 1925 and held that position for 26 years. He was town attorney for years and a deputy sheriff for a time. In 1932, he bought the *Courier* from Walter Perry, who was losing money and facing foreclosure because of his stand for the extension of Grand Teton National Park. With that, many Jackson businessmen canceled their ads in the *Courier*, and a group of Jackson's leading citizens, all opponents of park extension, launched a newspaper called *Grand Teton*, expressly to fight park extension. Thus, the propaganda war began: The old *Courier*, under editor Neilson, became the courageous defender of the Rockefeller project, and the 18-month-old bombastic and vindictive *Grand Teton*, under the editorship of William L. "Bill" Simpson, became the arch enemy of a larger Grand Teton National Park (see Trip 6c, Mile 11.1). The *Grand Teton* charged subsidization in its headlines: "Wilford Nielson heads the Rockefeller press." From then on, the two lawyer-editors traded editorial and personal blows.

Another 0.1 miles east is the Porter estate, where the **rifle pits** of the 1895 Indian scare are scarcely visible. Years of haying and trampling have reduced them to a section of rough ground. This is private property; permission is required from the Porter Estate to enter. By standing at the property entrance gate, however, and looking southeast beyond another gate into the next field, you can see a third gate near the territory of the rifle pits.

Mary Jane Wilson Lucas told about the rifle pits: "After the trouble with the Bannocks on Battle Mountain in 1895 everyone was afraid the Indians from the reservation would come here on the war path. On account of being centrally located and in an open flat, people from all parts of the valley came to our place. They brought their livestock and possessions and camped on our ranch. Mose Giltner brought his organ. In the evening, he played and the people sang. Rifle pits were dug. There was no war, but the people stayed until the Negro soldiers came—about three weeks. During that time, Father Wilson [Sylvester] died, and Mrs. George Pettigrew's daughter Ruth was born."

0.9 5.6 The road east is High School Road.

0.5 6.1 **Boyles Hill Road** (W). At this four-way intersection, turn left (W) on Boyles Hill Road to find the general location of the old Snake River ford and to locate the old trail that crossed South Park to Boyles Hill and the ford. Drive west 1.2 miles, past gravel pits (N) and marshy meadows (S), which offer good birding, to a three-way junction. Turn north (permission required to enter this private property), and drive another mile to the levees near the old ford area. This ford was used by Indians and trappers for more than 100 years, until the first steel bridge on the Jackson to Wilson road (N) was completed in 1922.

The Snake River was not always easy to cross. Usually it divided into several relatively shallow channels—belly-deep on horses—which were much safer to navigate than the single, deep, broad torrent. Father DeSmet crossed the river near this spot on July 10, 1840: "[It] intimidated neither our Indians nor our Canadians.... They rushed into the torrent on horseback and swam it. I dared not.... To get me over, they made a kind of sack of my skin tent; then they put all my things in and set me on top of it. The three Flatheads who had jumped in to guide my frail bark by swimming, told me, laughingly, not to be afraid.... In less than 10 minutes I found myself on the other bank, where we camped for the night." The next day, DeSmet and his party crossed Teton Pass.

Confronted with the Snake on June 12, 1860, Captain W.F. Raynolds sent two lance corporals to inspect the ford. Lance Corporal Lovett returned in 20 minutes with the startling news that Bradley had been drowned. Despite a reward offered to the Indians, Bradley's body never was recovered. After an improvised raft failed to survive the Snake's high waters, Raynolds tested the ingenuity and experience of Jim Bridger, the expedition's guide. Old Gabe made a bull boat by lashing a willow frame with rawhide thongs, covering it with an old rubber tarp smeared with pitch, and fastening a lodgeskin to the structure. Still, it took Raynolds and company four strenuous days of systematic labor to cross the Snake's three channels.

One day in the early 1970s, Dr. Dave Love, Wyoming's foremost geologist, apparently followed in the footsteps of a very early traveler. Dr. Love climbed halfway up the west side of Boyles Hill (el. 6,623) to a small limestone outcrop. There, tucked under a little overhang, he found a cache: a small quartzite hammerstone, a chert arrow point, about six preforms, plus several other chert tools and quartzite pieces. Early People had flaked all the cortex off the quartzite, chert and obsidian. They clearly were on foot, as suggested by the arrow point, in a time somewhere between 500 A.D. and the prehorse era. In the excitement of making the Snake River crossing, had the owners cached their workshop here and forgotten about it, never to return? Retrace your tracks.

Back at the three-way junction, several properties to the south and southwest have conservation easements set up between the landowners and the Jackson Hole Land Trust, whereby both parties cooperate to preserve the scenic vista and wildlife habitat permanently. To the west, Boyles Hill Road ends at the privately maintained Ely Springs Road, barring public access to the Snake and the public-maintained levees. Turn east on South Park Loop Road, and return to the four-way junction and continue east.

1.1 7.2 Jackson Middle School. Rejoin U.S. 191-189 (see Trip 1, Mile 46.5); turn left (N) to Jackson.

Trip 2

SNAKE RIVER (SOUTHWEST) ENTRANCE
Via Alpine, WY and Snake River Canyon
to Hoback Junction.
(23 miles)

Dynamite and the CCC boys blasted a road through the Grand Canyon of the Snake River in 1939, replacing the dim, treacherous, and seldom-used trail with a highway. Now U.S. 26-89 skirts Palisades Reservoir and travels through the twisting grandeur of the Grand Canyon of the Snake, into Jackson's Hole.

The first known explorers of the canyon, the westbound Astorian voyagers, were tired of horsepacking and eager to hit canoeable waters leading to the Pacific. The Snake at Hoback Junction looked good to them—until they saw its narrow canyon and whitewater rapids. On Oct. 2, 1811, they changed their minds and headed over Teton Pass instead.

Osborne Russell found good hunting here. In January of 1829, he and five buddies, along with seven lodges of Snake Indians, moved east from Fort Hall and hunted the ridges above the canyon. In Russell's words: "Here we found immense numbers of Mountain Sheep which the deep snows drive down.... We could see them nearly every morning from our lodges standing on the points of rock."

In 1863, the promise of gold lured 47 prospectors from Virginia City, Montana Territory into the area. Under the leadership of Captain Walter W. DeLacy, the party was following this canyon's "little-used" and difficult trail "about 100 feet above the river," when two pack animals rolled down the precipitous slopes into the river. "Colors," indicating the presence of gold, drew DeLacy's group through the Hole. They became the first men to pan its streams, and then continued on into the Yellowstone.

Next came the government men. In 1872, the Snake River division of F.V. Hayden's second Wyoming survey, under James Stevenson, swarmed south from Yellowstone. While in Jackson's Hole, they mapped, explored, and made copious notes before taking the trail through the Snake River Canyon.

The Snake River Canyon ended the adventures of Lt. Doane's 1876 winter boating expedition, when it ran into disaster and out of food here. Nobody attempted the Snake's tumultuous waters again until 1909, when Ivan Hoffer—the gold prospector at Pine Bar—dared the canyon in a boat steadied with ropes from the shore. Then, beginning in the late 1940s, a series of modern-day adventurers—Jim Huidekoper and Royal Little in 1947, Roger and Orrin Bonney in 1948 and Disney moviemakers Paul Kenworthy and John Hermann in 1956—ran these pre-Palisades Reservoir waters in light, kayak-type foldboats. Hermann was the photographer of the disastrous avalanche-shooting scene in Clear Creek, CO, that is shown in most avalanche-survival courses today. John was killed in that avalanche but his camera told the story.

Those fortunate enough to travel the Snake River Canyon during autumn will experience the multi-reds of the mountain maple—blushing delicate pink, flashing vibrant crimson—contrasting with the gold of the aspens. Each curve of the road brings more unforgettable colorful vistas frescoing the cliffs.

To reach the Grand Canyon of the Snake, you can begin in Idaho Falls (el. 4,710), 106 miles west of Jackson via Palisades Reservoir and U.S. 26. The mileage for Trip 2 begins at Alpine Junction, where U.S. 26 joins U.S. 89.

Big changes occurred at **Alpine Junction** when the old town of Alpine, a quarter mile west of the junction, and old U.S. 26 were moved to higher ground before the Palisades Reservoir was built. New Alpine, south of the junction, has become a busy recreation center. Because of its location, Alpine is the gateway to Star Valley (S), the Salt River—noted for its blue-ribbon fishing, and the Wyoming and Salt River ranges via Greys River Road.

McCoy Creek, across the reservoir (W) from Alpine, leads to the ruins of ghost towns. It was up this creek that Lt. Doane and his crew, stranded in the Snake River Canyon without food, struggled to get help during the winter of 1877. To get to these once-active Idaho mining settlements, take U.S. 89 south from Alpine four miles, then turn west across the Salt River and drive north on a dirt road seven miles to the mouth of McCoy Creek on the southwest side of Palisades Reservoir. Then go west.

Alpine has boomed because Jackson's Hole has become a millionaires' paradise with a shortage of low-cost housing, and folks have flowed west into Alpine and Idaho. Traffic has increased in the canyon, as has pressure to upgrade the road and make it safer. No matter the traffic and winding nature of the Snake River Canyon road, it is worth driving slowly in any season, taking time to examine the geology and applaud the grandstand views of the river.

0.0 0.0   Alpine Junction of U.S. 26 and 89. This is the confluence of the **Greys and Salt rivers** with the Snake River. The former rivers are separated by the Salt River Range, an overthrust range that extends south 50 miles.

When Robert Stuart arrived here Sept. 15, 1812—on his return trip from Astoria—he was lost and trying to find the route the Astorians had taken the previous year. He had been hired by the Pacific Fur Co. to locate fur sources and was heading back to St. Louis. Having traveled down the Salt River, he camped at its mouth on the Snake. The next day, Crow Indians attacked his party and captured all of their horses. Stuart would not allow his group to shoot at its attackers. With the loss of its horses, the party burned its baggage, improvised rafts and floated 91 miles down the Snake. Well off route, it was Oct. 7 before they made their way back through Pierre's Hole (Teton Basin) and across Hunt's Pass—present day Teton Pass—into Jackson's Hole.

0.3 0.3   Mouth of **Greys River**. Doane's party, stumbling westward, stopped here for a meager lunch of "rose pods." Later, when Hayden traveled through this area, he renamed the river for John Day, an Astorian party member. The name was changed back to Greys, however, when Western historian H.M. Chittenden raised a commotion. Old John Gray, an Indian and Hudson's Bay trapper, gained notoriety when he stabbed gallivanting Milton Sublette in

1832 over some real or fancied indignity to the stern chief's daughter.

2.3 2.6 **The Narrows**. This resevoir stretch of the calmed Snake River is a much less-exciting run today than in pre-reservoir days, when the violent water poured through the 20-foot slot in the rocky walls, forcefully spitting boaters into the foaming water below. Above the Narrows was the fearsome Churn, downfall of early boaters, though now gone. An early-day flimsy prospector's bridge once spanned the gap.

The Narrows area has much historical interest as well. Above its rapids, Doane's party lost most of its food and outfit on Dec. 12, 1876, when its boat capsized. Two days later, the men pulled their boat ashore above the Narrows, thinking it secure. After eating their last bit of horse meat, they took off afoot, heading downstream for the mines of Keenan City, on McCoy Creek in Idaho Territory. When five of the party returned to the boat on Dec. 27, they found it crushed into splinters by a floating 20-foot-thick mass of ice. What a bitter disappointment for these men who had found the Snake open all the way to Fort Hall.

0.7 3.3 **Sheep Gulch Takeout**. This takeout marks the end of the Snake's popular nine-mile whitewater run. Ferry Peak in the Snake River Range is visible to the north. Also visible from this spot is the Absaroka Thrust, where Arco-Sun once drilled an expensive well—the high cost of very complicated, overthrust geology.

3.5 6.8 **Lunch Counter Parking**. A good trail will lead you down the steep bank for a peanut-gallery view of Lunch Counter's watery jaws, as they munch a daily fare of rafters and kayakers out pushing their luck against nature. The first of the big upsetters in the climactic four-mile whitewater stretch is the big hole called Kahuna, a frothy boil a quarter mile upstream. While boaters can slip past Kahuna on river right, there's no way to sneak by churning old Lunch Counter below, so go for it! Below and around the next bend lurks twisty Rope, flicking its off-side kickers. Next comes the always bubbly Champagne—short and easy-looking, but don't believe it. Last but never least comes the Holy City/Cottonwood combo. Split by a huge rock, this region of shallow boulders, massive waves and ledges hiding man-eating holes, presents an awesome wall of white froth to kayakers, but its whiplash tail is pure play time.

Thousands of whitewater addicts play here each season with every type of water toy—rafts, dories, inflatables, kayaks, canoes, surfboards, and tubes—you name it.

The ominous threat to all this beauty and fun used to be the Bureau of Reclamation, because it favored the Narrows as a dam site. A dam at the Narrows undoubtedly would destabilize areas upriver, creating numerous landslides between South Park and the Narrows. These days, however, the threat is the Highway Department. Its plans to straighten, widen, and deface the canyon road were challenged, and opponents to the project charged the State of Wyoming with creating a workable compromise between maintaining safety and preserving the beauty of this unique canyon. Highway Department solutions don't always solve the problems. The wider and straighter the road, the faster people drive it.

2.6 9.4 The **Snake River Canyon**. Here, the river winds between the walls of the Snake River Range to the north and the Wyoming Range to the south, both forming part of Wyoming's famous Overthrust Belt—the source of an earlier oil and gas bonanza. A road/jeep trail follows the Snake's eastern bank from Hoback Junction south to Elbow campground; a trail then goes west five or so miles. But the best approach to the southside trails into the Wyoming Range is by boat.

2.1 11.5 **West Table Creek**. Recreational area and major boat-access point for commercial float trips.

1.3 12.8 **East Table Creek Campground**. Beyond the campground (W) is another popular river-floaters access point.

1.0 13.8 **Elbow Campground**. At this point, the Snake right-angles west, forming "The Elbow." Across the way lies Bailey Creek and, at its mouth, the 240-foot-thick gravel bar called Bailey's Bar. Chaos once occurred here when an old (Holocene) landslide flowed northwest out of the valley of Bailey Creek and dammed the Snake to create an enormous temporary lake that backed up nearly as far upstream as Jackson. Bailey's Bar is a remnant of the vast accumulation of gravel behind the landslide dam. Gold, originating in gold-bearing quartzites to the north, was carried down by the Snake's upper tributaries to end up at the Elbow. When the dam was created, the gold/gravel settled out. This "flour gold," however, is like micro-dandruff and not readily recovered by conventional methods, though men have been trying since 1870.

Enterprising souls, such as Uncle Jack Davis, mined Bailey's Bar for its gold. After killing a man in a drunken fight at Virginia City, MT, the 60-year-old Davis fled to Jackson's Hole in 1887. Until his death, Davis lived at Bailey's Bar in a one-room, windowless log cabin, hiding from his past. When he needed supplies, he skirted Jackson and headed for Menor's Ferry, 50 miles north.

Davis, a tall, blue-eyed, full-bearded giant, was one of the few to solve the riddle of recovering gold flour from the Snake's sands. He dug a ditch from Bailey Creek to bring water to his long sluice boxes. He shoveled pay gravel into the boxes, letting rock particles wash through. The fine, heavy metals sank and sifted through the steel-punched screens at the end of the box, then onto a series of barely sloping tables covered with burlap into which the gold and heavy concentrates settled. These, Davis swept into a tray then placed in a churn filled with mercury and warm water and operated by a homemade water wheel.

The gold and mercury amalgamated, like old dental fillings, and was poured into bars and sold. Davis' method was time-consuming, but 95-percent efficient. His take, which averaged a penny for each wheelbarrow full of gravel, gave him several hundred dollars a year—enough for his meager wants. Up Bailey Creek, you can still see the rows of boulders he piled to level his sluice boxes.

When Davis died, he was buried in one of the old boxes near Astoria. During his stay at Bailey's Creek, he became a changed man, killing nothing and befriending wildlife. He shared meals with his pets—Lucy the doe, Buster her fawn, two cats, squirrels, bluebirds, Dan the horse, and Calamity Jane the burro.

Since Uncle Jack Davis' days, others have made futile attempts to recover the flour gold. In 1965, Westinghouse moved its then up-to-date, but nonfunctional, million-dollar recovery equipment from the Gros Ventre River (see Trip 14, Mile 13.3) to this site. Again, its mining efforts failed. The U.S. Forest Service ordered the site cleaned up; when the operator tried to ferry the bulky equipment from the Bailey Creek side, the boat capsized. Today, Westinghouse's equipment rests at the bottom of the Snake.

0.9 14.7 Good view of the approximate position of the Bailey Creek slide remnant.

4.1 18.8 **Fall Creek Road.** This route takes you north to Wilson (see Trip 10). Here, in 1936, Civilian Conservation Corps (CCC) boys camped while they built the first canyon road. Today, it has become a winter feeding ground for elk; the nearby Pritchard Ponds (W) provide good birding. You can see an old irrigation ditch on the hillside above the ponds.

1.0 19.8   The old CCC bridge. Remnants of this bridge still are visible, and this area is popular for camping and accessing the river.

Across the river is another gold-bearing gravel bar, the 200-foot-deep and four-mile-long Pine Bar; it was created by the same landslide as Bailey's Bar. Here, Ivan Hoffer and L.M. Rosencrans also were after the gold flour that accumulated in this upper bend of the Snake as it had at the Elbow at Bailey's Bar.

0.4 20.2   Road cut. In the 1950s, entrepreneur Ben Goe, who owned the hot springs, dug an entrance into the black shale exposed by this road cut and installed benches. People paid 50 cents an hour to get irradiated, as this section of Phosphoria Formation contains uranium.

0.2 20.4   **Astoria Hot Springs** (E). The bridge that leads east to the hot springs once was part of the Wilson-Jackson highway; when the latter got a new bridge, this structure was moved.

These springs were known to prehistoric people, whose bones and those of the long-extinct buffalo species they hunted have been found on the site. Then, as today, wildlife and humans were drawn to the snow-free area, where the springs emerge from an old travertine-covered flat. The Doane party of 1886 noted "a small group of thermal springs in the cañon, but none of noticeable characteristics."

More recently, the springs were called Johnny Count's Hot Springs because of his homestead on these flats. Ben Goe next took over the springs. By the 1960s, Bruce Porter had acquired the spot, made improvements, and renamed them Astoria Springs, in honor of those early fur trappers—who, oddly enough, never mentioned the springs.

While the main pool's temperature hovers at 104 degrees Fahrenheit, the hot baths reach 114 degrees. You can test the waters during the summer for a fee.

1.9 22.3   **Rodeo Wall** (N). These cliffs have become a top rope climbing area; at least 10 routes have been established, most of which are direct and rated from 5.9 to 5.11b.

0.2 22.5   Fall Creek falls (N) was the site of at least two exciting boat scenes in the films *In the Pursuit of D.B. Cooper* (1981) and *A River Runs Through It* (1992). Breck O'Neil, coordinator of river stunts for the films, made the wild boat run over the falls himself in *Cooper.*

0.2 22.7   The hillside directly ahead above Hoback Junction is slipping slowly.

0.3 23.0   **Snake River Bridge.** Because of a destabilized landslide, this bridge has moved several inches downstream. U.S. 26-89 joins US 191-189 at Hoback Junction. Jackson is 14 miles north (see Trip 1).

TETON PASS (WEST) ENTRANCE
Victor, Idaho to Jackson, Wyoming
(25 miles)

The first pioneers took 11 days to haul their wagons over this historic hump; today, valley visitors cover the same distance in an hour. The gear-grinding switchbacks will, however, bring the same spectacular view that thrilled old mountain men and homesteaders alike.

The "Pass," the lifeline between Jackson's Hole and the outside world—specifically with Pierre's Hole (Teton Basin, Idaho)—was the well-beaten route of the early fur trappers. Oregon-bound, Astorian Wilson Price Hunt first reported crossing it on Oct. 5, 1811. Robert Stuart's party used "Hunt's Pass" on its return from Astoria on Oct. 7, 1812. Stuart's starving men became so desperate that one man proposed casting lots to see who would become the evening meal.

The rendezvous in Pierre's Hole caused a traffic jam on the pass as hundreds of men and thousands of animals headed for the gathering. Amiable Bill Sublette, on his way to the Rendezvous with trade goods, wrangled his pack train of 78 men and 150 horses over on July 7, 1832. Footing was difficult and horses slipped, rolling down the slopes; still others were lamed when their hoofs wore thin on sharp stones. At the summit, Sublette's group camped overnight, waiting for sick and inexperienced men to catch up. That night, a snowstorm struck and, by morning, they had to dig out from under a white blanket before descending into Pierre's Hole for the Rendezvous. When a cavalcade of westbound Gros Ventre Indians later crossed the pass into Pierre's Hole, they clashed with the trappers at the Battle of Pierre's Hole.

The early chronicles of Bonneville, Wyeth, Ferris, Zenas Leonard, Rev. Samuel Parker, and Father DeSmet mention the pass. In 1860, Jim Bridger guided the Raynolds expedition, on a rail-road reconnaissance, through the Hole; Raynolds would report that a railroad over Teton Pass would not be expedient. After 15 years' absence, the routes to Yellowstone had dimmed in Old Gabe's memory, but he managed to get them over Hunt's Pass. F.V. Hayden was along on that trip and, 12 years later, his survey parties would use the same route.

By the 1880s, people intent on homesteading Jackson's Hole began moving over the pass. Early settler Robert Miller horsepacked a disassembled wagon over the divide in 1885. After the first Mormon families built their own road over the pass, word spread and others began trickling over.

As early as 1883, ranchers were hazing bellowing herds of cattle over the pass. In 1886, Idaho sheepmen tried to get their flocks over, but were warned off. In 1895, the Whetstone Mining Co., wanting to get heavy sawmill equipment to an operation east of Jackson Lake, improved the wagon track by widening, corduroying, and building dugways and bridges.

One old-timer maintained that because the hauling costs over the pass were always added to the selling price of the goods at Jackson, Jackson Holers were buying the pass—rocks, ruts and red mire—a hundred times over, making it more expensive than the Brooklyn Bridge. But even when the supplies could not make the pass, everyone expected mail-delivery service to continue, despite blizzards, snow slides, high-centered horses, and nearly frozen drivers. The mailmen and freighters were early-day heroes.

In 1901, Uinta County put up $500 for a wagon road across the pass. Otho Williams surveyed the route with a crude level, fash-ioned from a donated oak table leaf. He essentially followed the old trapper trail, taking in 19-degree grades. The first auto, a Hupmobile driven by Ed Burton, actually chugged over the pass on its own in 1914.

It is 90 miles from **Idaho Falls** (el. 4,710) to Jackson (el. 6,209) via Swan Valley (U.S. 26), Pine Creek Pass (ID 31) and Victor, Idaho; the road log starts at Victor. Take ID 33 south at Victor. In Wyoming, it becomes WY 22.

0.0 0.0   **Victor, Idaho**. Founded in 1896 as an early railroad station, Victor (el. 6,207) is dominated by its wide main street and few houses. During the 1990s, it became Jackson's bedroom suburbia, taking up the overflow from Jackson's expensive home market; it also became the gateway to the Jedediah Smith Wilderness, on the west side of the Tetons.

Lying at the south end of Teton Basin, which the early trappers knew as Pierre's Hole, Victor was named for George Victor, who stalwartly carried the mail over the pass in 1895—despite the Indian scare of that year. Pierre's Hole was named for Vieux Pierre Tevanitagon who was an Iroquois Indian trapper for the Hudson's Bay Company.

The Battle of Pierre's Hole was fought just a few miles north of Victor, probably on Fox Creek, where artifacts have been found. On July 18, 1832, a caravan of Gros Ventre Indian families descended into Pierre's Hole via Teton Pass and the Moose Creek Trail. Trappers camped to the north saw the Indians and gathered to meet them; Antoine Godin and a Flathead Indian advanced as if to greet the chief, who was holding out a peace pipe. Instead, Godin and the unnamed Flathead killed him, touching off the battle.

The other rendezvousing trappers and Indians came racing down the valley preparing for battle. As they rode, Bill Sublette and Robert Campbell told their wills to each other. The fighting continued throughout the day. During the night, the Indians retreated over Teton Pass, leaving 26 of their warriors dead in the crude breastworks they had built.

Another major Indian battle was fought in Pierre's Hole on June 28, 1835, this time between 60 Piegans and 24 trappers. Relics, such as arrowheads and spear points, of these and other Indian battles still turn up occasionally.

The site of the Pierre's Hole Rendezvous of 1832 is about ten miles north of Victor. Trappers and traders gathered in a rousing carnival of sharp maneuvering and drunkenness that belied Washington Irving's polite description: "In this valley was congregated

Placer Mining (above) in Jackson Hole.

Nathaniel P. Langford (right), first superintendent of Yellowstone National Park, made the first ascent of the Grand Teton in 1872.

The Victor-Jackson Passenger Stage (bottom) at the road house on Teton Pass.

the motley populace connected with the fur trade. Here, the two rival companies had their encampment, with their retainers of all kinds; traders, trappers, hunters, and half breeds, assembled from all quarters, awaiting their yearly supplies, and the orders to start off in new directions. Here also… the Nez Perces… and Flatheads had pitched their tents beside the streams, and with their squaws awaited the distribution of goods and finery…. Such was the wild and heterogeneous assemblage amounting to several hundred men, civilized and savage, distributed in tents and lodges in the several camps."

In 1872, the Snake River Division of the Hayden Survey, out of Fort Hall and guided by Beaver Dick Leigh, camped on "West Teton Creek" (near today's Teton Canyon campground), and proceeded to discover that the Tetons were in Wyoming, not Idaho as previously believed, and to climb the Grand Teton. On July 29, a large party started out for the summit, but only four reached the Upper Saddle area of the Grand and only two reached the summit—James Stevenson, leader of the Snake River Division and Hayden's right-hand man, and Nathaniel P. Langford, guest of the survey and first superintendent of the newly established Yellowstone National Park.

When camp broke up, the division headed north into Yellowstone to join the rest of the survey, after which it turned south to explore Jackson's Hole.

3.1 3.1 **Targhee National Forest.**

0.4 3.5 **Moose Creek.** The road east follows the Moose Creek drainage to the southern Teton Range. At the campground two miles east of the highway is Moose Creek trailhead. This trail enters the Jedediah Smith Wilderness and climbs into the heart of the sedimentary Tetons. The 7.6-mile trail then connects with the Teton Crest Trail.

Before 1880, Indians, trappers, traders and the first settlers used two routes via Moose Creek to approach Teton Pass. The longer route took them along Moose Creek, Moose Meadows, Mesquite Creek, down Coal Creek, and up Trail Creek. The shorter, more strenuous course followed the current-day Taylor Mountain Trail, named for a successful Idaho sheep rancher. From Moose Creek campground, it climbed southeast up Taylor Mountain's west ridge between Moose and Trail creeks, to Taylor Mountain Basin, and across the shoulder of Taylor Mountain before dropping into Coal Creek to intersect with Trail Creek. Because of the steep, rough terrain, horses—never wagons—were used on these approaches. And both routes got you only to Coal and Trail creeks, far below the pass.

0.3 3.8 **Mike Harris Campground**. From the campground, take the little road left along Trail Creek to a trailhead. The trail up Mikesell Canyon goes five miles to Oliver Peak (el. 8,987) and connects with a web of trails in the northern Snake River Range that lead to Starvation Peak (el. 9,675) and Palisades Peak (el. 9,778), or Ice Cave Canyon.

2.3 6.1 **Trail Creek Campground**. This U.S. Forest campground lies just inside the Wyoming state line. The early wagon route up to Teton Pass followed Trail Creek, which loosely parallels WY 22.

3.4 9.5 **Coal Creek** parking lot and trailhead. The Coal Creek Trail north gives access to the Teton Crest Trail, Jedediah Smith Wilderness, Taylor Mountain (el. 10,352), Phillips Pass (8,932), Rendezvous Peak (10,927), and the south end of Grand Teton National Park.

To get into Jackson's Hole, horse-riding trappers had to make a decision at the mouth of Coal Creek. They could either continue east up Trail Creek to Hunt's Pass or take the alternate route to the southwest over Mosquito Creek Pass via Mail Cabin Trail. This trail, south of the road, follows Mail Cabin Creek west for six miles to Mosquito Creek Pass in the Snake River Range, then goes east down Mosquito Creek into Jackson's Hole. Nathaniel Wyeth's eastbound journal noted a crossing on July 17, 1832.

At Coal Creek, the historic Bircher's Roadhouse, built in 1905, provided an early haven for travelers. Writer Owen Wister remembered that clothes had been hung from ropes to partition the upper floor of the roadhouse into rooms. The barn and stables were across the road.

The roadhouse became a lifesaver when heavy snows and avalanches endangered mail and provision carriers alike. Old-timer Charlie Hedrick told how he was caught at the inn for three days. The inn was crammed with travelers waiting out an early-season snow storm, when the mail carrier stumbled in, having just escaped an avalanche that buried his team. Fed up with the pass, he trudged back to Victor. Later, Charlie and others found the horse team partly buried, weak but alive. After digging the horses out, they all shoveled and broke out the road into Jackson.

There are tall tales of the old Red Mud Hole, near the Bircher Roadhouse, its "bottomless" depths fed by a spring. With a bank on one side and a drop-off to the creek on the other, there was no way around it. One day, a wagon freighter came along and saw a hat floating on the surface of Red Mud Hole. Lifting the hat, he found cowboy Cal Carrington beneath its brim, his chin barely above the mud. "By gollies, Cal, you surely got into it; I'll go down to Victor and get some help." "Never mind," Cal says, "I'm a-horse-back and I think I'll make it."

Everybody who crossed Teton Pass had a story to tell, even the "Countess." Eleanor "Cissy" Patterson, the Countess Gizycka, her 11-year-old daughter, seven trunks, and her French maid had been met at Victor and loaded into a wagon for the trip over the pass to the Bar B C dude ranch in Jackson's Hole. At the base of the steepest part, the wagon stopped. "Them horses ain't elephants," the driver said. "They can't pull them trunks and y'all. You gotta walk!" So the Countess, in a beautiful tailored suit, her flaming auburn hair coiled up with jeweled hairpins, climbed up the pass ahead of the team in her custom-made walking boots, graceful as a deer and followed by an ecstatic daughter and a gasping maid.

From Coal Creek, WY 22 begins its looping switchbacks up the heavily timbered west-side slopes and through colorful red and yellow cliffs, gradually rising to the pass. The old horse-and-wagon trails followed a steeper route to the south, directly up Trail Creek. Cracking whips, lunging horses, and frequent rests accompanied freight to the top.

2.5 12.0 **Teton Pass** (BM 8,431). The pass and this parking lot lie between the Snake River Range to the south and the Teton Range to the north. Despite a straight-up, air-sucking trail, Mount Glory (10,086), immediately north, is probably your easiest way to bag a Teton peak. During the winter, Mount Glory and the ridges and bowls south of the pass provide some of the best skiing in Jackson's Hole, and you can't beat the price. The entire area is a snowbelt and powder heaven, thanks to the "cloud-milking" pass, where snow is released as clouds rise. Jackson's Hole and the Gros Ventres, in the Teton rain shadow, get what's left.

The trail south from the parking lot follows the divide of the Snake River Range, a crumpled, steeply tilted, sedimentary overthrust range. Depending upon the season, this 1.5-mile ridge hike, bike or ski leads easily upward through flowered or powdered bowls, to the Black Canyon overlook (el. 9,279). At the overlook, you can backtrack to the parking lot or take the trail that drops to the right, switchbacking three miles down Black Canyon to its junction with the Old Pass Road.

In October, 1889, Sylvester Wilson's clan lightened its wagon loads by caching provisions, then headed up Trail Creek, building a road as they went by cutting trees and piling brush ramps over fallen logs. With six horses helping on each wagon, the group pushed, tugged, and finally dragged their wagons up to the pass. After 11 days, families, wagons, and 80 cattle stood on the summit of the pass and saw the promised land—the lush hayfields and shining streams of Jackson's Hole. Then, as now, they looked upon West and East Gros Ventre buttes, the Fish Creek meadows, and the future site of Wilson.

Heartened, they turned to getting their wagons down the steeper east slope of Teton Pass. They changed wagon wheels, putting the larger back ones on the front axles to level the loaded wagon bed. They rough-locked the back wheels with chains and cut a large tree to drag behind; even after the "road" was built, this braking method was used.

Eventually, after a petition was signed, a mail route was established between Victor and the Hole. Those requesting the service carried the mail themselves for a year. In 1892, it took someone with endurance to carry those first mail loads into Jackson; he horsepacked in summer, snowshoed in winter, and was menaced in any season by fickle weather and snowslides. On the pass itself, carriers built a snow igloo; deep snows required a long slide down to the entrance. With coffee soon boiling, the snow began to drip on the mailmen.

The view from Teton Pass is both scenic and phenomenal—literally, one of phenomena. Amid the great beauty of the pass lies the story of an ancient geological collision that is still going on. Here, two structurally different mountain ranges, one rootless and the other rooted, came together: The "rootless" Snake River Range, lacking a Precambrian core, "crashed" into the "rooted" Teton

Range, with its solid Precambrian core. To demonstrate the power of this geological collision, it should be noted that the Cache Creek thrust and the Jackson Prospect thrust once lay 75 miles apart at Teton Pass; the two thrusts now are together. Geologists love the pass!

Moreover, your view from the pass also offers an idea of the magnitude of the ice river that once flowed through Jackson's Hole from the north. Ice moving southeast filled this area to within some 400 feet of the pass. From another perspective—standing at Wilson on the valley floor—the ice would have towered 2,000 feet above your head. That same ice flowed over the Gros Ventre Buttes and Snow King Mountain, visible to the east with the ski runs, but it never crested the pass.

0.1 12.1   From the east end of the summit parking lot, you can take a delightful hike down the switchbacking **Old Pass Road**, abandoned in 1970 in favor of the current highway. Wildflowers appropriate to their climatic zones offer a flowery paradise of seasonal display.

Descend Old Pass Road for 2.2 miles to reach **Crater Lake**, across the Mount Glory avalanche chute. In 1932, a slide swept down into Crater Lake and buried Harry Swanson, 14, in 40 feet of snow, where he stayed until the following spring. Others were luckier. Steve Leek described the experience of being caught in a pass snowslide. He said that when he heard the boom that erupted as the snow released, he wrapped his arms around a tree and hung on through a minute of sheer terror. He described the mist that followed the slide as suffocating and the noise as deafening.

During summer, Crater Lake had a more benign side: Old-timers drove cattle to corrals for overnighting by its waters, continuing on the next day to the Victor railhead. These days, people ski this section of the Old Pass Road, often a fast and slick track.

0.2 12.3 **Bucket Springs** (S). During the pass's heyday, horses were led to drink from these still-flowing natural springs. From the west end of the turnout, you can see the old springs below.

0.6 12.9 **Yellow cliff band**. At this pullout (S), this great yellow wall (N) across the road exposes one of the best fresh examples of mid-Cambrian Flathead sandstone and is the kind of roadcut on which geologists thrive.

0.1 13.0 **Mount Glory avalanche chute**. Where heavy rocks and dirt now fill this point below the narrow avalanche chute, state highway engineers first tried to straddle the gulf with a million-dollar steel bridge. Before the bridge could be used, however, avalanches of 1970 twisted it into a shapeless pretzel. Although avalanches are controlled in a variety of ways by the Highway Department today, slides block this entrance to Jackson's Hole every winter. The road's 10-percent grade also can act as a deterrent to free-and-easy travel.

0.6 13.6 **Phillips Canyon Road.** This bumpy road goes north two miles to a radio tower. It also accesses a delightful ski or hike, for those willing to follow vague signs and possibly misleading ski tracks. Both Ski Lake, a four-and-a-half-mile round trip, and Phillips Pass (el. 8,932), an eight-mile round trip, are popular destinations if you are looking for fantastic wildflowers and fine views. For a point-to-point excursion, continue down Phillips Canyon to Fish Creek Road, a seven-mile jaunt for hikers and bikers. Domestic sheep use the Phillips Pass area.

0.2 13.8 Parking for Phillips Canyon. Below this point and for the next 0.3 miles, the road cuts expose lava beds from an unknown source.

2.7 16.5 **Trail Creek Ranch** (S). This sharp turnoff to the south leads to the bottom of Old Pass Road. Early forest supervisor Louis Lockwood first built a roadhouse here. It was owned by Tom Lee when Owen Wister's daughter remembered the walls of the establishment papered in yellowed newspapers. Much later, Betty Woolsey—America's top woman skier in the winter "Nazi Olympics" of 1936—was skiing down the pass for the first time and saw this as the land of her dreams, so much so that she bought it from Nate Davis in 1943. It's been a popular dude ranch ever since. Today, the end of the road has ample parking for hike- or bike-ups and ski-downs.

0.8 17.3 **Elliott Cemetery.** The turnoff (S) leads to the burial spot of many Jackson's Hole pioneers. The cemetery was established on the Elliott homestead after the 1902 diphtheria epidemic killed two Elliott boys. Co-author of this book, Orrin H. Bonney, lies here, a natural chunk of his beloved Teton granite from String Lake marking his grave.

0.5 17.8 **Wilson** (el. 6,080 feet). Take the Fall Creek Road turnoff (S) to start Trip 10.

The Wilson Snake River bridge (above) during the 1925 Gros Ventre Flood.

Uncle Nick's Cabin (left) on Fish Creek.

The winter hazards of Teton Pass (below).

For years, the buildings at the bottom of Teton Pass have been the targets of out-of-control vehicles. In 1993, a dump truck loaded with rock careened off the highway and knocked Tom Waldron's old log cabin five feet off its foundation.

Once the promised land of the early Mormon families, Wilson has become a thriving special community with a mind of its own. It was named for Elijah N. "Uncle Nick" Wilson, who guided those first Mormons from Idaho. The village's first school stood just north of the highway. When it burned, a new one was built directly across from the Stagecoach Bar.

Today, "downtown" Wilson highlights include Sunday nights at the "Coach," cultural activities at the Snake River Institute in the Red Barn, breakfast at Nora's Fish Creek Inn, and shopping for everything from canoes to pins at old-timey Hungry Jack's.

0.2 18.0   **Fish Creek Bridge**. This area offers very limited access to excellent fly fishing after mid-July. Things were not always rosy in Wilson, though. The Gros Ventre River flood of 1927 submerged the small town under six feet of water; hundreds of cattle were lost, but no Wilsonites perished. The Wilson site has been flooded a half dozen times by the Snake because the valley floor tilts westward and Fish Creek is nine feet lower than the Snake River, which lies 1.6 miles east. Many folks question whether flood-control levees along the river can keep up with the westward tilt.

0.1 18.1   **Fish Creek Road** (Second Street), the turnoff to the north, was the early route to the valley's west-side ranches and Menor's ferry. It now dead-ends about five miles up Fish Creek and is a popular choice for running, biking, and horseback riding; the Phillips Canyon trailhead is located about 3.5 miles up the road, on a forested hill.

Turnoff (N) 0.1 miles to the site of Nick Wilson's homestead— the start of Wilson and the second cabin built on Fish Creek. Children once clustered around Uncle Nick to hear the exciting tales of his boyhood among the Indians and his Pony Express days, when he wore the red shirt, blue denims and leather boots of the legendary mail carriers.

Jim Imeson, husband of Susanah Wilson told how Uncle Nick wrote a book, using a two-finger system on an old typewriter, pipe clenched between his teeth as he slowly pecked out details of his life. Uncle Nick never went to school or learned to spell and probably a dude lady typed up uncle Nick's stories. The typewriter itself, an ancient model, had no ribbon; the keys had to be inked by hand before each word was typed. Jim read the original manuscript, full of apt expressions and Uncle Nickisms. All of his colorful language was lost when the book was edited by professor Howard Driggs and published as *The White Indian Boy.*

Wilson had a lot of firsts to his name: The post office (1898), run by his first wife Matilda; hotel (1899); store (1902); and "Wilson meeting house" (1902). He built a saloon and an eight-bedroom hotel across the street from his house, and ran it himself until his daughter, Edna Jane, and her husband, Abraham Ward, took over. The old Ward Hotel was razed in the 1980s as fire practice for the local fire department.

The Hardeman property north of WY 22, destined for development, and the Hardeman Meadows, to the south, part of a conservation easement, are part of the Nick Wilson homestead.

1.3 19.4 **Moose-Wilson Road**. This route north, WY 390, leads to Teton Village, the Jackson Hole Ski Area, and Grand Teton National Park (see Trip 11).

0.2 19.6 **Snake River Bridge**. There is access to the Snake River at both ends. Trappers crossed the river anywhere that looked good at the time, but they generally forded the Snake two to five miles downstream, between Boyles Hill and the mouth of Mosquito Creek.

In 1893, Ed Blair operated a ferry, but gave up the effort because the river kept changing channels and washing out approaches. In 1915, the settlers built a steel truss bridge in the area, but two years later, high waters washed out the soil and rocks, leaving the bridge unapproachable. For months afterward, communication was maintained via Menor's Ferry or by swinging a crate on pulleys and cable. When the water was low enough, a new ferry system was installed.

In 1922, the Snake was bridged permanently, and while that new structure held its own against the 1927 Gros Ventre flood, the approaches again were washed out. Since then, extensive levees have been built to confine the river and prohibit flooding to the west.

Crossing the Snake was never easy in the early days. When Idaho sheepmen first brought flocks over in 1886, Jackson Holers posted a warning and most herders turned back. One flock, however, reached the Snake and crossed on a wagon-bed bridge stacked with brush. Some 200 sheep were killed. The survivors were escorted east through the Hole and out over Union Pass.

East of the bridge, the highway bends south and directly ahead is Boyles Hill. The Skyline Ranch ponds (W), are a good birding stop; the local power company has even built a platform to encourage nesting osprey. The road then turns east, skirting the south end of West Gros Ventre Butte. Boyles Hill is south. The two Gros Ventre buttes were faulted and lifted at the same time as the Tetons and were subsequently whittled by erosion to an elevation of 700 feet, only later to become volcanically active.

3.2 22.8   Junction. **Spring Gulch Road** (Trip 3a), north.

0.4 23.2   **Antelope Pass**. This small rise in the road marks Antelope Pass, the break between East Gros Ventre Butte (el. 7,408) to the north and its southerly summit (el. 6,421). Both the Jackson and Cache Creek faults pass through this saddle before striking westward.

0.2 23.4   **The "Y."** The junction of WY 22 and U.S. 191-189 is commonly known as the "Y." The landslide developing below the highest house on the north side is not surprising. Inset into the hill, it and the other houses have been built on the unstable green clay of the Pliocene Shooting Iron Formation. The break in the slope between the butte and the valley floor is a fault scarp. A mild earthquake in this seismically active area probably would cause some property damage. Turn left at the junction.

1.4 24.8 **Jackson Town Square**.

Trip 3a
SPRING GULCH ROAD
(8.0 miles)

This scenic road, which contours along the base of East Gros Ventre Butte, should be driven slowly to appreciate its history and scenery—and for safety's sake. Spring Gulch Road, nestled between East and West Gros Ventre buttes, appears on a 1908 map. Even earlier, DeLacy's prospecting party, traveling north up this creek in 1863, described the valley as being large "and one of the most picturesque basins in the mountains," with "fine grass."

The Gulch was one of the first areas settled because it was lush with hay, was protected in winter, and had a good water source. Today, Spring Gulch has become a shortcut to Grand Teton National Park. It bypasses the town of Jackson and has good birding.

0.0 0.0 Junction of WY 22 and **Spring Gulch Road**. The road was partially blacktopped in the 1980s to access residential and resort development on East Gros Ventre Butte. Its pavement is great for biking and cautious rollerblading.

0.9 0.9 **Spring Creek Resort**. The road climbs eastward up a 2.3-mile grind, especially challenging in winter, to the top of the butte, where a hotel, restaurant, conference center, and a mass of row houses etch the horizon, all vying for a piece of the sublime Teton view.

0.3 1.2 **The Gulch**. This narrow valley, always rich in natural hay, attracted early ranchers like John Cherry, Lee Lucas and Bill Redmond (1893). Redmond sold to Bert Charter, who, in his youth,

75

was a member of the Butch Cassidy gang and, so the story goes, paid for the ranch with a bag of cash. P.C. Hansen ended up with the Redmond ranch. For the next few miles, the half dozen ranches you'll pass include that of former Sen. Clifford Hansen and his family (W)—one of just four Jackson's Hole ranches still run by those who started them. Here, you will find cattle, haystacks, high hay fences, irrigation systems and fascinating old-timey hay bailers.

Cliff Hansen was born in 1912 in Zenith, now a non-existent community to the north. "Wyoming is hell on horses and women," he says, and to prove his point, he tells of his mother, Sylvia Wood Hansen, washing diapers on a washboard, mending clothes, and caring for ailing family members, all by the light of a kerosene lamp or a "button bitch," a string stuck through a button floating in lard or oil. After completing those tasks, Sylvia took on the ranch chores.

1.5 2.7   Spring Creek Equestrian Center and Nordic Center. Coming up are 20-mph right-angle curves along the base of East Gros Ventre Butte.

0.5 3.2   The original 1908 road forked near here, the left fork heading north to the Gros Ventre ford and the Zenith area.

1.3 4.5   Spring Creek crossing. At this hard right angle, the 1908 road continued northeast across Lucas land, past the Warm Springs Ranch, and on to the Gros Ventre ford, where the U.S. 191 bridge now stands.

0.6 5.1   **John Cherry's Homestead.** Look east across the Lucas ranch to where John Cherry homesteaded—at the north end of East Gros Ventre Butte, near the old (Nickell) warm springs. The stories about and by Cherry are legendary. Due to conflicting records, not much is definite about his life prior to coming to Jackson's Hole. He may have been born on the Medina River in Texas, between 1853 and 1858; his real name might have been Ryan or Riley; perhaps he was brother of the notorious Nebraskan horsethief "Doc" Middleton and cousin to "Cowboy King" Buck Taylor, of the Buffalo Bill shows. Maybe a book was written about him and called *Life and Lies of John Cherry*. Old-timers talked about the book but nobody ever came up with a copy.

Some facts are reliable, though: Cherry settled in the Gulch in 1887 and proved up his homestead in 1901. He built a house, stables, corrals, and a racetrack (on the east end of the property, which now is under U.S. 191). He raised thoroughbreds, and ranchers liked to breed their mares with his registered stock. He was known to be "racehorse crazy." But where he got his fine stock was debatable: From his horsethief brother? Or maybe from his good friend and client Lewis S. Thompson, an Easterner whose father had "the strongest stable in the East?"

Because Cherry was a top hunter and guide with good dogs, his hunter clientele returned year after year. Thompson once took John to New York City, where John one day decided to walk into town. "Can you find your way back?" his host asked. "By gunnies, I shore can," Cherry replied. Imagine the consternation of the city dwellers as Cherry passed down the street hacking big blazes on their trees.

William Jennings Bryan and wife reportedly went hunting with Cherry. After cooking up a meal, Cherry called out: "It's all ready, by gunnies, let's eat," and he sat down. "We are not accustomed to eating with the help," Bryan reproved. "Oh, that's all right," John replied. "I'll be through here in a minute."

Cherry was one of Teddy Roosevelt's hunting guides in the Yellowstone. When bears wandered around camp, somebody offered $100 to anyone who could ride one. Cherry took the bet and hopped on a bear; they disappeared into the bushes. Some 15 minutes later, Cherry reappeared, scratched up and minus most of his clothes.

The stories about John Cherry followed him to Salmon, Idaho, where he spent 10 years fishing and prospecting beginning in about 1918. But he came back to Jackson's Hole and died at St. John's Hospital in 1931; he is buried in a plot east of the Henries' in Aspen Cemetery, at the base of Snow King Mountain. His stone, erected by friends, notes: John "Cherry" 1853-1931 Pioneer and Scout. His land now is part of the Lucas ranch.

In 1896, the *Wyoming Tribune* reported that promoters were staking out the City of Grand Teton at the northeast end of Spring Gulch, anticipating a population boom during the coming summer. The pipe-dream city—half a mile from the springs—may have been on or near Cherry's homestead.

The ancient gulch was not always so pastoral a scene, judging by the extrusive rock outcropping on the northeast corner of West Gros Ventre Butte (W). This vent once spewed lava, which soldified into basalt. Both the east and west buttes are *roches moutonnée*, overridden by nearly 2,000 feet of ice. Spring Creek is bounded on both sides by faults.

0.4 5.5 Cottonwooded floodplains of the lower Gros Ventre River.

0.3 5.8 **Gros Ventre River Bridges**. A pair of bridges cross the Gros Ventre River, now leveed beyond recognition. Because of irrigation demands, very little water makes it into these streams, except during high spring runoff. Alas, the lower Gros Ventre once supported blue ribbon fishing!

0.2 6.0 Kings Highway (W). This road enters a residential area west of the golf course. The old **Zenith Schoolhouse**, 0.2 miles west, now is a private residence, with a little sign identifying it. It originally was built between the Doug Price and Louie Waterman ranches, and constituted one of Jackson Hole's three school districts. That little one-roomer must have been typical; its one teacher, Mrs. Roberts, taught all grades. Small kids from ranches rode short-legged horses to school so they could get down and open gates. During winters, they rode bareback because the horses were warmer than the saddles. Much to Mrs. Roberts' consternation, moose used to bed on the school steps at night.

0.5 6.5 **Jackson Hole Golf & Tennis Club**. This resort comes complete with restaurant, swimming pool, tennis center, parking, and golf shop; the valley's most reasonable rates make this par-72 course popular, so make your reservations early.

The golf and tennis club covers the former Barber Ranches, originally operated by four brothers. John Barber married Cora Nelson (Price), who was the first white child in the valley. She rode across the pass behind her mother on a saddle horse, greatly annoyed by precious flatirons swinging from the saddle strings. Although the first Zenith post office was established by Harry Smith in 1902, the last was managed on the Barber Ranches, not closing until 1930. As with other post offices in the valley, the official "P.O." moved around from ranch to ranch. Zenith earned its name because of the altitude and because folks considered the area "the zenith of all places to live."

1.0 7.5 **Four-Way Junction**. To the west, little remains to suggest the existence of the lively community of **Zenith**. More recently, Zenith's old ranches along "Sagebrush Drive" have been subdivided into ranchettes with expensive houses. Some buildings on the old Price ranch—on the Snake's floodplain bench, two miles west on Sagebrush Drive—continue to be used by its current owners. The presidential entourage of Chester Arthur made its third Jackson Hole camp, Camp Teton, in this area. It was a dusty camp; dust blew into the presidential tent. A "banquet" was held here with Indians, and a "free tent" with all kinds of "liquid refreshments" was available.

The road north from this four-way junction passes several residential subdivisions and the less-junky backside of the Jackson Hole Airport.

Turn east from Four-Way Junction into Grand Teton National Park.

0.5 8.0 **Gros Ventre Junction**. From here, you can take Trip 7 north or south, or Trip 13 east. Near this junction, the first and only black family homesteaded in 1887.

Trip 4
TOGWOTEE PASS (EAST) ENTRANCE
From Brooks Lake Junction over Togwotee Pass
to Moran Junction
(32 miles)

In 1916, the first car struggled through the bridgeless streams, miring mud and chuckholes of the old wagon road over Togwotee Pass. Residents were congratulatory, but not overly impressed, believing the auto would never faze this country. They didn't foresee that modern roads would change the Rockies and Jackson's Hole forever.

Long before that first car traveled up the Wind River valley and across Togwotee Pass, prehistoric people were taking the same route to Jackson's Hole, the Yellowstone area, and beyond. The early Indians' presence is evidenced by the chippings from non-native stone found at their old campsites. At his camps, the Indian would take out his always-handy supply of rocks, found elsewhere, and start chipping out weapon heads to replenish his supply.

The first trappers did not describe Togwotee, so it was not as popular as the Hoback, Union or Teton Pass routes. In June of 1860, Jim Bridger tried to get the Raynold's expedition over Togwotee Pass into the Yellowstone, but the heavy snow forced them to take the Union Pass route farther south into Jackson's Hole. Even in June of 1880, when William A. Baillie-Grohman was at Fort Washakie, no one he spoke with had been to Jackson's Hole or knew of a route from the Wind River Valley.

Baillie-Grohman must have talked to the wrong people, because Charlie Hedrick came into Jackson's Hole via Togwotee Pass in 1896 and later described the experience: "We camped on top of the pass in the big meadow.... There was a trail... well-defined because it had been used for years by the Indians, and the tracks where they dragged their tepee poles behind the ponies were worn eight or 10 inches deep in the ground.... The Indians from the Wind River Reservation used to come over to Jackson Hole on hunting trips in the fall."

The Corps of Engineer's Captain W.A. Jones explored Togwotee Pass in 1873, as a route for an Army road. Returning east from the newly created Yellowstone Park, he had to bribe his rebellious guides to get the expedition from Yellowstone through Two Ocean Pass, down Lava Creek, and up Blackrock Creek, thus "rediscovering" the pass. He named it for his English-speaking Sheepeater guide, Togwotee, Shoshone for "Lance Thrower." In his 1875 report, Jones recommended that a wagon road be built across Togwotee and Two Ocean Pass into Yellowstone.

The early efforts of Captain R. A. Torrey of Camp Brown—present day Fort Washakie—to build a road in the area were stymied. In May, 1874, he was ordered to build a wagon road to the pass; he got within eight miles of the top and had to quit. In 1881, Wyoming's territorial governor, John W. Hoyt, also tried to get the federal government to build the road, but to no avail. Because of the 1895 Indian scare, however, Sen. F.E. Warren introduced a bill in 1896 to construct the road.

When the feds finally built the military road in 1900, between Fort Washakie and Fort Yellowstone, they took it via Union Pass (S) to Jackson's Hole and the Buffalo Fork River, and then west to Jackson Lake. Today, U.S. 287 and Trip 4, kept open by plow during the winter, is an integral part of the Continental Divide Snowmobile Trail.

From **Lander** (el. 5,357), via Fort Washakie, Dubois, and Togwotee Pass, it is 133 miles to Moran Junction in Jackson's Hole. Begin mileage log 100 miles west of Lander, at Brooks Lake Junction.

0.0 0.0   Turnoff (N) to **Brooks Lake Recreation Area**. This five-mile-long gravel road to the north follows old U.S. 287, ending up at the lodge and campground on Brooks Lake.

Wyoming Governor Bryant Brooks discovered the lake in 1889 by accident, while on a hunting trip. Studying the area through binoculars, Brooks spied a glistening lake surrounded by "fine primeval forests," its beach "dented by the innumerable tracks of elk and bear." At the lake, he also found great mountain trout lazing along, undisturbed by his presence. He described a smaller lake above, surrounded by rugged hills "whence burst forth countless springs."

The dramatic skyline of precipitous breccia "hills" around this valley are the southern end of the Absaroka Range. The cliffs to the west are topped by the Continental Divide and the Teton Wilderness boundary. There's a wonderful two-day hike around Pinnacle Buttes (E) via Bonneville Pass to Kisinger Lakes in the DuNoir Valley. It is best done counter-clockwise from the trailhead, which is a mile southeast of Brooks Lake campground, in an old clearcut east of Brooks Lake Road. The trail continues southeast, climbing around the south end of Pinnacle Buttes into the DuNoir. The trail north from Brooks Lake through Bear Cub Pass is a very popular entrance into the Teton Wilderness.

During the 1960s and 1970s, when the Forest Service started its "save-the-pines-from-the-pine-beetle-chomp-chomp" philosophy, Forest Service officials of the Shoshone National Forest allowed areas such as Jules Bowl, near Bonneville Pass, to be destroyed by clear-cutting. Next, oil and gas leasing became the threat to Brooks Lake, Pinnacle Buttes, Lava Mountain, and the DuNoir, much of which is critical grizzly habitat. Demonstrations and letters protesting the leasing gave the Forest Service pause, and Brooks Lake was withdrawn from consideration. With the fickle Forest Service, however, don't be surprised if you return to find oil derricks in the area, instead of pine trees.

Brooks Lake Lodge sits west of the campground. The lodge was built in 1922, to coincide with the opening of Yellowstone's South Entrance. The original Two-gwo-tee Inn was an overnight bus stop on the Lander-Yellowstone Transportation Company route. When the new open-aired, high-clearance White motor coaches, averaging 20-25 mph, rolled up with the first guests on July 1, 1922, the lodge was only roughly finished. The trip from Lander through Yellowstone to Cody, including meals and five nights' lodging, cost $158. When the trip became a one-day affair, the Two-gwo-tee Inn languished until the mid-1920s.

In 1924, Jim Gratiot bought the lodge and transformed it into the Diamond G, an incredibly successful dude ranch. In 1961, the Diamond G brand moved to the DuNoir and the building again became Brooks Lake Lodge. Twenty-six years later, Richard Carlsberg bought the lodge; with a facelift, Brooks Lake Lodge became a rustic mountain retreat, its walls hung with trophy heads from throughout the world—including a grand slam of bighorn sheep heads and a Siberian argolia sheep. He also restored one of the White Motor Co. buses. Carlsburg died in 1994. These days, the lodge is a busy feeding and relaxing station for summer and winter visitors alike.

After passing the lodge, old U.S. 287 circles back to U.S. 287. In the old days, the bus drivers' nightmare was skirting fearsome Barber's Point, a sharp turn with an exposed drop—wicked when wet. Driving below Barber's Point meant traveling on black gumbo; the upper road presented an equally exciting bentonite stretch. W.C. "Slim" Lawrence negotiated both routes as a Lander-Yellowstone Transportation driver. Today, the entire stretch of old U.S. 287 is used only by skiers, snowmobilers, bikers, and hikers.

0.4 0.4 View of **Brooks Lake Falls**.

0.4 0.8 Turnoff to **Falls Campground**, the site of an old tie-hack operation. Brooks Lake Creek cuts a neat little gorge where it pours over a hard ledge lip. This area was one of the locations for the movie *The Mountain Men* (1980), with Charlton Heston.

1.4 2.2 **Pinnacle Buttes** (N). The layered volcaniclastic rocks of these buttes to the north are dramatic because of dark beds of volcanic conglomerate interlayered with white tuff, some 45 million years old. Road cuts in this area expose more volcanic breccia and conglomerates.

0.9 3.1 Forest Service Road (S). This gravel road to the south accesses the heavily clear-cut Moccasin Creek area. From this vantage, the rounded, reddish cinder cone knob of Lava Mountain is south, the result of nearly 1,000 feet of horizontal lava flows derived from localized vents. South of Lava Mountain, the Wind River granites begin.

3.5 6.6 **Wind River Lake** (N). The turnoff north ends at a picnic area. Sublette Peak (N) is named for Bill Sublette, one of four brothers who trapped fur in Jackson's Hole. He and his Rocky Mountain Fur Co. partners—Jedediah Smith, the explorer, and

Davey Jackson, the field man—had half a million dollars worth of furs in 1827, which Sublette, the trading partner, took back East. To the south, old U.S. 287, a ski and snowmobile trail to Brooks Lake Lodge, rejoins U.S. 287.

0.6 7.2 **Togwotee Pass** (el. 9,658). This pass officially divides the breccia-walled Absaroka Range (N) from the Wind River Range (S), although the Absaroka breccias actually end at Lava Mountain (S), and the Wind River granites start at Fish Lake Mountain, 14 crow miles south. The tops of Two Ocean Mountain (SW) and Pilot Knob (three miles SE) define the Continental Divide, the boundary between Bridger-Teton (W) and Shoshone (E) national forests. From this watershed, the Wind River flows east and Blackrock Creek west. Geologically speaking, Two Ocean Mountain also is the southernmost remnant of the Wiggins formation, which comprises these gorgeous cliffs.

If you want to explore the Sublette Peak area during winter, take a Blue Diamond Ski Trail that goes east from Togwotee Pass, below the Continental Divide, through the saddle west of Sublette Peak, and then east down to Brooks Lake; return via old U.S. 287 to Togwotee Pass.

Old U.S. 287 and the pass have been the site of great hoopla. In 1900, National Park Service funds were used to realign, renovate and repair the Lander-Yellowstone highway (U.S. 287)—at the time considered in the "forest reserve." This set the stage for the official dedication of Togwotee Pass on Aug. 21, 1921. A barrage of publicity attracted all sorts of dignitaries from the National Park Service, city, county and state governments, as well as assorted politicians, Indians, reporters, and others. More than 160 cars thronged the pass, to gather for the dedication at 11 a.m.; the event touted the opening of a new era for the valley, meaning better highways and more tourists. As the services started, so did "great volumes of one-eighth-inch hailstones, snow and rain."

1.0 8.2 **Breccia Peak** (N) (el. 11,010). The highway travels below this notable wall of volcanic breccia, denoting the Teton Wilderness boundary and the rock basic to the Absarokas. The breccia makes for a miserable climbing rock, a crumbly "fruitcake" of volcanic pebbles and boulders mixed into the molten andesite lavas.

3.6 11.8 Bentonite-caused landslide. When the highway cut

through the old stabilized slide, its activity started again. Bentonite clay beds are the villain. During fall and spring, they slipped and swelled, opening cracks several hundred yards up the hill and often barred travel. When wet, bentonite becomes one of the slickest, gooiest materials imaginable. Because of this, it has a wide variety of uses in human industry, such as in drilling mud for oil wells, lining resevoirs, wine making, peanut butter and chocolate production.

0.3 12.1   Snowmobile paradise. Unfortunately, it is too easy for 'bilers to "crash" the low point of the Teton Wilderness boundary (N) between Angle Mountain on the west and the Breccia Cliffs on the east.

The small road north leads a quarter mile to the unsigned trailhead for **Holmes Cave**. The 12-mile round trip takes you north and northeast from the highway into the Teton Wilderness. To begin the hike, climb northeast for two miles to the low saddle in the ridge, the Teton Wilderness boundary. From this ridge, look NNE to get your bearings—a USGS topo map is recommended. Plot a route across the large meadow below (N) and directly toward a distant tree-encircled lake on a plateau off the north end of the cliffy ridge. The lake disappears as you descend a mile north across the meadow. Climb along a trail one half mile up to the plateau, which holds the lake. From here, the trail goes right or east of the lake. Continue another half mile past another lake south of Simpson Peaks to a big sink—more than five acres—in the center of which lies the small entrance to Holmes Cave.

The surrounding drainages pour into this hole, making it a place best explored in a dry season, with caving and climbing equipment. This tremendous underground labyrinth, winding 4,000 feet or more, consists of three chambers: the Wilson, Neda and Holland. The caves were discovered in 1898 by Edwin B. Holmes, John H. Holland and Neil Matheson, and were explored first in September, 1905.

2.4 14.5   **Flagstaff Road**. This logging and biking access road loops south through the Bridger-Teton National Forest (and grizzly bear habitat) before swinging back onto U.S. 287 at Hatchet Campground.

0.9 15.4   **Togwotee Scenic Overlook**. Take this turnoff north for the first panoramic view of the Tetons. Behind and above, to

Early Holmes Cave explorers inside the Holland Chamber (above), opposite the entrance.

Olga Mauger (right)—What Happened to her on her Honeymoon?

John Cherry (bottom) on his desert claim.

the northeast, is Angle Mountain, where the Precambrian core of the **Washakie Range** was buried beneath thousands of feet of volcanic debris from the Absaroka volcanic field, and only now is being exhumed.

In the 1930s, the southern margin of the Absarokas was a geological black hole and became the Ph.D. thesis project of young geology grad Dave Love. Certainly, Love did not expect to find that an entire granite-cored mountain range had been buried by the Absaroka's pyroclastic pile of Pinnacle Buttes, Breccia Peak, and the Ramshorn, to name a few. He traced the mountain range from the Owl Creek Range (south of Thermopolis) west through Togwotee Pass to this point. From here, it headed north through the Teton Wilderness, ending up at the South Arm of Yellowstone Lake. He named the buried range after the old Shoshone chief. The ancient range continues to be exhumed today, and its remnants can be seen handily in this spot and in South Fork Canyon to the north.

Another mystery in this area probably never will be solved. In September, 1934, Carl Mauger and his 21-year-old bride, Olga Schultz Mauger (sister of author Mrs. Bill [Edith] Thompson), spent their six-day honeymoon at a hunting camp in the Togwotee Lodge area. Hiking north one day, Carl headed up a steep hill, leaving Olga seated for a rest; when he returned in 20 minutes, she was gone, and so began one of the unsolved mysteries of the time. An intense search uncovered no clues to Olga's disappearance. Through the years, the story regularly turned up in the Sunday supplements, but nothing further ever was learned.

0.4 15.8   **Togwotee Lodge.** In the lodge, you'll find a restaurant, as well as guide services for hunting and fishing in the Teton Wilderness. The area is opened to snowmobiling and skiing in the winter. From the lodge area, a trail goes north into the wilderness to Angle Lakes and to the South Buffalo Fork Trail near the confluence of the North and South Buffalo forks. This is the shortest route to South Fork Canyon, where you can get a good view of the exposed Washakie Range.

Albert Angle opened the lodge in the mid 1920s. When he closed it on the first of December, taking his horses east over Togwotee Pass, he said he "pulled the pass shut behind me."

3.2 19.0   **Four Mile Meadow Picnic Area** (S). The turnoff north takes you on Turpin Meadows Road, the old U.S. 287 (see Trip 4a).

0.1 19.1 Dinosaur quarry in road cut. The south side of the highway yielded a mixed bag of fossils when this road was built—ceratopsian dinosaur fragments and remains of salamanders, fish, and alligators.

0.7 19.8 Overlook (S). Pull over for another view of the ever-impressive Tetons. The old Indian trail (S) was between Blackrock Creek (S) and the road.

2.4 22.2 Old landslides. The several slides along this stretch have given highway builders constant trouble because road cuts disrupted the once-stabilized slide. The culprit—quartzite pebbles. Geologist Dave Love believes the pebbles in this Harebell formation were carried here by powerful rivers that drained eastward from the now-subsided Targhee uplift, northwest of the Tetons in Idaho. No base rock like it exists in Jackson's Hole.

1.3 23.5 **Black Rock Ranger Station**. Now on the south side of the highway, the station once sat a half mile north. That earlier cabin was built in 1904 by the first ranger, Rudolph "Rosie" Rosencrans. It has been moved back to the station grounds, where you can examine skillful axe work that made the logs look as if they had been planed. Rosencrans, born in the Austrian Tyrol in 1875, graduated from Vienna University and was trained as an ocean navigator. He came to Jackson's Hole in 1903 and became a ranger of the Yellowstone Park Timber Reserve and, in 1908, the newly established Teton National Forest. The maps and plats he produced were invaluable through the years. He left Black Rock in 1927 because of failing eyesight and died in 1970 at the Jackson hospital. The prominent ridge with the summit beacon northeast of Blackrock Ranger Station is Rosie's Ridge.

North Jackson Hole originally was part of the Yellowstone Park Timber Reserve, the nation's first national forest. It was created on March 30, 1891 by President Harrison and was headed by the Interior Department's A.A. Anderson. In 1897, the Teton Forest Reserve was carved out of it. By Feb. 1, 1905, the forests were transferred to the Forest Service, managed by the Department of Agriculture. The name "Teton National Forest" became official in 1907. During Anderson's years, the forests were considered as timber reserved from exploitation for commercial gain. Today's more exploitive policy of multiple use on the nation's forests developed under later administrations.

In 1898, the Teton Forest Reserve required permits for grazing domestic animals within its boundaries. Such limitations caused outright resistance from stockmen. Breathing defiance, 40 armed men came up from Utah with 60,000 sheep, intent on grazing within the reserve. Anderson mobilized 65 armed rangers and met the invaders in Jackson's Hole. They served injunctions and issued fines for trespass. The flock was pushed over into the Green River country, where touchy cowmen killed 800 sheep and beat up a herder.

0.2 23.7 **Hatchet Campground Recreation Area** and **Spread Creek Road**. This gravel road winds and climbs its way south for 10 miles to a viewpoint of the distant Tetons, before entering the heart of the timber-covered prime grizzly habitat of the **Mt. Leidy Highlands**. It also is an approach to Mt. Leidy. The road was rebuilt in 1949 by Stanolind Oil Co., and has since become a confusion of junctions and two-tracks because of the numerous logging and oil-drilling roads. The Forest Service had to renumber these forest roads because so many had been added; for example, FS 014 now is FS 30160.

SPREAD CREEK ROAD

From U.S. 287 (Trip 4), turn south on **Spread Creek Road** (FS 30160) at the **Hatchet Campground**. Sagebrush Flat junction is 5.5 miles south. Here, you have two choices: 1) Either head east for Lily Lake and a roundabout driving approach to Mt. Leidy (el. 10,326), with a shorter climb to the summit, or 2) head south for a more direct approach to Mt. Leidy, with a longer climb.

1) For Lily Lake and the Flagstaff Road, take the left (E) fork another four miles to the lake (brook trout); the former fire lookout on Baldy Mountain was one mile north. From the junction east of Lily Lake, you can either continue northeast on Flagstaff Road (FS 30100) to U.S. 287, which makes a great biking loop, or turn east, then south up the South Fork of Spread Creek jeep trail about four miles to a second junction. Here, take the right (W) fork south a mile to FS 30250, which goes west up Leidy Creek to Leidy Lake.

Wells have been drilled throughout the area. At this point, you can take a track west a mile to climb Mt. Leidy (NW) by its southeast ridge; or take a track south a mile to climb the west ridge of East Leidy.

2) At Sagebrush Flat Junction, take the right fork south half a mile to Spread Creek (cutthroat, brook). Another 2.7 miles brings you to Skull Creek Meadows, named either for the numerous buffalo skulls found there, or for the alleged discovery of a human skull found near a bear trap, which had hand bones caught in it.

Continue 1.6 miles south, where the road ends at a drill site and old well, and the start of the climb of 10,326-foot **Mt. Leidy** by its long east ridge. The Mt. Leidy Highlands are a less-distinct mountain mass, with high ridges cut by deep stream drainages. This incredibly valuable roadless area had excellent wildlife habitat. Historically, elk migration went along this east side of the valley through the highlands. Development forced elk to migrate more through the park, which created elk-management problems. The entire area was omitted in the Rare II inventories because of ignorance.

Traditionally, Spread Creek and the Mt. Leidy Highlands have long been the site of fall hunting camps. In 1903, while accompanying her husband on such a hunt—outfitted by Frank Petersen and Henry Moser—the intrepid Mrs. Moser and her maid, both in full long-skirt regalia, made the first female ascents of Mt. Leidy.

(Return to U.S. 287 and Hatchet Campground.)

0.2 23.9   Hatchet Motel, coffee shop, film, gas, cabins.

1.5 25.4   The old **Hatchet Ranch** (S). Charlie Hedrick told about traveling up from Colorado in 1896 and over Togwotee Pass with his buddy, Smith, and arriving at the homestead of John Cherry and his partner, Jack Shive, at the bottom of the pass. Cherry—a talkative and friendly guide, prospector and trapper—welcomed the two men. He impressed Hedrick with his wild-looking hair poking out of the holes in his battered felt hat. Four or more Indian tepees stood around an uncompleted log cabin. When the first real snowstorm of 1896 struck on Nov. 1, Hedrick and Smith were still there to see what happened.

Hedrick described the scene: "As soon as the clouds broke... I climbed the lookout tower (used for locating horses)....I watched the elk coming out of the hills as long as I could see. That night there were five of us in that little cabin.... The elk crowded around the cabin so we had to shout to one another to hear.... It was one continual roar all night long. In the morning... elk were everywhere."

Because no survey had been done in the Hole, homesteads were staked out by "squatter's rights" until a survey of the valley was done. Cherry's homestead had a similar origin. He had two homesteads, one north of Jackson and a "desert claim" here. Under the Desert Claim Act of 1877, he "squatted" on a "dryland homestead" here, meaning no water was available and that there were no minerals of value and no timber. After five years, he could make his proof and receive a deed from the government after a survey. But Ed Hunter protested Cherry's claim, alleging there was coal on the land when there wasn't, and stating that the homestead had not been fenced. As a result, Cherry did not get his deed for 19 years.

When Jack Shive came into the valley in about 1889, he acquired a homestead adjoining Cherry's, by squatter's rights under the Homestead Act of 1862. The ranch was well-located for taking in wealthy Easterners for hunting in the Hole or the Yellowstone. But the Cherry-Shive partnership waned when Shive married Lucy Nessbitt in 1897. By 1917, Cherry had sold out to Shive.

The Hatchet Ranch, named for its colorful cattle brand, became the local social center. Frances Judge, granddaughter of John Shive, described the ranch and the life led by those early settlers: "When my people ranched here, there was no Grand Teton National Park; there was just the stupendous scenery.... And no one then would have dreamed of hiking anywhere for pure pleasure. You would have been considered completely crazy—and would have been. If there was time to go any place, you got into a wagon or on a horse and went fishing, huckleberry picking.... Hike? Hell no!"

And when folks tired of fishing, the Hatchet was the perfect place for many a night-long dance. Winter or summer, teams of horses jogged in from miles around, loaded with laughing people, food, and children, all ready to dance to the swingy calls of Grandma Shive, Hedrick's mouthharp, or the later rhythms of Hank Crandall's slide trombone and his wife, Hilda's, piano.

1.8 27.2 **Mount Leidy Highlands viewpoint**. To the south are the timbered slopes of the Mount Leidy Highlands, topped by the naked, fluted gravel ridges of Mount Leidy (el. 10,326). Professor Joseph Leidy was a comparative anatomist of the Hayden Survey. This dense pine and fir area provides a huge untouched home for animals, including the grizzly, but heavy timbering by the Forest Service threatens the habitat.

Geologically, this plateau-like upland is composed of Pinyon conglomerate, a gold-bearing quartzite that is between 1,000 and 1,500 feet thick; it is the oldest Tertiary formation in the area. Its summit ridges are stream gravel beds, once washed in by powerful rivers from the northwest. Subsequent earth movements pushed the summit 3,000 feet above the valley. Erosion and narrow drainage channels have continued to carve its higher ridges.

From this point, look SSW at the south edge of the floodplain traversed by the highway and you will see a draw emerging from the floodplain. Here are located several large seeps of flammable gas, the largest of which bubbles up through slightly sulfurous water in a 100-square-yard area. Another seep, when lighted, blows a continuous flare six inches high. It once was a favorite campsite for cattle-roundup wagons because wood chopping was eliminated: The cook merely put a vented metal barrel over the seep, lit the gas, and cooked meals on the barrel.

1.0 28.2 **Buffalo Fork River**.

0.1 28.3 Turnoff to **Turpin Meadows** (see Trip 4a). The turnoff north goes past Buffalo Valley summer homes and to Turpin Meadows and Turpin Ranch.

0.5 28.8 Abandoned coal mines. To the north are old tipples and dumps of abandoned coal mines. Some of the coal supplied the fuel during construction of the Jackson Lake Dam between 1910 and 1916.

0.3 29.1 **Lava Creek bridge**. An old road on the east side of the highway goes north for half a mile. The interesting cliff band upstream is Bacon Ridge sandstone and lies at the crest of the Spread Creek anticline. Some 20 miles long, it is the largest in the valley; it has seeps, but no oil or gas. A coal bed in the area also was mined by the Bureau of Reclamation between 1910 and 1916.

0.3 29.4 Enter **Grand Teton National Park**.

1.9 31.3 **Moran**. The school and post office are northwest.

The post office was moved in 1959 from its former site near Jackson Lake Dam; it was the Elk post office in 1931.

0.1 31.4 **Moran Junction**. (See Trip 6d, south to Moose and Jackson; Trip 6e, west to Moran, Grand Teton Park east entrance and Jackson Lake.)

Trip 4a
Turpin Meadows Road
(14 miles)

This detour, along an abandoned section of U.S. 287, has been known variously as the Atlantic-Yellowstone-Pacific (AYP) highway, the Lander-Dubois-Yellowstone road, and old U.S. 287. It wanders through the lovely valley of Turpin Meadows, where you might spot a grizzly and where old trapper trails take you to hunting and horse country, as well as to thrilling views of the Tetons.

Turpin Meadows provides access to the 565,000-acre Teton Wilderness, which was set aside by the U.S. Forest Service to be "preserved from commercialism." Lying south and east of Yellowstone Park, this wilderness abounds with big game, providing some of Jackson Hole's best hunting; within those preserved acres is the Jackson Hole elk herd's summer range. Turpin Meadows is an outfitting base for hunting camps, as well as the start of several trails into the Teton Wilderness.

In addition to offering cover to wildlife, this wilderness was the hangout of dinosaurs (their tracks have been found), and it is the hideout of the Washakie Range and horsethief trails. The Teton Wilderness was part of a major thoroughfare, as it lies on the Continental Divide and contains the headwaters of the Yellowstone, Snake and Buffalo Fork rivers. Early trappers knew it well, giving names to geographic features—such as Two Ocean Pass, Atlantic and Pacific creeks, and Bridger Lake—before 1872. Game-migration trails provided the routes that Indians and trappers followed, and the Forest Service had only to hang up the signs. A pack trip into this exciting country will reward you with scenery, adventure, good fishing, and a firsthand look at the results of a world-record tornado.

0.0 0.0 **Four Mile Meadows Picnic Area.** Turn north from U.S. 287 at the picnic ground (see Trip 4, Mile 19.0), and head north on a gravel road through a thick forest.

0.3 0.3 **Rosie's Ridge.** A road turns west and climbs the ridge to the summit with its beacon.

3.7 4.0 **Turpin Meadows Ranch.** The historical marker commemorates fiery-tempered Dick Turpin, who spent his first winter here in 1887, making the rounds of his trap lines.

By 1931, when Lester Leek owned the ranch, it was a different scene. That year, an all-expenses-paid tour of 40 people, mostly school teachers, was stranded at the ranch when its impresario guide skipped out with his clients' money. The news of stranded schoolmarms wildfired throughout the country, and cowboys, rangers, and other hopefuls stampeded to Turpin Meadows. It was a decided turning point in the social and cultural history of the valley.

0.2 4.2 **Buffalo Fork Campground.** The Buffalo Fork is one of the major forks of the Snake. The road west is oiled. Just north of the bridge, turn east to a junction: The left fork goes to summer homes; the right fork goes to public corrals, campground, parking, and a trailhead at the east end of the campground, for the North Buffalo Fork and South Buffalo Fork trails into Teton Wilderness. The latter trail leads to South Fork Canyon and a good exposure of the Washakie Range.

0.6 4.8 Box Creek Bridge.

0.5 5.3 Turnoff. Drive north for 0.6 miles to the campground, public corrals, and the start of the 14-mile (one-way) **Enos Lake Trail**. In August of 1987, the trail and lake both laid in the path of a fierce tornado that set a high-altitude record. Winds gusting up to 200 mph flattened timber along a northeasterly path between the Box Creek trailhead and Falcon Creek, destroying an awesome swatch of forest one to two miles wide and 20 miles long; some of the outfitting guides had some pretty interesting stories. You can study the tornado's swirling pattern of destruction from Enos Lake. In addition, the unexposed Washakie Range lies below the area.

2.8 8.1 Ranches, outfitters' camps, and homes. The view

Beaver Tooth Neil's Store (above).
A Ned Frost party in the Teton Wilderness, below Yount's Peak, on the Continental Divide.

opens on aspens, the Buffalo Fork, and Rosie's Ridge to the south. There's a turnoff south to a campsite and a shortcut road and bridge to U.S. 287.

0.3 8.4 **Tracy Lake**. This artificial lake is dammed and sits on private property. It was homesteaded by Randolph, who is the namesake of Mount Randolph (el. 9,180) and who caused ranger Rosencrans game-poaching problems.

2.0 10.4 **Lava Creek Trail** (N). The remnants of corrals and cabins at a horsethief hangout at the head of Lava Creek to the north still remained in the early 1900s. The old "Horsethief Trail" cut across Jackson's Hole some miles north of this road.

1.0 11.4 Overlook. Buffalo Fork valley, the Tetons, and Burro Hill to the south.

0.9 12.3 **Heart-Six Ranch**. Somewhere on this piece of private property, now packed wall-to-wall with outfitters, ranches, motels, gallery, and store is Charlie "Beaver Tooth" Neil's Buffalo River Ranch. He originally homesteaded this ranch and operated a store and gas station.

A valley character, Charlie Neil (1872-1936) stood six-foot-two, weighed 200 pounds, and was the "homeliest man" in the valley, according to Floyd Wilson, who worked for Neil. Black eyes puffed out like grapes, and a receding chin and prominent upper teeth earned him the name Beaver Tooth. One thinks of a Stetson hat and jeans as standard apparel for this frontier community, but when Beaver Tooth went to town, he dressed in a long black coat and derby hat, and carried a cane. He was kindhearted and generous, and no man was ever turned away from his door hungry or for want of shelter.

Despite these good qualities, however, his lifetime vice was his delight in outsmarting the law and diddling his hired help out of wages and his customers out of gas at the old pump. From the time he came to Jackson's Hole in 1908 until he died, Neil spent limitless energy trying to outwit the game wardens. He had a lengthy conviction record, mostly for poaching and, for two decades, he kept game wardens busy. Actually, the game wardens honed his talents. He learned the hard way never to plead guilty. The one time he did, he was taken to Evanston and Salt Lake City via train and jailed at county expense; when released, he had no money and had to walk home.

After that, around trapping season, wardens would pick him up—without cause—and take him south. Though Neil was not necessarily guilty, the season would be over by the time he walked home. This taught Neil to avoid being caught, so he became a master of trickery. He boasted of his tricks but never used the same ploy twice. He used his fertile imagination to get beaver pelts over Teton Pass.

For example, so the story goes: One day, Mrs. Neil arrived in Jackson on the stage, with her suitcases in tow. She was bruised, skinned up, and limping. She told everyone there that her husband had gone crazy and had given her a terrible beating. She was leaving. She told one game warden at the hotel: "You just watch that Charlie; he's coming down here in a few days with a big shipment of furs." The next morning, the warden helped her load her trunks on the stage, and over the mountain she went.

Four or five days later, old Charlie showed up with a little packsack for luggage. The game warden watched him closely until Charlie told him, "You can jist quit watching me; I don't have any fur. Mrs. Neil's already got it in Kansas City. You helped her load her trunks on the mail stage here, and they were jist full of beaver hides."

Charlie Neil knew all the poaching tricks too. Once, he confused his pursuers by wearing his snowshoes backward to make it look like he was headed in an opposite direction. It worked, but he recalled that he "nearly pulled the tail outta that dog teaching him to walk backwards." Another time, he fixed elk hooves to his shoes to hide his footprints. Yet another time, game warden Fred Deyo, trying to catch Charlie redhanded, came upon a trap with a beaver in it. At that moment, Neil came out of the willows with a witness and made much of catching a warden poaching.

Because the gas station brought in only minimal revenue, Neil began looking for a more profitable business. As he got older, such winter business as trapping brought on aches and pains, so Charlie advertised in sports magazines as a "buyer of furs," offering great prices for catches; the furs poured in. He kept no records and sent the furs on to a reputable buyer. Eventually, the scam roused postal inquiries because of missing mail. This time, Charlie outwitted the postal inspectors by dying. To close the case, Dr. Huff had to depose that indeed Beaver Tooth Neil was dead.

Above all, Charlie Neil provided Jackson Holers with a tremendous fund of stories. According to *The Courier*, he had for two decades "occupied a prominent place in the Justice Court's records."

The road west travels the bench above the Buffalo Fork valley, with a full view of the Teton Range.

The 1872 Hayden Survey described the Buffalo Fork's "Broad Valley"—which it ascended to the South Fork Canyon—in some detail, mentioning "These bottoms containing some large groves of Menzie's spruce, (Abies menziesii) whose peculiar cones were seldom seen elsewhere by us." [Editors note: this species is now known as Douglas fir *(Pseudotsuga menziesii)*]

1.4 13.7   Junction with U.S. 287, Trip 4.

YELLOWSTONE (North) HIGHWAY
From Yellowstone South Entrance
to Jackson Lake Junction
(23 miles)

This historic route is one of Jackson Hole's most fascinating. Hidden in the thick, dark pines along this highway lie the giant claw marks of past ice ages, the rutty tracks of Indian travois, the soft-scuffed trails of moccasined mountain men, and secret cabins hiding shadowy men from the law.

The first comprehensive study of Jackson's Hole was done in 1872 by the Hayden Survey's Snake River division, as reported by the division's chief geologist, Frank H. Bradley. Bradley's nutshell summary sounds like the study team went through the Hole like a dose of salts as it headed south from Yellowstone. It "examined all the headwaters of the main Snake River, and descended that stream, via Jackson's Lake and the Grand Cañon, to its emergence into the Great Basin..." in 24 days—from Sept. 12 to October 5. Fast-moving parties on horseback, with a pack horse or two, swarmed over Jackson's Hole on side trips—up major drainages and into the Tetons—gleaning a massive amount of data.

The Doane winter expedition of 1876 took this route. Lt. Gustavus C. Doane, Sgt. Server and five soldiers left Fort Ellis, Montana Territory on Oct. 11, 1876, equipped for an arctic environment. They had horses, 60 days' provisions, a tepee, buffalo coats, carbines, and material to build a boat when they reached

Yellowstone Lake. They planned to winter explore the Snake from Yellowstone Lake through Jackson's Hole to the Columbia River. U.S. 287, the Yellowstone Highway is plowed all winter and as such is the route of the Continental Divide Snowmobile Trail into Yellowstone.

0.0 0.0 **South Entrance to Yellowstone Park** and **North Entrance to the John D. Rockefeller Jr. Memorial Parkway.** In the 1920s, when the first tourists drove over Togwotee Pass to Yellowstone, they reached this point, only to learn that auto travel was a no-no in Yellowstone. Cars had to be hauled to West Yellowstone via freight wagon. If you look east across the Snake River and the grassy flat beyond, you can see the numerous hot springs that emerge from fossiliferous sandstone, about a half mile east. Others are a mile east.

Doane described them on November 18, 1876. "Most of the strongest springs were in the bed of the stream, all of them were Snake River Geysers. That is they flowed continuously from small craters. One jet was four feet in height and six inches in diameter; a boiling fountain, without impulsions. . ."

The Hayden surveyors camped here for five days, exploring the Snake's hot springs (E), the Upper Snake to its source and other drainages and ridges in today's north Teton Wilderness. Westward they discovered the Bechler and Falls rivers. "Beulah Lakes," and the heavily timbered "basaltic" Pitchstone Plateau.

Connecting Yellowstone and Grand Teton national parks, the **Rockefeller Parkway** memorializes the extraordinary efforts of John D. Jr. He rescued Jackson's Hole from the "progress" of predatory commercialism by buying 33,562 acres of private land and turning it over to the National Park Service in 1950 to create a larger Grand Teton National Park.

0.5 0.5 Parking and Snake River access (E). Later in the season, you can pick your fording spot along the river here to reach the hot-springs areas, half a mile and a mile east.

From this point south, U.S. 287-89 loosely follows the Snake and the "Military Road" of President Arthur's 1883 party. It also parallels the Teton National Forest and the Teton Wilderness, to the east. As the highway rolls through lodgepole-pine country, it's hard to miss the patches of blackened trees and new growth, the result of the 1988 summer of fire.

1.5 2.0 Turnoff (W) to the relocated Flagg Ranch, Flagg Ranch Campground, and the **Grassy Lake Reclamation Road** to Ashton, Idaho (Trip 5a).

Beginning in 1995, Flagg Ranch was moved from the lower bench, a tenth-mile to the south, to this higher bench in the trees. Flagg Ranch now has greatly expanded facilities, becoming a major supply point for the snowmobiler and auto visitor. Its amenities include horse rentals and float and fishing trips. All this expansion has, however, destroyed a lot of prime grizzly habitat. As part of this rinky-doo political game, the Grassy Lake Road, Trip 5a, is closed annually throughout April and May.

0.1 2.1 Rockefeller Parkway Ranger Station (W).

0.4 2.5 **Original Site of Flagg Ranch** (W)

0.1 2.6 Snake River Bridge

0.1 2.7 **Sheffield Camp** (W) and **Sheffield Creek Trailhead** (E). Sheffield's Camp, according to the 1911 Shoshone topographical map, was south of the Snake River bridge. Ever since Ed Sheffield opened the Snake River station, this area has been a camp and supply point for dudes and visitors. The station offered "a splendid accommodation for the tourist," and was the midway camp for the clientele of his brother Ben. Ben's dudes horse packed from Yellowstone down to Jackson Lake and motor boated to (old) Moran.

Hunting guide Ben Sheffield built his road along the old Military Road to transport wealthy clients to his camps. It twisted and pitched its way south along the western base of Huckleberry Mountain (E) to Jackson Lake. The brothers wanted the country to remain primitive to preserve good hunting. In 1910, however, the government condemned the road to use it in the reconstruction of the Jackson Lake Dam.

The unsigned road, to the east, is the Sheffield Creek Trailhead and fords Sheffield Creek (high in the spring), which forms the boundary between the memorial parkway and Teton National Forest, and enters the Huckleberry burn of 1988. The road provides access to the Teton National Forest, Teton Wilderness, Sheffield Creek campground, public corrals, and the Sheffield Creek trailhead (near the information board). The trail climbs east five miles to the **Huckleberry Mountain Lookout** (el. 9,615), on the wilderness boundary. This historic building was the valley's first pre-fab structure, built below and toted up the long timber-covered ridge (E). Even earlier, the mountain was an elk-tusker hangout, as evidenced by several log-gabled, earth-covered shelters, part of a string of six such huts across the country. A gun silencer (J.H. Museum) also was found here.

The Teton Wilderness, where dinosaurs once roamed—their footprints have been found—is the summer range for the Jackson Hole elk herd and the heart of Jackson Hole hunting.

0.3 3.0 **Snake River Day Use Area** (W). The turnoff west leads to this former campground. Its status was changed because this is prime grizzly country and because of the nearby Flagg Ranch campground.

1.0 4.0 From Yellowstone's South Entrance, the highway follows a geologic transition zone into Jackson's Hole. Beginning about here, the road is flanked by the tan-colored ash-flow deposit of the Pliocene Huckleberry Ridge tuff that came out of Yellowstone's vulcanism 2.1 million years ago.

1.3 5.3 Dime Creek Pullout (E). The highway parallels Dime Creek, which is in the little valley below (W). Also below is a trace of the old freight road (Trip 5a) that followed the creek from the Snake River ford just northwest of this point.

0.5 5.8 **Old Freight Road**. From the pullout at the top of the hill, you can see the old freight road cutting across the hillside to the southwest. The Dime Creek camp, built in this area in 1910, was a freight-wagon stopover between Ashton, Idaho (W) and old Moran (S). When heading for Ashton, freighters took a big shortcut at this point by fording the Snake west of here before joining the newly built Reclamation Road in Soldiers Meadows (Trip 5a); they then continued west to Ashton along a section of the old Marysville Road. One of the Hayden Survey side trips took the same route to Beulah Lake.

0.7 6.5 **Buffalo Glaciation**. At this point, the road passes through one of the numerous hollows grooved by an ice sheet of this second-to-last glaciation, which moved south from Yellowstone Park into Jackson's Hole.

0.1 6.6 Enter **Grand Teton National Park**.

About one mile west on the Snake, Lt. Doane's 1876 party came across hundreds of otter growling from holes in the bank as the boats passed by. The men shot several of the mammals for food. "Later, Starr cooked one of the fine otter," Doane reported. "The flesh was nice looking… fat and tempting. Baked in a dutch oven and fragrant with proper dressings, we anticipated a feast, were helped bountifully and started with voracious appetites. The first mouthful went down, but did not remain. It came up without a struggle…. The taste was delicately fishy, and not revolting at all, but the human stomach is evidently not intended for use as an otter trap. Like Banquo's ghost, 'It will not down.'"

2.9 9.5 **Lizard Creek Campground** and Fonda Point. The Point is used today for crossing Jackson Lake directly to the single trailhead for Berry Creek, Owl Creek and Webb Canyon trails. The Point got its name when Ranger John Fonda broke through the ice while skiing across.

Across Jackson Lake, the north end of the Teton Range becomes prominent, rising to the south but disappearing to the north, buried under the Pitchstone Rhyolite Plateau of Yellowstone Park.

0.2 9.7 Lizard Creek Crossing.

0.5 10.2 Pullout (W) beyond Lizard Creek Crossing. The mouth of Lizard Creek is just north, marked by willows. This creek is unidentified on the *Shoshone* Quad of 1911, but the next creek, three miles to the south, is labeled Lizard Creek on the 1901 *Grand Teton* Quad. On today's maps, it is Arizona Creek. Somewhere down the line, the name Lizard Creek was switched. Historically that puts the Edwards Ranch freight stop on Lizard Creek actually on Arizona Creek, which is more of a midway stop, mileage-wise, between Dime Creek and old Moran than is today's Lizard Creek.

0.9 11.1 Pullout (W). According to the *Grand Teton* Quad of 1901, you are looking at the route of the Indian-Trapper Trail where it forded the Snake. At this point, the trail, coming up from the south, headed west, employing the long-used prehistoric ford to connect with the Berry Creek/Owl Creek/Webb Canyon trailhead (W) at the mouth of Webb-Owl creeks.

North Tetons

A. *Eagles Rest.* B. *Doane Peak.* C *Wilderness Falls.* D. *Waterfalls Canyon.* E. *Ranger Peak.* F. *Colter Canyon.*

0.4 11.5 **Jackson Lake** viewpoint, with a park sign of the 1974 Waterfalls Canyon fire. In pre-dam days, this point overlooked the marshy Snake River floodplains; the natural north end of Jackson Lake was two miles south. Arizona Island (S) probably was part of the mainland. The old Trapper Trail/Military Road passed along this bench.

Looking west, three canyons drain the west side of Jackson Lake. The most southerly one that swings left is wild and beautiful Webb Canyon, where Johnny Graul operated his mystery mine. Even his good friend, Slim Lawrence, who took him supplies, didn't know what Graul was mining. For 23 years, Graul slowly chiseled away solid basalt to carve an opening and shaft. On a rare trip away from Jackson's Hole, a misstep pitched him to his death in a Colorado mine shaft—on a Sunday, a day he reportedly never worked.

Deeply cut Owl Creek forms the central canyon of the three. It holds not only the Owl Creek drainage, but has eaten behind Elk Ridge (el. 8,470) in the foreground, to steal Berry Creek, which once flowed through its own canyon to the north. Berry Creek is the third northern canyon.

0.4 11.9 **Archaeologic Overlook**. Picnic site (pit toilets). When Jackson Lake was lowered to its natural level for intense repair work on the dam in 1983, a five-year archaeological project took place, under National Park Service archaeologist Melissa Connor. A gold mine of artifacts from 109 sites, the traces of the bygone summer campers, were located on the lake's exposed edges. Fire rings, bone fragments of bison, elk and rodents, and hundreds of stone artifacts pointed to a way of life after the glaciers disappeared. (Please note that it is illegal to remove archaeological finds.) The different obsidians indicated that these people had connections with trade sites in Idaho and on the plains to the east. The largest campsite was near the old Snake River ford and the lake's natural inlet.

Traces of **prehistoric hunters** are found throughout Jackson's Hole, even 400 feet below the summit of the Grand Teton, and archaeologists have been piecing together a fascinating story about the "Early People" who used the valley after the last ice age, based on evidence at some 1,100 sites.

Research shows that the glaciers retreated about 15,000 years ago. Earliest evidence, a Clovis point, suggests that people have been using the valley for 11,000 years. There was scattered use between 1,500 and 9,000 years ago, and "relatively consistent use"—meaning relatively little use—thereafter. According to Charlie Love of Western Wyoming College in Rock Springs, the valley was more a stopover than a destination; few large mammal bones were found in the Jackson Hole sites. Why? The valley probably was too cold and barren to support the large prehistoric herds. Just consider the Early People's lifestyle: small family bands of 50 or less, with children and traveling on foot, necessarily taking the easiest route—along low passes, with no snow and shallow river fords.

This is the view Early People enjoyed. The most massive peak north of the Grand is Mount Moran (el. 12,605), with its obvious north-side Triple Glaciers. At the base of the Tetons, the break in slope marks the Teton normal fault, movement of which began less than 9 million years ago; it's still moving. Looking SSW, gray Madison limestone cliffs intersect the lake and are cut off by the Teton fault; a half-mile-long series of hot springs (135 degrees Fahrenheit) emerges from the fault trace at the rate of 2.4 million gallons a day.

The Teton mountain front is the youngest (less than 9 million years) and the steepest of the Rocky Mountain chain. The unique Teton/Jackson Hole scenery is a product of an unusual geologic history. The record of sedimentation, volcanism, and tectonism shows one of the thickest, most complete, and most complex sequences in North America. Tectonism is still occuring, which explains the fresh, jagged appearance of the Tetons, the anomalous drainages, the abundant landslides, the narrow canyons.

0.5 12.4 **Arizona Creek Trailhead** (E). Drive 0.4 miles to the old corrals. The trail takes off to the left of these, and goes north five miles to Bailey Meadows and another four miles to the north end of Brown Meadows, where it meets Rodent Creek trail (going east), and Sheffield Creek Trail, near the wilderness boundary. The latter trail climbs the wilderness ridge north another three miles to the Huckleberry Mountain Lookout.

Arizona George wintered on Jackson Lake in 1888-89. Amateur archaeologist and historian W. C. "Slim" Lawrence found a carefully hidden log cabin in timber along Arizona Creek. The

Slim Lawrence at Ed Sheffield's Snake River Station (top), built in 1905-06 of material from the Soldier Station, just a few miles to the west, when it was abandoned.

Fire Ring campsites (above, left) on the Pre-dam shoreline of Jackson Lake.

Tusker Cabin (above, right).

Ed Harrington, alias Ed Trafton (left), after the robbery of 15 Yellowstone coaches, with his wife and daughter.

The building of Sheffield Lodge (below), of Moran.

building had no doors or windows, just a 14-inch-by-20-inch opening in the south wall and a roof constructed with expertly hewn boards. When Lawrence touched two gunny sacks wired to the ceiling, they crumbled, spewing out dishes and a can of staple foods. A moldy-smelling remnant of an imported cashmere shirt hung on a nail. Lawrence recognized the site as a tusk-hunter cabin. The Lawrences trapped in this area until 1950, operating two trap lines with some 150 traps.

0.1 12.5 **Arizona Creek Crossing** gives only a quick view of its little canyon (E). This creek was called Lizard Creek on the 1901 *Grand Teton* Quad. Pull up in 0.1 miles at an open patch on the shoulder of the road. To the west is the remains of an old road in a large clearing, site of the Edwards Ranch, as located on the 1901 *Grand Teton* Quad. The ranch, on the old Trapper/Military Road (W), was the third night's stop on the rigorous Ashton-Moran wagon road. Lacking other amusements, this small tent settlement, clustered around Edwards' log cabin, became a mecca for practical jokers, outrivaling Jackson's "jobbing" fame. For example, the dam's electrician once rigged two glass marbles like eyes peering through two peepholes into the women's latrine. When the battery button was pressed, they "blinked," as if a bobcat was staring in at the occupant.

According to the 1901 quad, Lizard (Arizona) Creek did not flow west into the Snake, but flowed southwest two miles across the marsh into Jackson Lake itself. (In the very dry year of 1994, this checked out.) The Trapper/Military Road cut across the creek a short distance below (southwest of) today's road. Traces of the old bridge logs have been found. Arizona Island was either a peninsula or a high piece of marshland. It also was a prehistoric and pre-dam site. At a two-room cabin site found on the island by the archaeologists, was garbage—broken beer, wine and soda bottles, bullets and cartridges for a minimum of 17 types of weapons. Obviously the cabin was used by hunters who target-practiced a lot!

1.1 13.6 Obscure short gravel road (W) leads to a steep trail down to a small bay (locally called Arrowhead) and a lakeshore fishing site. This bay was an Early People campsite. It was also the site of the Lakeview Ranch, established along the old road (W) on the point of timber on the bay's north shore. Its foundations might still mark the spot. An old outhouse was there in 1989. The ranch also was on the northeast shoreline of the pre-dam Jackson Lake. The outfit turned out to be an aborted attempt by G.H. "Herb" Whiteman and the Heighos to get into the dude business in 1896. Beside this roadhouse, Cora Heigho (pronounced Hee-oh) opened the Antler Post Office from March 23 to Dec. 1, 1899.

1.1 14.7 **Arizona Lake Trail** (E). Drive 0.5 miles to parking. This two-mile trail follows the dim tracks of an old road east a mile—downfall forces little detours—to a ridge overlooking a large willow/grassy swamp. To avoid the swamp, the road or trail descends some 100 feet, then swings north 0.1 miles to jog east again across a ford and through forest and willow patches. East of the meadow, the faint road or trail, almost obscured by downfall, turns north a mile to Arizona Lake, following a little valley scoured by a large ice sheet, which moved south from Yellowstone Park during the Buffalo glaciation. From the air, the huge south-trending grooves between Pilgrim Creek and Yellowstone Park look like giant claw marks. This ice sheet was 1,500 to 2,000 feet thick and probably covered more than 1,000 square miles in Teton County alone.

0.5 15.2 **Overlook** and picnic area (W). The view below through the trees is the upper end of Sargents Bay. There's a trail northwest down to the north shore, where John Sargent had his little store along the old Military Road.

1.1 16.3 Turnoff (W) to a fork: Left is **Leeks Marina** and to the right is the **University of Wyoming-NPS Research Center**. Leeks Lodge was the tent-cabin hunting/fishing camp of **Stephen N. Leek** (1858-1943), who homesteaded in South Park in 1888 (Trip 1, Mile 45.4). One of the valley's first guides, he explored and was instrumental in placing the **Trappers Monument**—just south of the marina fork in the road—marking the old trail that passed this point. It forded the Snake at the north end of the natural Jackson Lake (at Mile 11.1) to join the Berry Creek trail. Leek had a hunting lodge on the north end of Leigh Lake and "used to... feed his dudes raw meat... [because] he imagined they were out to exemplify the crude lives of the early" explorers. They were not disappointed.

The private road leading right (N) from the Leek marina area goes to the **University of Wyoming-NPS Research Center**, which conducts environmental research on the Jackson Hole/Yellowstone

Park areas. The center is located on the former Marymere/Mae-Lou/AMK (Berol) Ranch, which became park property in 1976.

The Berol Ranch started out as Marymere—"a hotel for the accommodation of travelers." The original lodge was built in 1890 by remittance man John Dudley Sargent, the black sheep of a wealthy Maine shipbuilding and lumber family that included artist John Singer Sargent. Sargent, a Jekyll-and-Hyde type bordering on genius, madness and sickness, was a manic depressive who had drifted into the Hole twice before settling on the site. In 1890, he brought his wife, Adelaide, and baby, Hemingway, into the valley via the Conant Trail. His partner in the enterprise was Robert Ray Hamilton (descendant of Alexander Hamilton), a 37-year-old lawyer, a New York legislator, and "a wealthy young club man." In 1889, Hamilton clandestinely married Evangelina Steele, an actress with an unsavory background, and thus was ostracized by his friends and family. In a family squabble, Eva tried to stab Hamilton, and the ensuing investigation revealed that he was a victim of a conspiracy by Eva and her common-law husband, which involved convincing Hamilton that a newborn baby was his.

On a hunting trip west in May, 1890, Hamilton met and became the partner of Sargent, and together the two hired a crew to build a 10-room lodge (22 feet by 70 feet). Two Swedish log workers from Ashton finely whipsawed the logs and pegged the corners. The lodge was elegantly furnished, and everything—including a classic library, one of the best in the valley, a piano, and a sailboat—had to be horsepacked across Conant Pass at the north end of the Tetons. Hamilton was, however, drowned in the Snake that same August (Trip 6a, Mile 4.0). Hamilton's estate went to the child; Eva sued from prison for her share. Newspapers questioned whether Hamilton was indeed dead, pointing out that it had been impossible to identify the body after 12 days in the water; that Hamilton had trouble proving his case for annulment; and that his wife was countersuing. In 1891, the questions prompted officials to exhume the body, buried near Marymere, and return it to New York, where it was positively identified as Hamilton's.

Unfounded rumors of foul play—that Sargent killed Hamilton to gain sole possession of the ranch—persisted. The valley's opinion was summed up in a diary entry of Dr. J.K. Mitchell, who later traveled through the Hole with Owen Wister: "All Jackson's Hole, a community of scalawags, renegades, discharged soldiers and... predestined stinkers, unite in the belief that Sargent killed H." At the time, however, the Hermit of Jackson Lake was in Idaho, getting supplies and mail. Sargent had alienated many locals with a crusade that named violators illegally killing elk on the Forest Reserve in Jackson's Hole.

The lodge was an attempt at dude ranching, which failed. Sargent had registered cattle, and even kept hogs on Hog Island, which doubtless gave the island its name. It took him years to prove up on his land, probably because of the lack of a survey. In the 1900s, Sargent operated a small store—a self-serve establishment limited to candy, tobacco, milk, and, of all things, Victor talking machines and RCA records, for which he had the RCA sales contract—in a cabin next to the Military Highway-Freight Road. As the northernmost homestead in the valley, Marymere became a travel stop and roadhouse, because the Trapper Trail (over Conant Pass to Idaho) passed just to the west of the Sargent homestead, and the Yellowstone Military Road passed just east. Travelers used a short secondary loop, which went right by the Sargent cabin, to access campsites south of the ranch buildings.

But the undisciplined wilderness was no place for Sargent's civilized vices; he was "brought before the public" several times in the next few years. Then, in May of 1897, some soldiers skiing down from Yellowstone passed Marymere and heard a woman screaming. Nobody answered their knocks so they reported the matter in Jackson. Upon checking, Mr. and Mrs. D.C. Nowlin, and Mrs. Sam Osborne found Mrs. Sargent badly beaten, "while Sargent, steeped in the fumes of opium and morphine, calmly awaited the moment of her death." They loaded Mrs. S. on a sled and took her to Jackson. In the few days she lived, she said Sargent had beaten her and also "repeatedly assaulted one of the little daughters." She was buried in Jackson, and the five children were sent to Eastern relatives. There were threats of a lynching party but Sargent disappeared. Two years later, he turned himself in at Evanston, where he eventually was tried and acquitted.

Marymere again became the source of stories in 1906, when Sargent married Edith Drake. At various times, she was seen wandering naked through the forest, sitting in a tree taking sunbaths, or playing her violin. Rumors abounded: Was she mentally ill? Or did Sargent keep her clothes from her? Did he get paid to care for her? She eventually was returned to a New York mental institution. The violence and rumors all came to an end in 1913 when, in the living room of Marymere, with the Victrola playing "Ye Who Have Yearned Along," Sargent sat before the fireplace, "placed the barrel of his 40-90 rifle in his mouth, tied a string to the trigger then to his big toe, pulling the trigger in this manner." Marymere subsequently was sold for $746 in unpaid taxes.

The second major owner, Lou Johnson, built a fine, New England style house near the Sargent cabin; it was two stories, as Mrs. J. wouldn't sleep on the ground floor because she was afraid of bears. After the Johnsons died, the estate administrator, Irving Trust Co., ordered Slim Lawrence—under threat of being fired as caretaker—to tear down the unique Sargent cabin, in order to bury the Johnsons on the site. Lawrence hated the job: "A 10-room log cabin with a sod roof built in 1890. People would've gone crazy over that nowadays. Just to let them walk through there with all those race horses and prize fighters on the wall, with John L. Sullivan and that old bunch."

In 1936, Alfred Berolzheimer, of the Eagle Pencil Co., bought the Johnson-Sargent property, and it became the AMK/Berol Ranch. In 1937, the Nelson boys started construction of the new Berol lodge—an elongated, single-story structure covering some 5,200 square feet. The Berols were big entertainers, with such notable visitors as publisher Alfred Knopf and labor leader John L. Lewis. All original ranch structures, except those built by Sargent, are still standing and represent some of the largest and finest examples of local work remaining in the valley.

W.C. "Slim" Lawrence (1899-1986) became caretaker of the Johnson/AMK from 1929 to 1982, a job that included cutting firewood for 10 fireplaces. In the ensuing years, Lawrence also became an expert in and collector of Indian artifacts and the fur trade. He and his wife, Verba, collected more than 5,000 Indian artifacts from the Lawrence site on Jackson Lake. These valuable finds now are in the Jackson Hole Museum, founded by Lawrence and Homer Richards. Lawrence was a voracious reader during the winter months, and his fine 2,000-volume library was the basis of the Teton County Historical Center collection. Among his other firsts, Lawrence made the first ascent of Eagles Rest Peak and the first successful moonlight climb of the Grand Teton, with the Exum group in 1933. And he was tireless in locating and marking the Trapper's Trail.

Sargent, the Johnsons, and Verba and Slim Lawrence all are buried on the AMK/Berol Ranch. Sargent's grave is 500 yards north of the loop parking near the Berol house, on the west side of a track road that probably once was the Old Military Highway. A hundred feet north of his buck-fenced grave are the remains of a huge Douglas fir, near which a dim trail heads west down the hill to the Johnson grave. The Lawrences' ashes are buried near there. A few mounds indicate the site of the Sargent cabin, in the clearing some 100 feet east of the Johnson grave and a bit north of the path. The "violin tree" where Edith often sat—a dead pine propped up by Slim Lawrence, with steps made of the hacked-off branches—is northwest of the Johnson grave some 300 yards or so, on a bluff overlooking Jackson Lake.

0.9 17.2 **Colter Bay.** The turnoff west takes you to this large tourist center, complete with campground, large-group camping sites (reservations required), trailer village, tent cabin village (bring or rent bedding and cooking utensils), and cabins. During the tourist season, accommodations here are among the least expensive. Among the amenities are a gas station, restaurant, gift shop, taproom, grill, fountain, laundry, showers, post office, public phones, ice, and horses for rent.

The **Colter Bay Visitor Center and Museum** offer other amenities, including a variety of ranger naturalist programs that explain the area and include walks. Additional illustrated programs are given each evening in the amphitheater. A tour of the Indian Arts Museum is a must.

Located at the marina is a lake-shore picnic spot and swimming area, as well as a dock and launching ramp for boats. The tackle and boat shop rents a variety of watercraft for cruises on the lake; fishing guides are worthwhile, but reservations are required.

Jackson Lake is the largest glacial lake in Jackson Hole and was the second largest natural lake in Wyoming until it was dammed. The lake has a very complex origin: It formed by a deep glacial groove cut by ice flowing south from Yellowstone Park and the westward tilting of the valley floor, combined with waters

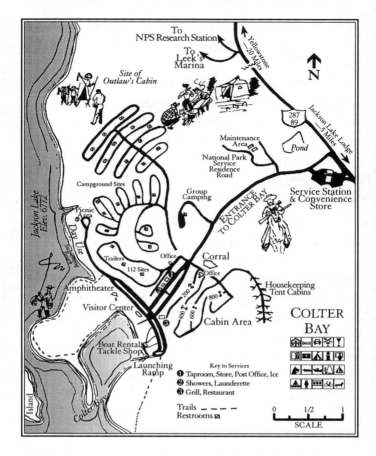

To
NPS Research Station
To
Leek's
Marina

To
Yellowstone
—20 miles

N

Site of
Outlaw's Cabin

287
89

Jackson Lake Lodge — 5 Miles

Maintenance
Area

Pond

National Park
Service
Residence
Road

Campground Sites

Group
Camping

ENTRANCE
TO COLTER BAY

Service Station
& Convenience
Store

Jackson Lake
Elev. 6772

Picnic
Area

Day Use

Trailers

112 Sites

Office

Corral

Office

Amphitheater

200

Housekeeping
Tent Cabins

Visitor Center

400

600

800

Cabin Area

COLTER
BAY

Boat Rentals
Tackle Shop

Launching
Ramp

Island

Colter Bay

Key to Services
❶ Taproom, Store, Post Office, Ice
❷ Showers, Launderette
❸ Grill, Restaurant

Trails – – –
Restrooms

0   1/2   1

SCALE

dammed by moraines pushed eastward by Teton canyon glaciers.
It has had many temporary outlets. Its high water shoreline en-
compasses some 52 miles, containing 25,730 acres.

Over the years, several names have been attributed to this lake:
On Clark's 1814 map, it was Lake Biddle (Riddle), while trapper
Joe Meek called it Lewis Lake, and W.A. Ferris of the American
Fur Co. called it Teton Lake. Jackson Lake it has remained.

This heavily fished lake has a good supply of mackinaw and
cutthroats. Spring visitors can shore fish for Macs after "ice-out,"
trolling for them after they go deep. Shore fishing for cutthroats
and browns works in summer because the fish are feeding on a
large minnow population; recommended lures include Krocodiles,
Pixies, or red-spotted yellow Wonders. You can catch winter whitefish after lake-trout spawning is over in November.

The presence of fish other than cutthroat and whitefish in
Jackson Lake is historically recent. In August, 1889, Jack Shive and

Wilson, a scout, planted mackinaws from Lake Superior in Sho-shone and Lewis lakes; the Lewis and Snake rivers connect those lakes to Jackson Lake. The fish—300 two-and-a-half-inchers in containers—came by rail from Michigan and were hauled by wagon from Cinnabar, MT to Old Faithful. From there, they were mule-packed 18 miles to the lakes. The motion of the pack animals and the splashing in the cans kept the fish alive on that final journey.

Mackinaw continued to be planted in Jackson Lake until 1916. They reproduced well and spread via the connecting tributaries. One of the largest fish caught in Jackson Lake weighed more than 30 pounds.

Jackson Lake has been attractive to more than fish. In 1829, after the rendezvous on the Popo Agie River near Lander, the trap-pers broke up, and Bill Sublette, with the main body, pushed west into Snake River country; he was searching for his long-absent partner, Jedediah Smith. Sublette followed the Astorians' trail—Wind River-Union Pass-Hoback River—into Jackson's Hole, where he met Davey Jackson, another of his partners. They waited for Smith on the shores of Jackson's lake; when he didn't appear, they went out to find him. Trapper Joe Meek finally located Jedediah Smith in Pierre's Hole.

West across Jackson Lake is Waterfalls Canyon, with Wilder-ness Falls in its upper recesses. Ranger Peak (el. 11,355) lies to the north, and Doane Peak (el. 11,355) is on the skyline. The nine-foot-high summit cairn was built Sept. 10, 1931 by surveyor E.M. Buckingham, who made the first ascent. Named for Lt. Gustavus C. Doane (1840-1892), the mountain originally was called "Cairn Peak."

Doane commanded the Fort Ellis military escort of the 1870 Washburn Expedition through the Yellowstone and wrote the first official report of the area's wonders. The report described Yellow-stone factually, making it credible by taking away the fantastic and tall-tales aspect of the region. Doane's report was instrumental in establishing Yellowstone National Park in 1872. That same year, Doane served with the Hayden Survey and later took charge of the 1876 winter exploration of the upper Snake through Jackson's Hole.

Looking across Jackson Lake, Eagles Rest Peak (el. 11,258) and Bivouac Peak (el. 10,825) are south of Waterfalls Canyon, with immense Moran Canyon filling the gap beyond. For Jackson Lake, Doane's party had split: Part of it made good time by boat; the rest took a beating by horsepacking over rocks and through tangled fallen timber along the west side of the lake. When Doane killed a deer near Moran Canyon, the shot created much excitement as it echoed and re-echoed. Testing the echo, the party had fun during the next few hours. Finally, Doane wrote, "I then tried Starr's tremendous voice alone, and had him call, 'Oh Joe!' with a prolonged rising... and... falling inflection, repeating it at intervals of 30 seconds.... The first call had not ceased when a hundred exact repetitions were reflected to the little bay. Then a rush of hoarse exclamations followed up the gorge, and the fusillade of calls on every rock and cliff answered 'Oh, Joe!' And these sounds echoed and re-echoed a thousand times, reaching higher and higher along the mighty walls, till faint goblin whispers from the cold icy shafts and the spectral hollows answered back in clicking notes and hisses, but distinctly always the words, 'Oh, Joe!'.... We named this inlet Spirit Bay." It now is called Moran Bay and, alas, the echo, for some reason, is gone.

When in trouble, outlaws had a penchant for high-tailing it to Jackson's Hole. Edwin H. Trafton, locally known as Ed Harrington, had a hideout in this area—north of the Colter Bay campsites—the remnants of which Slim Lawrence found in 1931. Trafton's notorious adventures began with horse-stealing operations based in Teton Basin, Idaho and Jackson's Hole and covering Idaho, Wyoming and Montana. He served two prison sentences for horse theft and one for robbing his mother of $10,000. Owen Wister drew on some of Trafton's character when plotting his novel, *The Virginian*. Trafton liked to claim he was the hero, "The Virginian," but Wister's readers will recognize the villain Steve Trampas as Trafton.

Trafton won notoriety as the man who single-handedly robbed 15 Yellowstone stagecoaches on July 29, 1914. The long, tourist-laden train of Concord stages, separated by 100 yards because of the dust, was passing Shoshone Point when the first driver pulled his four horses to a sudden, rocking halt in a cloud of rising dust. Blocking the road, a lone masked robber warned them not to "make any false moves because my partner in the timber has you covered." The victims were ordered out and told to deposit valuables in a sack on the ground. The bandit knelt oddly, his rifle across his

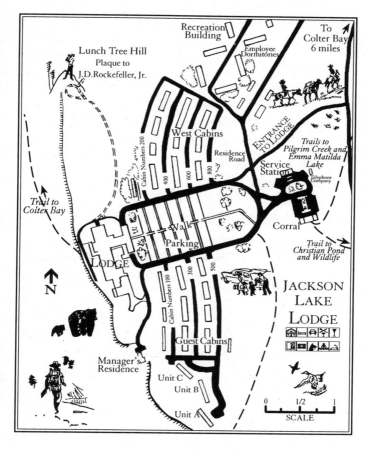

right knee. As each of 15 coaches drew up, passengers were systematically robbed. The unseen driver of the 16th coach, suspecting a holdup, wheeled his rig around to warn oncoming drivers and to spread the alarm. The bandit, with $915.35 in cash and $130 worth of jewelry, disappeared into the timber, where tourists found some emptied cans of off-brand tomatoes. Later, scouts picked up tracks of two horses half a mile south and, farther west, the tracks of a man on foot. They followed the footprints to Charles Erpenback's cabin on Conant Creek in Idaho, 100 miles from the crime. Charged with the robberies, Erpenback posted bail and returned to his cabin.

As various reports began to filter in, the pieces of the puzzle soon began to fit: Trafton, with an old gunshot wound in his right leg, could not kneel on it; he had taken two horses from Ben Sheffield's camp at Moran on Sept. 22; two days later, a Mexican sheepherder was robbed of several cans of off-brand tomatoes on

Conant Creek; then Erpenback caught Trafton trying to ambush him and plant a fake suicide note that confessed the robbery. Erpenback notified the U.S. Marshal that Trafton was the bandit. Trafton was arrested, tried at Cheyenne, found guilty and, on Dec. 14, 1915, sentenced to five years in Leavenworth.

In 1919, the 68-year-old Trafton was released, at which time he moved to California, where he tried—unsuccessfully—to sell his life story for a movie. Five years later, at a soda fountain and roaring with laughter, Trafton was telling the soda jerk how he robbed 15 stagecoaches in one day when a sudden, violent heart attack cut the laughter off. The last, great Western stagecoach robber pitched forward, dead on the counter.

1.9 19.1 **Pilgrim Creek Road.** Looking east from this turnoff, you will see Grand View Point, an old basaltic volcanic center. This northeast-traveling road will not lead to suitable fishing, but flour gold has been discovered in the quartzite beds. At 1.6 miles, have a closer look, through the trees, at the old volcano crater. Another 0.7 miles leads to parking, corrals, Pilgrim Creek (not suitable for fishing), and a trailhead. Pilgrim Creek Trail goes north into Teton Wilderness. **Pilgrim Peak** (NW) is the rounded hill with timber patches on it. A quarter mile east, across the creek, vertebrate fossils, including those of oreodonts—extinct cud-chewing hogs—and a camel were found.

The Pilgrim Creek Trail connects with other trails, such as Coulter Creek (NE), East Rodent Creek (NNE), and Wildcat Ridge (N).

1.5 20.6 **Grand View Point Trailhead**. Turn east and go 0.2 miles to parking for a trail that goes north 1.3 miles to a fork; the trail east climbs to join the Two Ocean Lake Trail. For Grand View Point, however, drive another mile to more parking at the end of the road. The trail north from here joins the Two Ocean Lake Trail, and climbs—steeply—first to a minor summit, then to the Point summit and a view of the crater (W), of Jackson Lake and the Tetons (W), and Mount Leidy and its highlands (S), where obvious clearcuts appear. Two Ocean Lake is below (NE), and a piece of Emma Matilda Lake (S) shows as well. The trail descends north to a fork: Either continue north to Two Ocean Lake, or turn west to circle the Point and join the first trail described.

0.9 21.5 **Jackson Lake Lodge**. Turn west to reach Jackson

Lake Lodge, with its complete tourist-related services, including saddle horses. The lodge offers a variety of scenic Snake River float trips throughout the day. A boat and bus trip includes a complete park tour and picnic lunch on Elk Island. Check the Jackson Lake Lodge activity desk for details and other outings.

Originally known as Amoretti Inn, this lodge was built in 1922 and was one of the largest of the early tourist resorts. It had seven tent camps in Teton and Yellowstone parks, and all but one were reached by horseback. Accordingly, Amoretti had 300 horses. The Inn became Jackson Lake Lodge as part of a campaign by Lander and Casper forces to develop the eastern approach to Jackson's Hole through Lander. The 1955 opening of the later Jackson Lake Lodge, built by John D. Rockefeller, Jr., found 5,000 visitors inspecting architect Gilbert S. Underwood's work. They saw $6 million worth of modern reinforced concrete motel on this plateau of Pinedale-age glacial moraine overlooking Jackson Lake. The monolithic lodge included separate guest cottages to house some 800 visitors.

John D. Rockefeller, Jr., who operated the Grand Teton Lodge Company, chose the site so that the main lounge's magnificent picture window—60 feet wide and two stories high—could frame the Tetons. Before construction, Rockefeller had a temporary scaffold erected to the exact level of the lounge floor. He wanted to make certain that America saw the Tetons from his perspective, with nothing cutting the view.

Opinions flew that day as to whether the lodge architecture was appropriate for its setting. It probably is safe to say that the 1955 scene would have made 19th century intrepid trappers and mountain men gasp.

Regardless of the reaction to the architecture, lovely trails spider out from the lodge's grounds. The Rockefeller family had its first good look at the lake and Tetons beyond from the easy Lunch Tree Hill trail to the north. Other worthwhile trails include the old Swamp Road heading north to Colter Bay, or others going east via the horse trail under Christian Creek bridge and the highway to Grand View Point Trail, Christian Pond, and Two Ocean and Emma Matilda lakes in the hills east of the lodge.

0.2 21.7   Christian Creek Bridge. If you look east at Christian Pond, you might see a pair of trumpeter swans.

0.3 22.0 **Willow Flats Overlook.** The pastoral view to the west overlooks an extensive freshwater marsh created by Christian Creek, which provides excellent habitat for birds, beavers and moose. Near this point, Robert Adams—with the 1872 Hayden Survey—used a canoe to take the first soundings in Jackson Lake; before a squall drove him off the lake, he measured a depth of 258 feet. In about 1910, the *Titanic*, a log-hauling tugboat operated by Captain MacDermott, plied its way between the north end of Jackson Lake and the dam (S). In its final days, it was docked at Pilgrim Creek, just west of Willow Flats, where it was used as a diving platform.

You can hike down past the pond to catch Ben Sheffield's old Swamp Road north to Colter Bay; or hike south along Christian Creek toward old Moran. Sheffield built his "Swamp Road" from old Moran, across these swamps, to bypass his competition—Amoretti Lodge, now Jackson Lake Lodge. The road, even when later oiled by the National Park Service, kept sinking into the swamp and finally was abandoned in 1960. A new road—the current one—was built by Rockefeller to the east, along earlier and higher wagon roads.

Opposite the Willow Flats turnout is the turnoff east to the old **Allen (Moran) Cemetery.** Drive past a residence and turn south half a mile to the cemetery, which overlooks the Snake River. Some of the names found here are Budges, Charles J. and Martha Allen, Marie and Emile Wolff, Otto Nelson, and Herb Whiteman. "Grandpa" Allen (1853-1937) could claim 100 direct descendants in his lifetime. When he sold his 340 acres (S) to Ben Sheffield, he reserved three acres "for the old cemetery." It only required half an acre, so he leased the rest for tourist cabins and a dude ranch. When Rockefeller's men bought the Allen homestead from Sheffield, they had to bargain again, finally paying more for the 2.5 acres than they had for the original homestead.

0.5 22.5 **Jackson Lake Junction.** U.S. 287 continues left, east (see Trip 6e). Teton Park Road goes right, south (see Trip 6a).

Trip 5a

Grassy Lake Reclamation Road
(9 miles to Grassy Lake; 50 miles to Ashton)

Originally a well-traveled Indian route, trappers and settlers used this old trail across the north Tetons as well. Its eastern portion now is covered by the north end of Jackson Lake, though you can boat to the westside portion or hike south 10 miles from this road to reach it.

Osborne Russell used the Grassy Lake route, crossing here Sept. 1, 1839 on his way from Yellowstone to Fort Hall. The 1872 Hayden Survey party took it to the Falls and Bechler rivers and "Beulah Lakes." It also was the route of choice for elk tuskers and horse thieves out of Idaho. Using this route, outlaws slipped in and out of the Hole in half the time it took U.S. Marshals to circuit through Teton Pass. Owen Wister mentioned the trail in *The Virginian.*

As more permanent settlement began, the Grassy Lake road saw more use. Willis L. Winegar said he drove the first wagon over in 1883, heading for Yellowstone—probably along the old Marysville route out of Idaho. The Reclamation Bureau built the Ashton-Moran Freight Line Road in 1910, during the reconstruction of Jackson Lake Dam. The original dam on Jackson Lake was a Rube Goldberg affair of log cribbing, which washed out July 4, 1910. Another dam had to be built immediately. It became engineer Frank Crowe's problem to rush men, materials and heavy machinery into remote Jackson's Hole before snow closed the valley. That's when he learned of the old horse-thief route. Unsurpassed planning and energy had the wagons rolling the 75 miles from Ashton into Moran by August, hauling freight—cement, housing material, food, and supplies—by wagon or sleigh. Roadhouses were built or set up along the route at Squirrel Meadows, Cascade Creek, Dime Creek and the Edwards Ranch on Arizona Creek.

Describing the climatic feat, Joe Markham wrote in 1972: "Finally on October 15, 1927, George Osborne Jr. and Charley Myers delivered the last loads of freight to Joe Markham at Moran. After 17 years of rain, mud, dust, thunderstorms, snowstorms, blizzards, avalanches, snowslides, and temperatures ranging from 63 degrees below in early February of 1915, to 100 degrees above, the Ashton Idaho-Moran Wyoming Horse and Wagon Freight Line was terminated." It may have been the last such road used by wagons in the United States.

The first car into the Hole, a Cadillac, ground its way over the Grassy Lake route in 1911, driven by Bill Dunn, with Al Austin along to repair tires. The road still is not a super highway, remaining unpaved and decidedly rocky; no trailers or large RVs are allowed on the western one-lane portion. Because of snowy, unplowed roads, the reclamation road is closed during April and May until warm weather clears it. Unplowed in winter, it becomes a snowmobiler route between Flagg Ranch and Ashton, Idaho.

0.0 0.0   Turn west from U.S. 287 at Flagg Ranch (Trip 5), two miles south of South Yellowstone Entrance, on Grassy Lake Road. This road through the Rockefeller Memorial Parkway has several small forest campgrounds along it, usually full during busy summer months.

0.5 0.5   **Polecat Creek.** North a half mile is the skiers' delight—the hot springs of moonlight treks, champagne and strawberries. It's hard to find, but worth the effort. Road turns south along the Snake.

0.5 1.0   Old entrance to the former Huckleberry recreation area. The Park Service bought the popular fun site and razed it.

1.7 2.7   Cross creek. In the woods (S) was a hidden corral where the author found parts of an old iron pot (J.H. Museum). This area (N) was called **Soldier Meadows** because of a post maintained here in the years to 1917 when Yellowstone Park was under Army administration. President Arthur's 1883 Cavalcade made its last stop here in Jackson Hole on its way to Yellowstone. The weary Yellowstone-Jackson Hole travelers would stop at this Snake River

Military Station, which actually was mislocated two miles outside the Yellowstone boundary. "A soldier-cook would prepare a great feast—Snake River salmon trout, French friedpot, lima beans, well-boiled rice, bread, butter, loaf sugar (unusual), brown sugar and condensed milk." At this point, the historic freight road shortcutted by coming in from the southeast and Dime Creek (see Trip 5, Mile 5.3) to join the 1888 Marysville road going NW to Grassy Lake.

1.8 4.5 **Berry Creek Trailhead** (S). This trail leads south to the north end of Jackson Lake and Harem Hill (five miles). From there, it turns west to and up Berry Creek for six miles to a junction (patrol cabin in area) east of Survey Peak (el. 9,277), which is on the hydrographic divide. Near here (S), on the north side of Forellen Peak (el. 9,776) was the old asbestos mine that was commercialized slightly; it was a spot where Indians also obtained soapstone (talc) for pipes and utensils. The old mine still is connected by the Hominy Trail—an old road that crosses the divide at Jackass Pass—to Ashton, Idaho. Tailings and old machinery mark the spot. Slim Lawrence was one of four men who filed on the mine, but nothing ever came of it.

Berry Creek Trail splits at this junction, the north fork crossing the divide north of Survey Peak and meeting the South and Middle Boone trails west. The south fork passes south of Survey Peak, following the old mine road west two miles to the divide at Jackass Pass (el. ca 8,460); there it intersects the north/south Teton Crest Trail and connects with Hominy Trail/old mine road, which continues west 5.3 miles to the trailhead at Jackass Road. The outlaws used both routes. It is 20 miles west to Lamont, Idaho.

0.5 5.0 **Glade Creek**. W.C. Lawrence found the remains of a smokehouse used by an elk poacher to smoke elk meat or 'jerky,' which then was sold in Idaho. The log cabin, now crushed by a tree, was 14-by-8-by-7 feet high, had a dirt roof, no floor, and was lined inside with small pole shelves. A firebox, eight feet outside the south wall, had a flue going under the wall to the center of the floor. Smoke drifted up around the shelves where the elk meat lay—all illegal, of course.

4.0 9.0 The road crosses the hydrographic divide of the Teton Range at the east end of **Grassy Lake Reservoir** (small campground, rainbow, brook, cutthroat); the divide also forms the boundary between the Targhee National Forest (W) and the

Mt. Moran Plane Crash of 1951 (above). The first visit to the site after the winter rescue attempt by Petzoldt and Vande Water, to hold a service for the victims. The DC-3 struck the boulder on top of which are (L to R) Glenn Exum, Paul Petzoldt and Blake Vande Water.

The lounge — Jackson Lake Lodge (below, left).

Tusk hunter Charles Purdy, right, at a tusker headquarters at Loon Lake near Ashton, Idaho (below, right). During prohibition Purdy switched from tusk hunting to bootlegging. The skis are handmade.

Roy Osborne drove the last freight outfit from Ashton to Moran (bottom). Taken on Pilgrim Creek, 1902.

Rockefeller Parkway, which we leave at this point. Here too, the Beulah Lake Trail goes north four miles into Yellowstone.

The road passes north of Grassy Lake, which was built on the upper Falls River, about two miles to its northwest corner and the dam. At this trailhead point, the Old Marysville Trail goes northwest into Yellowstone; the Grassy Lake Road turns southwest across the dam (campsite), following the route of the old freight road, which headed for the Cascade Creek roadhouse, two or so miles west of the reservoir. Cascade Creek was mid-station for husky Mormon freighters with loaded Studebaker wagons and six-horse teams. Beyond Cascade Creek is the signed turnoff (S) to Lake of the Woods and Scout Camp Loll, on the north boundary of **Jedediah Smith Wilderness**. From this point west, one section of the road is one-lane; *trailers and large RVS are not allowed on this section*. The Grassy Lake road continues west between Jedediah Smith Wilderness (S) and Winegar Hole Wilderness (N), through beautiful country to Gibson Meadows and a junction. The two-lane Reclamation Road continues right (W) at this junction and on to Squirrel Meadows, where another freighters' roadhouse stood. Charlie Purdy, the elk tusker who was kicked out of the Hole, lived here. The road emerges into foothills for five miles, and then travels 20 miles to Ashton.

There are two access points into the **Winegar Hole Wilderness**: the Calf Creek Trail turnoff (N) 4.5 miles west of the reservoir; and Loon Lake Road (N) and Trail, at the North Boone Creek road crossing, 8.5 miles west of the reservoir. Willis Winegar, early freighter and butcher from St. Anthony, Idaho, hunted this obsure corner of Teton County. The Wilderness area is noted fertile grizzly country and for nesting sites for trumpeter swans, sandhill cranes and loons.

At the Gibson Meadows junction, the left fork, Jackass Road, goes south some four miles to Jackass Meadows and provides three access points into the Jedediah Smith Wilderness: Middle Boone Trail, South Boone Trail and Spring/Jackass Pass Trail. From Jackass Meadows, the road heads west toward Ashton or Lamont.

North and South Bitch creeks to the south— accessed by Coyote Meadows Road—are the wildest area in the Jedediah Smith Wilderness. The north slopes of the wilderness are about the wettest area in Wyoming—a superb habitat, but wildlife is scarce. Erosion of sheep and cattle trails is a big problem, as is poaching.

THE PARK LOOP

The Park Loop, a 45-mile must for visitors, is packed with outstanding scenery, colorful stories, and unsuspected points of interest. You can travel the Loop in either direction. If your time is limited, try the west side first, and hear the exciting story of the mountains.

Trip 6a

TETON PARK ROAD
Jackson Lake Junction south
to Jenny Lake Road
(10 miles)

0.0 0.0 **Jackson Lake Junction.** Turn south on Teton Park Road and cross the south end of beaver-created Willow Flats, a swampy habitat for moose.

To the east is the site of the old Research Station, until it was moved to the AMK/Berol Ranch (see Trip 5, Mile 16.3). On the same site here was Captain Smith's big log hotel. According to an 1896 parenthetical entry in Dr. W.S. Webb's diary: "'Captain' because he owns and operates a row boat on the Lake, and 'Smith' because … he doubtless modestly wishes to conceal his identity." In winter, the section of road between Jackson Lake Junction and Signal Mountain Lodge is kept open and becomes part of the network of the Continental Divide Snowmobile Trail, as is the unplowed Park Road to the south and the Signal Mountain Road.

0.3 0.3 Cross the heavily willowed Christian Creek.

0.1 0.4 **Signal Mountain Landslide**. Parking (E) gives access to the Snake River. Trees east of here mark the north edge of a landslide that flowed northwest off Signal Mountain, damming the Snake and forming Willow Flats. The river later breeched the landslide dam.

0.5 0.9 **Old townsite of Moran**. Turnoff (S) to parking area, restrooms, and fishing access to the Snake below the dam. Within the swampy area, the town drilled an artesian well, the site of "aphrodisiac spring." For reasons known only to themselves, moose, elk and deer prefer this swamp water just before their rutting time. According to Dr. Dave Love: "They honk and holler and carry on," crowding in, pushing and shoving to get at it.

In 1903, hunting guide Ben Sheffield (1863-1946) bought the Frank Lovell place here and started a dude business. His hunting and fishing camp developed into Teton Lodge, noted worldwide for hospitality, its excellent table, and efficiency. Government officials, wealthy men, and European royalty were regular guests.

Four years later, Sheffield became the Moran postmaster when he moved the post office equipment by boat from the Allen place (Trip 6e, mile 3.7). He remained postmaster until 1929, when Charlie Fesler took it over in his store, which burned in 1950. Sheffield brought the first gas launch into the valley, hauling it in by wagon. Gradually, a picturesque village built up, with Sheffield's post office, log cabins and lodge as a nucleus. In 1921, his ranch was chosen for RCMP headquarters in the movie "Nanette of the North," which represented the first film location in Jackson Hole.

Unhappy when the Reclamation Bureau started building dams, Sheffield forced the Bureau to obtain his land by condemnation. In 1928, he sold out to the Snake River Land Co. for $100,000 and retired. He lost most of his fortune, however, in the 1929 stock-market crash, and ended up as fire guard on the Signal Mountain lookout.

By 1959, the Park Service had dismantled the old town of Moran "to restore the spot to its natural beauty." Many log cabins were moved to Colter Bay for further use; the rebuilt Fesler store/post office was the last to go.

0.3 1.2 **Jackson Lake Dam**. The dam is built across the outlet of Jackson Lake. Fishing in the Snake starts 200 yards below the dam. Glaciated ice advanced out of the Teton canyons to this point, blocking the southward flow of the Snake with a great moraine and diverting the Snake east around Signal Mountain, away from its former southward channel. Melted ice behind the moraine created the natural Jackson Lake.

In 1902, Frank Lovell built a toll bridge to replace the ford at the outlet of Jackson Lake. From 1903-1910, Sheffield operated the bridge, until the wooden dam at the outlet broke and swept the bridge away.

The first government dam raised the natural Jackson Lake by three feet. On July 4, 1910, the swollen volume of melting snow swept away the dam's flimsy cribbing. The released water rampaged down the river, tearing out bridges and ruining Menor's Ferry, 40 miles downstream. To meet the emergency, 400 men, horses and heavy material were rushed to the dam site before the snow fell; as they came, they built a wagon road across the northern Tetons from Ashton, Idaho (see Trip 5a). By the spring of 1911, a substantial earth dam was completed, raising Jackson Lake by 10 feet—at a cost of $50,000, according to one source.

No sooner was that dam completed than a larger dam was needed. In 1914, work began on the new dam, which was completed in 1916 and raised the lake level another 39 feet. The accompanying dredging of the outlet channel was finished in 1917.

Many folks have been unhappy with the Jackson Lake Dam, including writer Owen Wister: "...And here let me pause to lay my ineffectual but heartfelt curse upon the commercial vandals who desecrated the outlet of Jackson's Lake with an ugly dam to irrigate some desert land away off in Idaho!"

The 847,000 acre-feet of impounded waters "belong" to Idaho lands, having been given away by early Wyoming legislatures. Wyoming retains only two percent of the Snake, though Jackson Hole could use more. Idaho's huge, wasteful irrigation network gobbles up Wyoming water either in ditches, such as the Egyptians used, or by spraying Wyoming waters into hot winds.

Wallace Stegner's opinion of the "water engineering" of the West was pretty low. He called it "intemperate tinkering" and the "original sin." He said it brought death into the world—loss of rivers and lakes, and desertification of our oasis civilization faster than in Africa.

At one time or another, most of the valley's lakes—including Jenny, Leigh, Emma Matilda, and Two Ocean—have been eyed by Idaho's politicians and farmers for their use. The local reaction to such efforts is typified by a sign that used to be in the men's restroom at the old Jackson courthouse: "Please flush the toilet; Idaho needs the water."

In 1983, the dam was declared unsafe, so another dam repair began in 1984. It turned out that the earthen dam had been built not on bedrock but on "saturated unconsolidated fine-grained sand and silt." It had been built between the Teton (W) and Spread Creek (E) faults. Fearing the dam could not withstand a major shock, i.e. that the soils underlying its structure would saturate and liquefy, as happened in the Mexico City earthquake of 1985, the Reclamation Bureau began a five-year repair job that would cost $79 million.

To effect the repairs, the old earthen dike was removed and the new foundation was strengthened with dynamic compaction, i.e. pounding by dropping a 30-ton weight repeatedly from 100 feet. The Japanese experts called in used mammoth 100-foot-high augers to finish drilling several hundred holes. These holes were stuffed with a sand and concrete mix called "soilcrete," which further was tamped for stabilizing pylons to reinforce the soggy foundation. Not everyone was certain the dam was worth the money and, for a while, an ironic joke circulated the valley about pure dollars being pounded into the bottomless pit/dam.

Theoretically, the new dam can withstand an earthquake that registers as high as 7.6 on the Richter Scale, but it somehow reminds one of the 1925 Gros Ventre Slide dam, which engineers had thought would block that river forever (see Trip 14, Mile 4.7). Faith may be the key word here.

Reservoirs behind the earlier dams killed thousands of trees with no mitigation, other than the CCC boys cleaning up the mess, years later during the 1930s. For this latest go-around, the BuWreck paid for the necessary archaeological study.

The Jackson Lake outlet has been the site of other historical events. In 1839, Osborne Russell spent his second July Fourth in Jackson Hole, under happier circumstances than he had four years earlier, when he was dunked while crossing the Snake. This time, he and his trapper friends dined on 20 "salmon trout,... fat mutton, buffalo beef and coffee, and the manner in which it was served up constituted a dinner that ought to be considered independent even by Britons."

From the dam, the old road went straight up the hill, on a grade that a Model T Ford could not make. "It took a four-horse team to drag a car up that hill," former Yellowstone Park Superintendent Horace Albright recalled. "Occasionally, Ben Sheffield would let me have a team to pull my car up the hill and thus avoid the long, hard drive east to the old Buffalo Fork crossing and Menor's Ferry." In 1921, the Forest Service built a good road, which since has been replaced.

0.1 1.3 **U.S. Bureau of Reclamation** facility manager's residence. This federal agency, also known as the BuRec or BuWreck, is located in one of Sheffield's old cabins, east of the road.

0.1 1.4 Small glacial pond (W) with some beaver activity. Academy Award winning actor Wallace Beery bought one of R.F. McConaughy's cabin's, located near here, to be his "ranch" during the 1930s and 1940s. Here, he vacationed and worked on *Wyoming* (1940) and *Bad Bascomb* (1945), two MGM films made in the valley.

0.3 1.7 **The Brinkerhoff "Blue House."** Ben Sheffield first had a summer home on this site. After his death, R.J. McConaughy of Salt Lake City bought it—in 1946—but an unusually heavy snow collapsed the cabin to its foundation. Zack K. Brinkerhoff, Jr. then bought it in 1947 and rebuilt it on the Sheffield foundation. His geologist created the massive stone fireplace out of rock from the Wind River Canyon near Thermopolis. It represents the geological ages, with Cambrian rock at the base, moving to Cretaceous rock at the top. The U.S. government bought the cabin for $70,000 in 1955 and did some remodeling in 1969 and more over the years. Today, this government "blue house" is used by the Park Service as a retreat and for lodging distinguished guests, including President Jimmy Carter, George Bush, Walter Cronkite, senators, judges and other VIPs.

0.2 1.9 **Jackson Lake Overlook**. The pre-dam natural lake was nearly 400 feet deep, with the deepest sections nearest the mountains and the active Teton fault.

0.5 2.4 **Chapel of the Sacred Heart**. This Catholic church was called Our Lady of the Tetons until 1964, when it was realized what "Tetons" meant. Take the turnoff (W) to the chapel and picnic ground.

0.6 3.0 **Signal Mountain Lodge and campground**. This resort first was known as Wort's Lodge, boasting a fishing camp with 25 cabins, plus a lodge and small store. Sold in 1940, it now is a full-service lodge, offering float trips, fishing guides, and windsurfing lessons. The Park Service's **Signal Mountain Campground** has a 14-day limit and includes facilities for trailers.

To hike the three-mile **Signal Mountain Trail** to the summit of the mountain (el. 7,593), park at the campground entrance and hike the "Boat Launch" road for 200 yards. The well-marked trail goes east, crosses the highway, and climbs another 0.2 miles to and across Signal Mountain Road. Continue east past the Moose Pond (campground to this point 0.5 miles) to a junction: The left fork, the Ridge Route, goes a mile to a second junction; the right fork, the Lakes Trail, takes the low route past several ponds and Keith Lake (campground to Keith Lake 1.5 miles) to join the Ridge Route at the second junction. Both head east 0.2 miles to a third junction marked by an old sign. At this point, the left trail turns north and ascends Signal's south gully 1.5 miles to the Jackson Lake Overlook. The right trail, dimmer and unmaintained (downfall) but marked with red painted dots, heads south and east, crossing the lower south gully drainage. It contours east and north below the cliffs of Huckleberry Ridge Tuff (east side) to rejoin the Cattlemen's Bridge trail (three miles) of Trip 6e, Mile 3.5.

1.0 4.0 **Signal Mountain Road**. Parking is 0.1 miles down this turnoff; no trailers are allowed on this narrow road. The five-mile round trip takes an hour, but the side trip is worth the superb view of Jackson Hole.

The winter road south of the lodge is not plowed and is open to snowmobilers, as is the Signal Mountain Road.

Early photos show Signal Mountain denuded of timber. It was burned off in the great forest fire of 1879, which swept through Jackson Hole and burned thousands of acres. Only August rain and early snowstorms finally put it out. Because of the lack of forage, animals starved to death that winter.

It was during that fall that painter Thomas Moran, in Teton Basin, Idaho, wrote: "It is so very smoky that the Teton Peaks can scarcely be seen and at times are entirely obscured so that sketching is out of the question."

Signal Mountain earned its name in August of 1890. On a

hunting trip, Robert Ray Hamilton was headed for Marymere on horseback (see Trip 5, Mile 16.3). When he didn't turn up, his alarmed partner, John D. Sargent, who had returned from Idaho on Aug. 27, called out search parties. After a week, one party found Hamilton's dog and horse, alive, two miles below Jackson Lake outlet. The men built a log canoe to search the river; some distance below their camp, they found the body under the shelving bank. People speculated that Hamilton, on horseback, had tried to ford the river at night—his watch had stopped at 9:30—but in the wrong area. A good swimmer, he had cast himself off the horse to swim ashore, only to have his huge spurs tangle in weeds and his full cartridge belt weigh him down. As prearranged, this party climbed the highest point and built a signal smoke for the search to end on Sept. 2.

At 4.0 miles is **Jackson Lake Overlook** and parking. As several Hayden surveyors studied Jackson Lake from this point in 1872 they wondered why the Snake had "deserted" the broad valley that extended southward from Jackson Lake and instead, had "turned off so far to the east to find another outlet." They concluded that glaciers out of the Tetons and their moraines had caused the diversion. During another Hayden Survey in 1878, photographer William H. Jackson took his first east-side photographs of the Tetons, having taken his famous west-side photo of the Grand in 1872. From this spot, he took only a few photos "because of a smoky haziness that filled the air" from forest fires.

At 4.7 miles is **Emma Matilda Overlook**, with a parking spot 0.2 miles south. Take the short path to view the Absaroka Range, Teton Wilderness, and Emma Matilda Lake to the northeast. Emma Matilda was named by surveyor William O. Owen for his wife (see Trip 6e, Mile 1.3). Both glaciated Emma Matilda and Two Ocean (not visible) lakes were the subject of Idaho irrigation schemes but national-parks director Horace Albright stopped their inclusion in such projects.

At 5.0 is **Ranger Lookout** and summit parking area. The trail south leads to an information display and a fine view of Mount Moran, Jackson Lake and the Snake River plain.

The timbered patches to the south are glacial moraine—rock piles bulldozed by slow-moving glaciers and left when the ice melted. Water has filled some of the pits in the outwash plain, forming small lakes, such as Cow Lake. Remember that Signal Mountain was completely overridden during the valley's next-to-last glaciation—the Buffalo Glaciation—by at least 2,000 feet of ice; as a result, its summit is capped by glacial gravels and cobbles. The various buttes to the south, including Signal Mountain, are fault-bound uplifts, and each is an aborted attempt at forming a mountain.

(Return to Teton Park Road.)

0.3 4.3 **RKO Road** (E). This old road east to the former Upper Bar BC was used as a location site by the RKO movie studio for the films *Big Sky* (1952) and *Far Horizons* (1955). It provides a 16-mile mountain-bike trip along the Snake River to the old Bar BC Ranch. The entire loop trip is 27 miles and is best done starting here at the north end (see Trip 6c, Mile 8.2).

1.3 5.6 **The Potholes** (E). East of the road is parking for the "Potholes." This conspicuous knob-and-kettle topography was formed by melting leftover ice masses that remained embedded in morainal debris long after the glaciers melted. This great flat looks like an inland sea bottom, with sunken holes—some filled with water. Once the favorite bear-hunting grounds for Ben Sheffield's clients, these days it's among the most-favored snowmobile country.

0.6 6.2 **Mount Moran Scenic Turnout** (W). This old outlet channel of Jackson Lake cut through the lake's most recent recessional moraine, created by the Pinedale Glaciers.

From this excellent vantage point, the huge mass of **Mt. Moran** (el. 12,605) dominates the Teton Range with its impressive Black Dike, Falling Ice (S) and Skillet (N) glaciers. Moran's summit, large enough for a tennis court, is capped by a fascinating patch of light-colored Flathead sandstone, deposited by a Cambrian sea. Its matching layer, far beneath the valley floor, is 30,000 vertical feet and six miles, horizontally, from its mate.

Dr. F.V. Hayden named this stately peak for his friend and famous artist, Thomas Moran (1837-1926). While the name first appeared on Bechler's map in the 1873 Hayden report, other expedition members were calling it Mt. Leidy. Moran first saw the Tetons—from the Idaho side and in very smoky conditions—in 1879. His field sketches later were used in his Teton landscape paintings, including his famous studies of Mt. Moran. He never set foot in Jackson Hole.

For the climber, massive Mt. Moran offers no easy route. Despite a long trek to its base, it has become increasingly popular and now has more than 24 routes up its 3,000-foot sides.

LeRoy Jeffers hoped to make the first ascent of Mt. Moran. Leaving his wife near Skillet Glacier, Jeffers raced time and weather to reach Moran's north summit at 9 p.m. on Aug. 11, 1919, only to discover a higher summit south. Sleet, darkness, and common sense barred him from claiming it. Descending by the same route, he found his wife gone and the area where he had last seen her swept by a great avalanche. After a frantic search, he caught up with her; she was on her way for help. Three years later, Jeffers returned with ranger W.H. Loyster to finish the climb he had begun; to his dismay, he found the south summit record of Dr. L.H. Hardy, Ben C. Rich, and Father Bennet McNulty, who had claimed the first ascent just 10 days earlier, on July 27, 1922.

When Norman Clyde, the "Old Man of the Sierras," solo-climbed Skillet Glacier in 1926, he used only a miner's pick. He would swing this tool over his head into the ice above and then pull himself up to it.

These days, the regular and easiest route is up the northeast ridge. Climbers on this ridge always receive a shock. Tragically, on Nov. 21, 1950, a DC-3 plane, off course with a group of New Tribes missionaries—men, women and children—crashed into the northeast ridge at 11,000 feet, the same elevation as the lower end of Skillet Glacier handle. All 24 passengers and the crew were killed. Because it was impossible to remove the bodies or wreckage, this climbing route was closed for five years, until the remains had weathered away. Even today, climbers who are unaware of the accident are startled to stumble onto the shiny remnants of the plane. They can also be seen mornings with binoculars from Jackson Lake Lodge.

Moran's north side is flanked by **Bivouac Peak** (el. 10,825). Like Moran, its flat crest has the same peneplain remnant of Cambrian Flatstone sandstone. Its easy east summit was first climbed in 1916 by Arthur C. Tate and try-anything-once "Wild Bill" Scott, a reformed horsethief who served as Ben Sheffield's hunting, fishing and climbing guide—the valley's first. It was one of the few Teton ascents before 1923. Then, in 1930, ranger F.M. Fryxell, Theodore and Gustav Koven reached the higher west summit. The late hour forced the Kovens to bivouac below while Fryxell bush-whacked back to Jenny Lake that night. Thinking of his bivouack-ing friends, he so named the peak.

0.5 6.7 **Burned Ridge**. The prominent timbered ridge to the south is a moraine left from the Pinedale glaciation. You can see more potholes in this area as well.

1.7 8.4 **Spalding Bay Turnoff** (N). This narrow, steep, rough road leads to the bay and a small boat launch. RVs and cars are not advised, and trailer parking requires a permit.

1.0 9.4 **Mountain View Turnout** (W). On Moran's sunny southeast flank, Falling Ice Glacier tumbles between West Horn and East Horn, whose shadows preserve it from extinction—though it is receding greatly. Above the glacier is the 150-foot-wide diabase "Black Dike," which extends through the mountain and west seven miles. It projects 300 feet out of the east face, forming the difficult Dike Route climb. Clearly visible on Moran's south side is the great South Buttress, its complex faces and ridges a mass of difficult climbs. Its best approach is by boat across Leigh Lake to Leigh Creek and Canyon.

Thor Peak (el. 12,028), a major summit, loses its distinction because of its obscure position behind the massive South Buttress of Mt. Moran. Thor has several routes from Leigh Canyon, not eas-ily reached. Paul Petzoldt and Bruton Strange made the first as-cent of Thor Peak in August, 1930.

South of Mt. Moran and Leigh Canyon is the lone hulk of **Mt. Woodring** (el. 11,590), named for the park's first superintendent, Sam T. Woodring. Not technically difficult, it is a long one-day or nice two-day trip from Paintbrush Canyon and has an interesting knife ridge summit.

0.3 9.7   North Jenny Lake Junction. Jenny Lake Road goes west; Teton Park Road continues south.

Trip 6b

JENNY LAKE ROAD
(4.4 miles)
Speed limit, 25 mph

0.0 0.0   North Jenny Lake Junction. Turn west from Teton Park Road. This is a two-way road to String Lake, and one-way from there to South Jenny Lake Junction.

0.6 0.6   **Cathedral Group.** This cluster consists of the highest peaks in the Teton Range, topographically and structurally, with the greatest total displacement on the Teton normal fault, which mostly is buried along the east base of the Tetons. Due west, at the base of the mountain front, note the slightly arcing shadow. It is a 150-foot-high postglacial fault scarp; the alluvial cones with their bright-green vegetation cut through the scarp, a sure sign of movement in the last 9 million years.

The Cathedral Group is not the historic "Trois Tetons" as named and seen from eastern Idaho. This noteworthy combination includes, from left to right, Teewinot, the Grand Teton, and Mt. Owen, with Mt. Owen's parapets and snowfields all but blending into the Grand's upper walls. Visible on the Grand's north face are two of the slanting ledges so vital in the difficult north-face climb.

At 12,928 feet, **Mt. Owen** ranks as the second highest of the Teton summits, only 842 feet lower than the Grand; it is, however, unsurpassed in beauty and climbing interest. It was named for early surveyor W.O. "Billy" Owen, who surveyed the first homesteads in the valley and organized the Grand's 1898 ascent. On July

16, 1930, Bob Underhill, Kenneth Henderson, Phil Smith and F.M. Fryxell, outstanding climbers of the day, conquered this last of the mighty Teton peaks. Reaching the base of the 60-foot summit knob, which had stopped previous attempts, they corkscrewed around from east to west and found it split by a chimney, which led them to victory.

At least 15 routes, plus variations, now lead to Owen's summit. The ice and spire pattern on Owen's northeast face forms one of the formidable mountain slopes in its 5,000-foot sweep out of Cascade Canyon. These snowfields, first soloed by Paul Petzoldt in 1931, provide the range's most interesting summer snow climb.

Mt. Owen has seen its share of tragedies as well. One occurred on Aug. 24, 1947, almost at the top of the east ridge, on the left skyline. Bill McIndoe was 100 feet off-route, clinging desperately and trying to find a grip in the pattern of smooth granite. As heavy storms buffeted the peak, the 20-year-old park employee—after celebrating half the night in Jackson—had left for the climb without registering and with friends protesting. The next day, his body was found on a ledge, crushed from a fall.

The old Square G, a well-known and loved dude ranch owned by the Gabbys, was located in this area.

1.0 1.6 **String Lake Recreation Area**. The turnoff will take you to parking, picnic area, the Leigh Lake trailhead, a small boat dock with a 0.3-mile paved handicapped-accessible trail connecting it to the picnic area, a horse unloading area, and swimming. String Lake, once called Beaver Dick Lake, fills a narrow, meandering depression—possibly an old river channel—that connects Leigh and Jenny lakes. It is shallow and warms up enough for good swimming, but poor fishing; you'll get suckers if you try. No motor boats are allowed.

To reach Leigh Lake and its outlet from the parking lot trailhead, hike north a mile. If you're using a boat (no motors allowed), be prepared for a quarter-mile portage. This lake has the best fishing before July 1, especially from either the abrupt northwest banks or close to the inlet. Winds can turn an otherwise placid lake into a dangerous challenge, so be prepared.

Leigh Lake was named for one of the last of the mountain men. Richard "Beaver Dick" Leigh (1831-1899), who lived in Teton Basin, Idaho, trapped mostly in westside Teton canyons but sometimes guided into Jackson's Hole. Born in Manchester, England, he came to the United States with his sister when he was 7 years old. He fought in the Mexican War, trapped for the Hudson's Bay Co., came to the Rockies in 1859, and even made a vague attempt to climb the Grand Teton on horseback. He sold his furs mostly at Eagle Rock—present-day Idaho Falls—and at Fort Hall.

Leigh earned the name "Beaver Dick" because he could "trap beaver where there warn't any." He guided for the 1872 and 1878 Hayden Surveys, for Teddy Roosevelt in 1892, and for others. He was described by Wister's friend, John K. Mitchell, as "a round-shouldered, long-bearded, big-nosed old man, with a clear light blue eye... & drops his H's like a hansom cabby in the Strand."

His first Shoshone wife, Jenny, and their six children, died of smallpox in 1876. Later, when he was more than 50 years old, Leigh married a 14-year-old Bannock girl, Sue Tadpole. A friend of her parents, he had assisted at her birth. Sue and Leigh had three children. Leigh died in 1899 on his "Hog Hollow" homestead in Idaho, and is buried on the bluff overlooking the Teton River where, as he wished, "I can see the Teton Peaks, and see who is the sonovabich who gets my land." His wife, Sue, lived until 1927.

TRAILS AROUND STRING AND LEIGH LAKES
(see map)

A well-marked, four-mile trail goes around String Lake, crossing bridges at the lake's outlet and inlet.

Leigh Lake Trails. Leigh Lake has five campsites on its shores, all accessible by boat and all requiring reservations. The eastside trail from the String Lake parking lot started out as a road to Forest Service summer-home leases on Leigh Lake. The Park Service eventually closed the road and turned it into a trail. Today, it has become an elk highway, while areas east and north of the lake have become spring calving grounds. The trail forks near the trail cabin at the north end, the right trail continuing north toward three campsites at Bearpaw and Trapper lakes. An unmaintained trail continues along the base of Moran, from which others split off west for various parts of Moran's east-face routes.

The unmaintained left fork involves bushwhacking and deadfall as it tries to follow an enticing but frustrating old trail west to

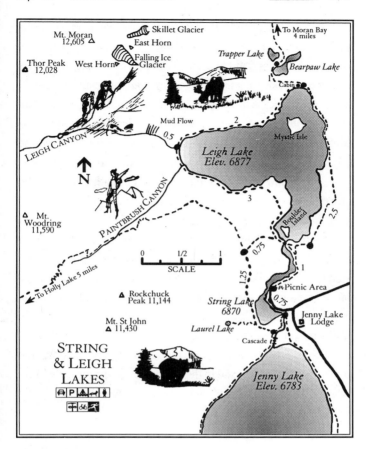

the mouth of Leigh Canyon. Here, in 1941, a tremendous mud avalanche swept down. On Aug. 9-10, cloudbursts supersaturated the north side talus slopes a half mile up canyon, converting them into mud, which slid down canyon a quarter mile and wiped out brush, scrub forest and trees. It was the largest of several mudflows that summer. For something that once caused quite a commotion, today the site, overgrown with brush, goes unnoticed. Climbing tracks can be found heading for the Horns, far above, and for the South Buttress. A loose trail network leads high along the north canyon wall toward Thor.

Paintbrush Canyon Trail to Holly Lake (5.5 miles, one way) takes off from the String Lake parking lot. Hike the mile north to the Leigh Lake outlet and a trail junction. Cross the bridge and take a left, westerly fork for three quarters of a mile, to a well-signed junction. Go right, through enticing huckleberry patches, switchbacking sharply across the steep faces of three glacial "stairsteps," or benches. Glaciers ground the lower canyon walls into rounded, polished surfaces. Above the former ice level, the rocks are rough and angular, more likely to break off. Five miles from String Lake, turn north on a faint trail; in a half mile, you'll reach Holly Lake, which lies in an old cirque facing south. The glacier melted so rapidly at the end of the Ice Age that little morainal debris surrounds the lake. If you are considering crossing Paintbrush Divide (el. 10,645) between Holly and Solitude lakes, be aware of snow conditions and cautious of weather changes. An ice axe and good boots also will be very handy. Folks on horseback should only cross late in the season.

August is best for the glorious thrill of these high-country views. Continue west from Holly Lake junction (or traverse south from Holly and back to the main trail) above timber, crossing snow patches for another three miles. If snow covers the trail, work right, above trail to the rock wall; don't get on the steep snow to the left. From String Lake to this Divide is 8.5 miles.

The trail continues west across the divide, descending into upper Cascade Canyon and to the north end of Lake Solitude. From the Divide, via Lake Solitude and Cascade Canyon, it is 12 miles to Jenny Lake Campground.

Back at **String Lake Junction**, continue south on **Jenny Lake Scenic Road**. It is one-way southbound for cars, two-way for bikes.

For the next 2.5 miles (S) to Jenny Lake, the road traverses the moraine that dams Jenny Lake; it was formed during the late Pinedale glaciation. Here, you'll find pure stands of Douglas fir— some mixed with the smaller alpine fir, which is replacing the earlier stands.

0.2 1.8 **Jenny Lake Lodge** (E). The guest facilities here offer a luxurious setting from which to ride horses, study original paintings, and dine sumptuously; reservations are required for the stunning six-course dinners.

In 1922, Tony Grace started up the small Danny Ranch for dudes, selling it eight years later to Rockefeller's "Snakes," who renovated it. A 1935 fire burned the lodge, and the gutted building has formed the nucleus of today's prestigious Jenny Lake Lodge, which was again remodeled and expanded in 1987. Such notables as Princess Grace and family have been here.

1.6 3.4 **Jenny Lake Overlook**. The U-shaped canyon directly west is Cascade Canyon, with Mt. Teewinot in the foreground, Mt. Owen beyond, and the Grand Teton barely visible behind Teewinot. A lake shore nature trail below the overlook leaves the Jenny Lake campground and takes you to String Lake.

Jenny Lake is the second largest lake in the park. At one time, others were less conservative-minded toward its water. In 1919, state engineer Frank Emerson proposed a dam at the outlet of Jenny Lake; it would have raised Jenny's water by 20 feet and Leigh's by 10 feet. A small group became incensed and opposed the construction. When the Forest Service did nothing to stop it, the newly appointed Yellowstone superintendent, Horace Albright, used executive order to prevent the project in 1918.

From the shallow, rocky shoreline of Jenny Lake, its blue waters deepen to a maximum of 225 feet. This natural lake is surrounded by a classic example of the youngest moraines in the region, which defined the limits of a glacier that flowed down Cascade Canyon. The lake also gives proof of other geological forces at work. In 1983, divers found two Engelmann spruces with five-foot diameters rooted in the lake bottom—standing upright and enclosed in 80 feet of water. Long after the ice was gone, the valley floor, still unstable, continued to drop. These big spruces went down with it, to be enveloped in the Jenny Lake waters.

Early-morning photographers will be rewarded by the mirror views of rugged Teewinot, reflected in Jenny Lake. This photogenic gem is named for Jenny Leigh, the Shoshone wife of Beaver Dick Leigh. His was the first wedding ceremony with an Indian performed according to white men's law in this region. Unhappily Jenny and their six children died Christmas week, 1876, amid a smallpox epidemic that swept Idaho's Snake River valley. A young squaw, widowed by the disease, with a 3-year-old child and another one due, had fled the plague in terror. The Leigh family kindly gave her aid, but smallpox and childbirth killed her, leaving the Leighs to care for the infected 3-year-old.

After contracting smallpox, Jenny also gave birth. Describing his wife's death, Beaver Dick pathetically wrote to his friend Dr. Josiah Curtis: "She was layeng very quite now for about 2 hours when she asked for a drink of water i was... Keeping them [his daughters] downe with the fevor i told Anes (Haines) what she wanted and he gave hur a drink and 10 minuts more she was ded Dick turned over in bed when he hurd the words and he sade to me father maby we will all die...."

In addition to the good photographic opportunities, Jenny Lake offers fishing. Cutthroat and Mackinaw trout are best sought here in spring and fall. Early-season shore fishermen do best if they hoof it along the trail to the mountain side of the lake, while the trolling is better later in the season. John Cherry always said he was the first man ever to fish Jenny Lake. According to his tall tale, he fished from a raft because the fish he caught were so big they pulled him and his raft around the lake all day.

Teewinot (el. 12,325) rises a sharp vertical mile above Jenny Lake, so dominating the view that visitors mistake it for the Grand Teton. Some say Teewinot means "Many Pinnacles" in Shoshone and once was applied to the whole range. But Osborne Russell (1835) disagreed, saying that tribe called the Tetons, "The Hoary-Headed Fathers." No matter the origin of its name, Teewinot is an essential part of this uplift range. Look along the mountain base for "fault scarps;" these traces of the Teton normal fault are best seen in late afternoon.

This is the only Teton summit rising to an actual point, one no bigger than your thumb. Because of a marvelous view of the Grand, it has become a favorite: It is an overly long one-day climb. It first was climbed on Dec. 15, 1915, from "Mirror" (Jenny) Lake, by three soldiers from the Army camp at Jackson Lake. In the early-morning darkness, Major J.D. Reardan, Sergeant Haske and Private Keen thought they had climbed the Grand Teton.

Fritiof Fryxell and Phil Smith definitely climbed Teewinot on Aug. 14, 1929, via the great east-face couloir. It was a harder climb than it now is because, in 1934, the upper third of the east face tumbled all summer, rolling into and filling the couloir below; more rocks rolled the night of the 1959 Hebgen Lake, Montana, earthquake. Cliff glaciers have gouged out the shallow cirques in the high-hanging gullies of the east face. In early season, snow packs the great couloir, where at least two people have died.

Although Teewinot is not difficult for experienced alpinists, like all the peaks, it is not for the foolhardy. In July of 1957, Richard P. Holleman, 20, grasped a projecting rock and swung from it. The rock pulled out, and Holleman fell into his climbing partner,

James Rast, also 20. Both tumbled 50 feet to a snowfield. A rolling rock hit Rast, shattered his back, and hurled him another 200 feet down the snowfield, where he plunged head-first into the rock outcroppings.

Two years later, Parshall Terry, 43, was climbing, unroped, with his two sons. On a short slabby pitch, he found himself unable to climb up or down, so he jumped. Terry lost his footing and fell 80 feet to the moat of the central snowfield, where he died of a broken neck and a fractured skull.

That same summer, Yvon Chouinard had a nonfatal accident on Teewinot's Crooked Thumb, on the peak's right skyline. A loose handhold caused Chouinard to fall 160 feet from the overhanging north face. The climbing rope, tied to a band of one-inch sling wrapped several times around his waist, stopped his fall. Miraculously, Chouinard escaped with only bruises.

Ice-carved **Cascade Canyon**, north of Teewinot, slices through the Tetons, forming the deepest, yet most accessible of the canyons. Its south fork circles behind the Grand, while its north fork goes to Lake Solitude. It was the "Great Cañon" of the Hayden Survey where "Mr. Taggart found a cluster of falls and rapids about 250 feet high, with lofty, precipitous walls on either hand." It is these walls that belong to a number of popular climbing peaks up this canyon. Let's look at them from south to north.

Storm Point (el. 10,054), overlooking Cascade Canyon on the north, seems almost dwarfed by the other peaks. But its superior rock climbing—within easy hiking from Jenny Lake—and the promise of an eagle's view of the faces of the Cathedral Group make it a popular destination. F. Fryxell and Frank Smith made the first ascent of Storm Point on Aug. 13, 1931. They so named it because this peak bears the brunt of storms sweeping down the canyon.

Adding to its popularity is Guides Wall. On their days off, the guides play here, and the Wall is always echoing with climbers' shouts. In 1992, this wall was the scene of a heart-stopping helicopter rescue in a deadly storm. Dr. Roland Fleck of Jackson had tested the in-site piton, which, he said, should have held a horse. Believing the piton secure, Fleck tied into it and leaned back to survey the route above. But the piton pulled out and Fleck fell past his lower belayer to a ledge 40 feet below; because of anchors, his belayer was unable to stop him sooner. With numerous and severe broken bones and a punctured lung, Fleck clung to life at the pleadings of his daughter. Finally, in the teeth of the storm, the park's rescue rangers were able to load him into a helicopter—after several tries—with the copter's blades whirring just 10 feet from the wall.

Ice Point (el. 9,920) is the tiny pinnacle on the ridge north of Storm. After climbing from Jenny Lake to the ridge, you'll look down breathtakingly vertical walls into Cascade Canyon from here. The vertical distance to the canyon floor seems deceiving and can lead to deadly mistakes. To James B. Ayer, crossing north of Ice Point in August, 1952, it looked like a few yards, a shortcut down. He fell 200 feet down the 500-foot walls, and his body was carried out in a sewed-up canvas bag.

Symmetry Spire, (el. 10,560), the next peak north, has become another favorite one-day climb. It boasts more than 20 distinct routes, ranging from classes 3 to 5.7 in difficulty, and including the darkly shadowed Templeton Crack, which gouges the southeast side and is flanked by the famous Durrance and Jensen ridges.

Cube Point (el. 9,600), a pinnacle on the east ridge of Symmetry Spire, also has been the site of tragedy. In August of 1960, Janet Crane, 18 years old and one of a party of four led by a guide, was descending near Cube Point. Unroped and standing on a ledge waiting her turn to rappel, she suddenly lost her balance, pitched over the head of the guide who tried to catch her, and fell 90 feet to her death.

To many, nearby Hanging Canyon is the most photogenic spot in the range. This glacial valley, hidden between Symmetry Spire and Mt. St. John (N), holds three lovely cirque lakes, above which towers a circle of pinnacles with names including Rock of Ages, Canine Tooth, Grinders, and Needle's Eye Spire.

Mt. St. John (el. 11,430) crests a serrated ridge, the highest point of which is difficult to determine from below. After several tries and using a Brunton transit, on Aug. 20, 1929, the park's first rangers—Phil Smith and F. Fryxell—determined that they had reached the summit, the first to do so. They named the mountain for Hayden Survey geologist Orestes St. John.

In 1933, the north face fell out, bouncing huge rocks off the slopes, shaking the valley below, and raising a hovering dust cloud. Today, you can reach St. John's via Class 3 climbing up Hanging Canyon and the ridge above the Lake of the Crags.

Rockchuck Peak (el. 11,144) was named for its little inhabitants. The north-south arcing shadow near its base is the Teton Fault. Probably the shortest major peak climb, Rockchuck has six routes and is recommended for knowledgeable beginning climbers or as a "conditioner" (Class 3) for other climbers. The last few hundred yards of the climb straddle an airy knife edge that drops vertically on both sides. The peak is best approached from west of String Lake. F. Fryxell made the first ascent of Rockchuck on Aug. 16, 1929.

0.4 3.8   Junction. The road turns east to join the Park Road, while the bike trail continues south to the campground. At 0.6 miles, the trail passes "erratics"—gray, angular boulders plucked from the high canyons and carried here by glacial ice. These **Jenny Lake Boulders** have become climbers'"practice rocks," with near-impossible routes to throw even the best of them. The Jenny Lake moraine marked the original 1929 east boundary of the park, which then embraced only the Tetons and the lakes at their base.

0.6 4.4   Junction with Park Road at South Jenny Lake Junction.

TRAILS AT JENNY LAKE
(see map)

Grand Teton National Park has more than 245 miles of trails, including the easy stroll to Hidden Falls, a hike around Jenny Lake, or the 27-mile hike up Cascade Canyon and down Death Canyon. Take your pick.

We'll go clockwise around Jenny Lake, on the **Jenny Lake Trail,** which is a 7.5-mile trip that begins at the south end of the lake, at the boat dock bridge over Cottonwood Creek. This hike takes you through the devastation of a freak hurricane that, in late 1973, blew down most of the trees along the lake's south end; the scars have healed slowly. Look for moose and beaver activity—dams, ponds, slides and aspen cuttings—at the Moose Pond Overlook, a mile west of the boat dock. By skirting the base of pinnacled Teewinot above, the lake trail loosely follows a section of the 50-mile-long, mostly buried Teton fault, which created the range 10 million years ago. The trees along here are large mossy, lichened Douglas firs, alpine firs, and Engelmann spruce. The shadowy shapes of twisted debris, results of the winter avalanche of 1950, still are visible in the lake's blue depths.

At the junction with Hidden Falls Trail (see below), continue right, or north, across Cascade Creek, past the floating boat dock, and around Jenny Lake 1.75 miles to the junction with the String Lake Trail. Continue right, crossing the String Lake outlet, and take the right fork at the next junction. From this point, the trail follows the hummocky Jenny Lake moraine 1.75 miles to Jenny Lake Overlook. *(See Jenny Lake Road for details)*. The trail continues south to the boat docks.

The trail to **Hidden Falls**, **Inspiration Point** and up Cascade Canyon undoubtedly is the Park's most popular—with good reason. Either take a 15-minute boat shuttle and save 2.2 miles, or hike the previously described trail to its junction with the Cascade Canyon Trail.

You should be duly impressed because, when you step off the boat dock, you are crossing the Teton fault, where a major earthquake split the landscape. When that occurred some 10 million years ago, the west block rose, creating the Tetons, and the east block sank to create Jackson's Hole. From the dock, hike 0.5 miles toward Hidden Falls, passing some unique layered rock—banded gneiss (pronounced "nice"), Precambrian core—the oldest exposed rock in the Tetons. When it was formed, the only life around was blue-green algae. The trailside polished bedrock exhibits the rounded and fluted "footprints" of glaciers.

At Cascade Creek bridge, turn left to a photographic point. Here, Cascade Creek plunges over a glacial bench to form Hidden Falls. Hayden surveyor Bradley's assistant, William Taggart, hiked up Cascade Canyon and found "a cluster of falls and rapids about 250 feet high." Perhaps you will see one of the climbing classes using the rocks left of Hidden Falls.

The main trail continues right, switchbacking up three glacial benches and 0.05 miles to Inspiration Point (el. 7,200) and a marvelous view from the top of the bench. The next four miles west go under Storm Point's famous south face, Guides Wall, past avalanche slopes and favorite moose delights, including willow, huckleberry, honeysuckle, and spirea.

When you reach the **fork of Cascade Creek**, five miles from the boat dock, the North Fork Trail splits off and continues north-

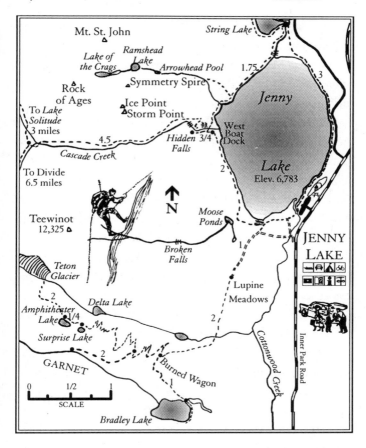

west for three miles along the creek to the reflective **Lake Solitude**; fishing is good in July and August. Lake Solitude fills a glacial basin, carved by a heavy body of ice, snow and rock, but because the ice melted rapidly, there is no terminal moraine. From the north side of the lake, a 2.5-mile trail climbs the north side of the canyon to **Paintbrush Divide** (10,640), then descends past Holly Lake, through Paintbrush Canyon eight miles, back to String and Jenny lakes.

For a long, hard one-day loop trip of 27 miles—unless you make it into a two- or three-day trip and enjoy the beautiful backcountry of the Tetons—try the South Fork Trail. From the Cascade Canyon forks, five miles west of the boat dock, take the left (SW) trail past the Whitebark Forest 3.8 miles to a faint junction. The dimmer left fork is the abandoned Skyline Trail, which dead-ends at the Cascade-Avalanche Canyon Divide, overlooking upper Avalanche Canyon and The Wall area (brookies in the lake below). The South Fork Trail continues right (W), switchbacking past **Schoolroom Glacier** (S). This glacier displays classic glacial features in miniature: bergschrund, crevasses, little lake turquoise-colored from rock flour in suspension, severed ice blocks, morainal rock debris bulldozed ahead of the snout, and a stream outlet.

At **Hurricane Pass** (el. 10,320), 6.5 miles from the Forks, you are at the highest point of the **Teton Crest Trail**, which you now join. Head south across the back of The Wall and descend into the snow-meadow-rock mosaic of Alaska Basin, studded with jewel-like lakes and glacial striations. Half a mile south of Sunset Lake (brookies), leave the Teton Crest Trail—unless you want to do the "Teton Death March" south past Basin Lakes, over Mt. Meek Pass, along Death Canyon Shelf to Fox Creek Pass, Marion Lake, and Phillips Pass, exiting at Coal Creek at the base of Teton Pass. Our less-adventurous trail climbs southeast out of Alaska Basin over **Buck Mountain Pass**, the divide southwest of Buck Mountain; it is 5.5 miles from Hurricane Pass to the divide.

When you're over Buck Mountain Pass, the trail skirts below Static Peak. You might as well bag easy **Static Peak** (el. 11,303), via a walk up the southwest ridge. Then, head south down the Death Canyon switchbacks, through another whitebark forest to the patrol cabin and junction at four miles. Continue left down Death Canyon Trail, below the popular canyon walls, famous for climbs like The Snaz (IV, 5.9). Save energy for the unexpected kicker climb up to the Phelps Lake Overlook, 2.5 miles from the cabin, and the final two miles to the Death Canyon parking area. Not to be recommended for the untrained, this point-to-point hike covers 27 miles.

TETON PARK ROAD
Jenny Lake North Junction to Moose
(11.4 miles)
45 m.p.h, enforced

In 1992, the Park Service widened and curved this road, formerly called the Straightaway; the wider shoulders have made the entire stretch bikeable. In the spring, after the first four miles are cleared of snow to Cottonwood Creek, the Teton Park and Jenny Lake roads are closed for a month to motor vehicles, making an ideal loop for hikers, bikers and rollerbladers to enjoy.

0.0 0.0 **North Junction Jenny Lake Road** (Turn west for Jenny Lake Road, Trip 6b). Continue south on Park Road.

0.4 0.4 **"Dry Hollow."** Locals named this abandoned channel of Snake River "Dry Hollow." It begins at a gap in the Jackson Lake moraine, which may have been a temporary outlet of Jackson Lake or a tributary of Jackson Lake glacier. This impressive channel goes south four miles to Timbered Island and is terraced on its west bank. During the hard year of 1897-98, 25,000 elk wintered here.

1.2 1.6 Scenic Turnout. See the Jenny Lake Road (Trip 6b) for the story of the view to the west.

1.0 2.6 Brush-covered flats. This area is the glacial outwash of earlier Ice Ages, brush-covered because the soil is too porous to support other vegetation. The highway in this section skirts the tree-covered Jenny Lake moraine to the west.

Building Jackson Lake Dam, 1910 (top).

Beaver Dick's First Family–L to R–Leigh, John, Ann Jane, Jenny with William, Dick Jr. on mule.

Amphitheater Lake (above, left).

St. John (I), Rockchuck (J) and Climbing Route (R). Note Teton Fault on lower right (right).

Crandall Studio (below, right) at Jenny Lake, now the Jenny Lake Visitor Center/Museum.

Tetons from Signal Mountain–L to R: Mt. St. John, Rockchuck, Paintbrush Canyon, Mt. Woodring, Leigh Canyon, Mt. Moran with West Horn, East Horn and Skillet Glacier on East Face, Moran Canyon and part of Bivouac Peak (bottom).

0.1 2.7   One-way Jenny Lake Road rejoins the Park Road.

0.3 3.0   **Jenny Lake Campground** (W). Ancient glaciers flowing east out of the range carried the large, angular Precambrian rocks—erratics—seen along the road. The campground is west of the highway, hidden in the timber.

1.0 4.0   **Jenny Lake Area** (see map). Here, you will find a campground, two big parking loops for regular and oversized vehicles, a ranger station, store/gift shop, visitor center, museum, vault toilets, trails to Jenny Lake, the boat dock, and the Exum mountain-guide service at the far end of the lower parking lot.

Some of the buildings in this area have historical significance. **The Jenny Lake Ranger Station**—moved to the Jenny Lake area in 1930 from Lee Manges' place at Windy Point—was the park's first ranger station and museum. Now it is the center for voluntary registration, and a place to get information about weather forecasts and route conditions. The climbing rangers have very good photos of the more popular climbing routes of various peaks.

Near the Jenny Lake Store, built in 1992, sits the **Jenny Lake Visitor Center and Museum**, which was the old Crandall Studio that stood for years on the shore of Jenny Lake and now is in its third location. In 1929, artist Harrison Crandall established himself as the park's greatest publicist, taking thousands of pictures and selling them as postcards or turning them into paintings. What he built as his studio in 1927, Crandall transformed into a store and gift shop in 1959, an operation that continued after his death. The visitor center now unfolds the fascinating story of the park's geology.

Beyond the restrooms are trailheads for the boat dock and Jenny Lake Trail to Hidden Falls and Cascade Canyon, as well as the lakeshore return trail (see Trip 6b). Other facilities include one of two of the fine climbing schools in Jackson Hole. The offices of the Exum Climbing School and Mountain Guide Service, the nation's first guide service, are near Jenny Lake and those of the Jackson Hole Mountain Guides are in Jackson.

Since long before the park's establishment in 1929, the **Jenny Lake Campground** has been a favorite gathering place for artists, photographers, climbers, and visitors. It was devastated in the fall of 1933, when the first recorded cyclone in the Hole whirled down the mountain and slashed a half-mile swath, uprooting hundreds of trees, snapping their trunks like match sticks. The CCC cleaned up the mess. Another freak hurricane struck in November of 1973, during which the campground and most of the large trees at the south end of Jenny Lake were flattened.

When F.M. "Doc" Fryxell came to the Hole in 1926 to work on his doctorate about the glacial geology of the region, he had no idea the influence he would have in the valley. In short order, he would make a dozen first ascents, name the mountains, and write

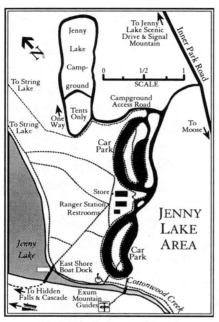

the first guide book. When Grand Teton Park was created in 1929, he became its first ranger-naturalist, setting up the first museum and starting the popular Jenny Lake campfire lectures. Known as a superb lecturer, he could talk about any aspect of the park, but was foremost a geologist. Fryxell also had a healthy sense of humor. One evening, he was talking about the glacial history of the Tetons and valley, telling his listeners that they couldn't put their sleeping bags anywhere without putting them on a hard rock deposited by the glacier. When a man asked where the glacier had gone, Doc thought a moment and then replied that it had gone back for more rocks!

0.7 4.7 **Lupine Meadows to Glacier Trail**. Take the turnoff west and cross Cottonwood Creek to a junction; the right fork goes to **Jenny Lake boat dock** for boat trips, boat rentals or public boat launching.

It also takes you to the site of the old CCC/Climber's Ghetto, slightly south of the boat-dock area, where the dregs of the old CCC camp (outhouse and water tank system) separated the "fun hogs"—noisy, dirty climbers—from the "dude campers" at the Jenny Lake campground. Here collected the brash, penniless, young tigers from Yosemite, today's famous and reputable citizens—Yvon Chouinard, Tom Frost, Al Steck, Royal Robbins, and et al—all searching for cool granites and new routes. The Gunk's bad boys of climbing, the notorious Vulgarians, were here too, looking for novelty and mean rock. Added to the scene were the Bonneys in their tepee, Bill Briggs and his guitar, nightly Teton Tea parties/campfires/all night singing, and cop-ranger Jules T. to make sure paradise wasn't! For various administrative reasons (upset rangers?), Climber's Camp was closed and bulldozed back to sagebrush—but never forgotten!

Take the left fork south and west for a mile to get to the Lupine Meadows parking area, complete with vault toilet. From Lupine Meadows, the Glacier Trail climbs six miles and 3,000 feet to Surprise and Amphitheater (el. 9,698) lakes. During this hike, you will pass through four life zones: Transition, Canadian, Hudsonian, and Arctic-alpine.

The Glacier Trail starts by climbing a morainal ridge two miles to the Valley Trail junction. (The left fork goes south to Taggart and Bradley lakes). Continue right. Beyond the junction, you will find the last spring water for several miles. From here, it's five long switchbacks and four miles from your car to the Garnet Canyon junction (take the left fork up Garnet Canyon to climb the Grand). Take the right fork another two miles, up 14 ever-tightening switchbacks, to Surprise Lake, which is stocked with cutthroat. Climbing Surprise Pinnacle, to the east and 260 feet above the outlet, presents a fine panorama of Jackson's Hole and the Tetons. Another 10-minute hike gets you to Amphitheater Lake, a campsite for climbers intent on Disappointment, Owen, Teewinot, and the east and north sides of the Grand. North of the trail, look high for a plaque dedicated to Theodore Teepe, the first to die (1925) climbing the Grand.

The **Teton Glacier**, the largest such body in these mountains, lies another strenuous two miles beyond Amphitheater Lake; until late in the season, an ice axe is recommended for this hike. To reach the glacier from the lake, hike another 0.2 miles to where the trail angles up to the low point in the ridge to the north, overlooking Glacier Gulch and the Teton Glacier moraine in the distance (NW). Whitebark pines uprooted by strong winds mark the spot on the ridgeline. Teton Glacier sits in the cirque at the head of Glacier Gulch. Follow the trail west around the base of Disappointment Peak, over steep snow banks—no glacier yet—to the bowl between Disappointment and the Grand. From there, go north up the moraine at its left or western edge, making a left traverse to the hard-to-identify glacier, a level area of dirty flat ice.

Above, you will see the hard pack, the ice falls and crevasses of the active glacier, as well as the upper bergschrund crevasse separating the moving ice stream from the stagnant frozen accumulation, still clinging to rock above. The glacier has receded considerably from its terminal moraine. In the early 1900s, it was about 3,500 feet long and 1,200 wide, with its central ice moving about 28 feet per year.

0.3 5.0   Former site of the Jenny Lake post office and store. Nell Roach and her sister and brother-in-law, Mr. and Mrs. Bill Novotny operated the store—once famous for milkshakes—for years. The post office, which opened in 1926 for summers only, originally was housed in one of Homer Richard's buildings south of here; eventually, it was moved to the Jenny Lake Store on the J.D. Kimmel property. The old cabins to the west now house park personnel.

Northern Jackson's Hole, west of the Snake River, was not opened to homesteading until much later than the south end because of a lack of survey to lay out the 160-acre homesteads. Once surveyed, though, folks began moving in, trying to turn rocky glacial outwash plains into hayfields. By the 1920s, private irrigation claims were staked in this area, with hopes of diverting water from Leigh and Jenny lakes for Idaho use.

This site once was called the "Nest," but with its dance halls, speakeasies, filling stations, and tent cabins, it more aptly would have been termed an early example of "intense visual clutter." In those days, the Jenny Lake dance hall housed rough and wild memories for teenager, and future famous climber, Glenn Exum. On the Saturday in 1931 when he soloed the first ascent of the splendid route on the Grand that later was named for him, he wasn't even late for his evening performance playing clarinet. From then on, his climbing and guiding career continued upward; he ran the world famous Exum Guide Service until 1978.

0.6 5.6   **Disappointment Peak** (11,618). At this point in the drive, Disappointment comes into view as a separate peak from the Grand.

0.2 5.8 Parking. **Grand Teton**. Follow the Grand's left sky-line down to Teepes Pillar, and below it to the triangular snowfield called Teepes Glacier (although it melted out one summer). Both features were named for Theodore Teepe, who fell to his death on the glacier in 1925. Tired from making the 13th ascent of the Grand and the long descent, he slipped near the top of this snowfield, rolling and crashing down before striking his head against the large, central rock in the glacier. Seeing the hole in Teepe's head, the size of a fist, probably helped convince his guide, Gibb Scott, never to climb again.

0.7 6.5 **Glacier Gulch Scenic Turnout**. From this spot, you'll get an excellent view of the range from Buck Mountain (S) to Teewinot (N).

In 1876, Lt. Doane described this country as a "wide valley... seamed with rocky channels and heaped with moraines... a grim ruinous landscape. There are no foothills to the Tetons. They rise suddenly in rugged majesty from the rock strewn plain. Masses of heavy forests appear on the glacial debris...."

The Tetons rise 7,000 feet from the sagebrush plains to their highest summit, the Grand Teton. Today's park visitors may wonder why early maps and reports listed them as the Three Tetons, when they actually see many more summits. The original name derives from the Idaho side, where three distinct summits stand out—the South, the Middle and the Grand.

Nez Percé (el. 11,901), pronounced "nay pursay," and once called Howling Dog, is named for an Indian tribe that once hunted the Yellowstone and customarily pierced their noses for ornamentation. You can climb Nez Percé's summit from four compass directions and many routes. F.M. Fryxell and Phil Smith, the park's first two rangers, made the first ascent in July, 1930.

Like so many Teton peaks, Nez Percé has seen its share of tragedy. In August, 1948, Winthrop L. Akin, 20, had reached the craggy west summit and stepped out to photograph his chum signing the register. Suddenly, the slab on which he was standing came loose, and unroped Akin fell backward through the air and onto rocks 100 feet below. Although he was killed instantly, his body tumbled further. Evacuating his body was a monumental task for the Park Service's rescue team, requiring 21 hours of work. After being raised 600 feet to the summit, the rescue team lowered the body by stretcher 4,000 feet into Garnet Canyon; from there, they packed it by horse another six miles.

In August, 1960, seasonal park rescue ranger Tim Bond, 24, waved as he passed the authors' tepee; he was bound for a successful, off-duty climb of the strenuous north face of the Grand. Two days later, however, this experienced climber clambered on to the steep south walls of Nez Percé with his new bride, Sally, and two others. A loose foothold pulled out and pitched him 60 feet into space, where he dangled with Sally holding his rope. He talked to Sally for 15 minutes, finally dying as the rope tightened on his injured chest.

Behind Nez Percé, astride the long ridge leading to the **South Teton**, are—from east to west—Cloudveil Dome, Spalding Peak, **Gilkey Tower** and Icecream Cone.

Many people have honed their climbing skills in the Tetons and gone on to attempt the highest peaks in the world. One such person was geologist Art Gilkey, an Exum guide who lost his life on the third American K2 expedition of 1953. He had developed thrombophlebitis but, while being evacuated, was swept off a ledge by an avalanche during a raging snowstorm. A cairn was erected at the base of K2. Forty years later, in 1993, a British expedition found his remains.

Though the fifth-highest peak in the range, the **South Teton** (el. 12,514) hides modestly behind Nez Percé. Now climbed by at least six routes, Albert Ellingwood and Eleanor Davis made the first ascent on Aug. 29, 1933. Technically easy, though long, the regular route follows the north skyline from the South Saddle.

Just below the north end of the South Saddle, a member of the Chicago Mountain Club got into trouble on July 21, 1948. Art Tielsch and four other club members were descending the Middle. They had only one ice axe between them and little snow experience. At about 11 p.m., the tired group started across a snowfield, holding hands instead of roping up. One climber fell, colliding with the others. The exhausted Tielsch was swept off his feet, and slid 200 feet to his death.

The next summit north is the **Middle Teton** (el. 12,804), which divides the forks of Garnet Canyon. The third-highest Teton peak, it is climbed by 12 routes. Albert Ellingwood soloed the first ascent in a snowstorm on Aug. 29, 1933. A more spectacular climb

Theodore Teepe Memorial Stone (top, left).

The Belly Roll, Spaulding-Owen Route, Grand Teton (above).

Hidden Falls (left).

Camping at Lake Solitude. West faces of Mt. Owen and the Grand (below, left).

Schoolroom Glacier (below, right).

Teton Range (bottom). A) South Teton. B) Avalanche Canyon. C) Nez Perce. D) Middle Teton. E)Lower Saddle & bivouac. F) Garnet Canyon. G) Grand Teton. J) Gunsight Notch. K) Mt. Owen. L) East Prong. M) Teton Glacier. N) Glacier Gulch. O) Teewinot. P) Crooked Thumb.

is the Black Dike of the Middle's Dike Pinnacle, while the shrinking Middle Teton Glacier on the northeast side provides yet another route.

The towering, ice-patched **Grand Teton** (el. 13,770) is Wyoming's second-highest peak, conceding 34 feet to Gannett Peak (el. 13,804) in the Wind River Range. The Grand, believed climbable for 31 years by one route only, now has at least 27 routes up its rugged sides. These climbs range from the regular, though often icy, Spalding-Owen route and the splendid rock climb of the popular Exum route to harder chimney climbs on the West Face and icy routes of the North Face. Most Grand climbs require two days, with a bivouac on the Lower Saddle between the Middle and Grand, and with the climb made early on the second day. Binoculars leveled at the Lower Saddle will pick out the hut used by the Exum guides.

Nathaniel P. Langford, the first (unpaid) superintendent of Yellowstone National Park, and James Stevenson, assistant director of the Hayden Surveys, made the first ascent of the Grand on July 29, 1872. The pair started at a campsite near the present-day Teton Canyon campground, 11 miles east of Driggs, Idaho (see Trip 3, mile 0.0). A trio of soldiers—Captain (Dr.) Chas. Kieffer, and two soldiers from the Yellowstone Garrison—made the second ascent on Sept. 10, 1893.

Controversy erupted, however, when W.O. Owen's party, led by Bishop Franklin Spalding, climbed the Grand on Aug. 11, 1898. Owen's group found no sign of earlier ascents and claimed theirs as the first. Initially, Langford won the bitter controversy that followed. But after Langford's death, Owen revived the controversy and, on Feb. 21, 1929, the Wyoming Legislature ruled in Owen's favor (See Bonney, *The Grand Controversy*, for the full, exciting beginning of Teton climbing). Eleanor Davis was the first woman to climb the Grand when she and Albert Ellingwood reached the summit on Aug. 27, 1923.

No controversy revolves around the first ascent of the popular Exum route, which follows the left, southerly, skyline. Glenn Exum, head of the park climbing concession until 1978—but then a mere beginner in the climbing game—soloed the new route on July 15, 1931. Paul Petzoldt and he were taking clients up the regular route when Paul told Exum to check out the southeast ridge, which Exum did. Exum admits to leaping the spectacular exposed gap at the end of the "Wall Street" ledge; today, the pitch is done with rope, belays, and prayers.

Three principal snowfields cling to the upper left (SE) walls of the Grand. Near the top is the summit snowfield; follow it down to the distinctive "Otter Body Snowfield," which presents the unmistakable outline of that mammal. The final snowfield on this southeast side is "Teepe's Glacier," the top of which is barely visible from the valley floor.

From the Glacier Gulch turnout, notice the almost-perpendicular skyline of the Grand on the right; this is the North Face. To its left rises the long East Ridge. Bob Underhill and Ken Henderson conquered this route on July 22, 1929; it was so formidable a climb that five years later no one had repeated it. Then a shocked suspicion of tragedy came when friends of Fred Ohlendorf, 29, and Helmut Leese, 28, called the ranger station on July 7, 1934 to express anxiety over the pair, missing more than 32 hours. With smooth leather-soled shoes, without ice axe or rope, without registering, and without experience, the pair had started for the East Ridge, waving good-bye to four friends. Rangers began a search. On July 8, field glasses picked out a sprawled figure high up on Teepe's Glacier. It turned out to be Leese, who had been dead 24 hours—face up and head downslope—his body greatly mutilated and one shoe missing. The rangers speculated that he might have fallen from the Molar Tooth, the first great gendarme on the East Ridge, 1,000 feet above.

The search for Ohlendorf continued; two days later, his body was found on Teton Glacier, below the North Face but on the opposite side of the mountain from Leese. It was suspected that he, too, had fallen from the Molar Tooth, 1,500 feet above. Their deaths are still shrouded in mystery: Who fell first? And how did they end up on opposite sides of the Grand? Their deaths were the first to be recorded in the newly created park, but many more would follow.

The worst accident in the annals of Teton climbing began to unfold early on July 26, 1962. Ten Appalachian Mountain Club members, dressed for a one-day thrill of climbing the Grand, instead became caught up in 72 hours of terror, requiring the most technically difficult mountain rescue in Teton history.

On that day, the AMC (Appy) party of seven men and three women, ages 18-65, were being led by the experienced Ellis Blade and his assistant, 21-year-old Stephen Smith. The group left the Petzoldt Caves in upper Garnet Canyon at 4 a.m., heading for the isolated and little-used Otter Body route. Blade planned to be at the top of Teepe's Glacier by 8 a.m., at the Grand's summit by noon, and back to the caves by 5 p.m.

By noon, however, the party had only reached the top of Teepe's Glacier and was already in trouble. The group had divided into two ropes and was being slowed by rock fall, which had swept away an ice axe and crampons. Next, an electrical storm struck, and the party sheltered in a moat.

Smith and Charles Joyce wanted to turn back, but Blade felt that was more dangerous than continuing. The party's progress up the long, rotten rockfall gully leading to the Otter Body Snowfield was further slowed by waterfalls, frequent rockfall and electric shocks; one member, Charles Kellogg, was hit. That night, nine members of the party bivouacked in the couloir, sitting on and tied into a huge boulder. Blade was two pitches above. Although June urged Blade to return, he refused, saying they were committed.

Dawn revealed three inches of wet snow. The climbers were soaked and had no dry clothes and no food. It took all of July 27 for the party to get up the icy couloir's last three pitches. Lester Germer, 65, helped belay the others and then collapsed; he looked as if he was dying. Blade decided a three-man party would continue up to get help; he asked Joyce and Smith to join him.

The rest of the group occupied a small sloping ledge and tried to keep Germer alive. The trio continued up the couloir to the Otter Body tail. Worn out and climbing slowly, Blade took a fall; Joyce insisted they bivouac on a small ledge. At this point, Smith began ranting; by the next morning, he was very weak. While Blade was exploring the route above, Smith died. Blade came down and he and June tried artificial respiration. But it was hopeless. After tying Smith to a rock, Blade and Joyce turned back.

In the meantime, at about 3 p.m. on July 27, rescuers far below on Teepe's Glacier, spotted three climbers stranded near the Otter Body Snowfield and heard shouting; unprepared for the storm, however, they had to turn back. District ranger Doug

McLaren called for a major rescue operation and, late that day, dispatched a pack team with rescue supplies to Petzoldt Caves. At 4 a.m. on July 28, rangers Pete Sinclair, Sterling Neale, and Jim Greig left the caves for Teepe's Glacier; they would be followed by another rescue party with equipment and food.

By about 1 p.m., Sinclair and Greig reached the stranded party. What they saw appalled them: Only John Fenniman could stand; the others couldn't even realize the enormity of the rescue problem. While the rangers fed the group, it began to snow. The radio stopped working, so the rangers could not alert McLaren of the desperate situation.

With little recourse, Sinclair and Greig began the slow belaying-lowering routine: Tie a body in tightly, push it like a sack of grain over the cliff, anchor it in below, then leave it shivering for half an hour to deal with others. Between pitches, the slow-moving victims staggered, slithered, stumbled, fell, and slid down through water and ice. By dark, they had been lowered 400 feet, at which time Blade and Joyce caught up and told them Smith was dead.

The nightmarish descent continued—an hour for each of the five pitches. Despite the risk in the dangerous couloir, four Exum guides and Sterling Neale climbed it with miners' lights attached to their helmets. Pete Lev and Al Read, the first to reach the group, were shocked by the smell of death. With their help, the nine survivors were within one pitch of Teepe's Glacier. As Sinclair and Greig headed down, the new troops took over.

Lev and Rick Horn were dealing with Fenniman, who had "cracked up," imagining his rescuers as "one-eyed demons." Finally, they knocked him out, removed his wet clothes, put him in a sleeping bag, and tied him into a litter. By dawn, the party was at the bottom of Teepe's Glacier. While helicopters evacuated Fenniman and Germer from the Meadows in Garnet Canyon, the others rested and recuperated at the caves; all had frostbitten hands and feet. The body of Stephen Smith later was buried in a moat on the mountain.

After that came the recriminations. Why hadn't the party signed out according to federal regulations and averted the tragedy by being warned off the isolated route? In the American Alpine Club's annual *Accidents in North American Mountaineering*,

Doug McLaren wrote: "It cannot be understood why Mr. Blade did not turn back at the top of Teepe's Glacier when the storm first hit and the party was progressing so slowly.... Blade said that he decided to continue the ascent because of the lack of snow and ice experience; however, if he had studied the route beforehand, he would have been able to see that the amount of snow climbing above him was almost twice what the party had encountered on Teepe's Glacier." It was a hard lesson for Ellis Blade and the Appalachian Mountain Club.

Hard to distinguish, **Disappointment Peak** (el. 11,618) blends in so well with the Grand that it goes unnoticed. Only when the shadows are right can it been seen. It was so named because an early ascent party thought they were climbing the Grand's long east ridge. Up, up they went, only to find themselves on this minor summit. They had a fantastic view of the Grand's north face and the massive Teton Glacier but they were cut off from their objective by a tremendous chasm. A bitter disappointment indeed.

The peak itself is not a difficult climb from the south side of Amphitheater Lake. But false trails can mislead would-be climbers into cliff bands, a mistake which has taken its toll—one death and numerous injuries from falling in the enticing major snow gully above Amphitheater Lake, which only looks easy.

Glacier Gulch Turnout also gives a good view of **Timbered Island** to the east. Its name is appropriate, as its timber supplied logs for many pioneer homes and for the Chapel of the Transfiguration. From a distance, this glacial-moraine remnant looks like a wooded island in a sagebrush sea. You can hear elk bugling there in the fall.

0.3 6.8　**Old Lucas Ranch**. The turnoff to the west takes you to the homestead of another colorful Jackson Hole character, Geraldine "Aunt Ger" Lucas (1865-1938). The Hole's first "female" homesteader, Aunt Ger also wanted to be the first woman to climb the Grand. But she could only claim to be the second. No matter, it was quite a feat, at the age of 59, with Paul Petzoldt and two other men hauling her to the summit, where she waved the Stars and Stripes. When they showed her the name of the first woman to climb the Grand—Eleanor Davis—she refused to believe it.

On her ranch, she got up at daylight and went to bed at dusk. "That's why it gets dark, ain't it?" She bathed daily in the icy stream outside her cabin, and drove a dog sled in winter (Ferry Exhibit).

When friends overstayed their visit, she would say, "Our visit's up now. Good-bye."

Against park extension and the Rockefeller purchases, Aunt Ger said: "They'll never get me off this land." She fought it and them until she died. "You stack up those silver dollars as high as the Grand Teton," she told Rockefeller when he offered to buy her ranch, "and I might talk to you."

After her death, her son, Lt. Russell Lucas, hurried back and sold out to neighbor J.D. Kimmel, who sold to Rockefeller. Her ashes are buried under a plaqued rock on the property. So, in a way, she was true to her word; they didn't get her off the land. Until he died, Homer Richards placed flowers on Aunt Ger's grave. Ironically, her chief adversaries, Harold and Josephine Fabian, president and secretary of Rockefeller's Snake River Land Co., next occupied Aunt Ger's cabins.

The now-modernized cabins at the Lucas homestead are fine examples of carpentry. They were built by Paul Imeson, whose work demonstrates old-time dovetailing and log fitting at its best. Unused these days, the homestead is one of the few remaining historical landmarks.

0.2 7.0   Photo vantage. From this turnout, you can see **Mt. Wister** (el. 11,490) separating the two forks of Avalanche Canyon. This lesser-known Teton peak was named after Owen Wister, author of the Western classic, *The Virginian*. Mt. Wister's first ascent was made by park ranger Phil Smith and Oliver Zierlein, in 1928; it now is accessible by seven routes.

This turnout also affords an excellent view of the Black Dike on the Middle Teton. Caused by an intrusion of liquid igneous rock—diorite—into an earthquake fissure, this dike splits the mountain from base to summit, forming the hard-to-distinguish, but sharply separated summit of Dike Pinnacle.

0.4 7.4   American Alpine Club's **Climbers Ranch** (W). The turnoff takes you to the site of three early guest ranches: The Highlands, now used for Park Service personnel; the X Quarter Circle X, now gone, and the old Double Diamond, operated by the American Alpine Club as a climbers' ranch. The latter offers a very reasonable bunkout and is handy to the start of the Glacier Trail.

0.5 7.9   **The Wall** (W). From this spot, you can view The Wall, which runs like a cornice along the head of Avalanche Canyon.

Skyline Trail once went below its limestone columns but continual bombardment from falling rock, pried loose by ice, forced the park to relocate the trail.

0.3 8.2   **Bar BC Ranch** (E). The bumpy road east takes you down the hill to the floodplain of the Snake and the Bar BC Ranch. In 1910, two Easterners began searching in Jackson's Hole for the perfect site for a dude ranch. Writer Struthers Burt, a Princeton grad, and Freudian psychiatrist, Dr. Horace Carncross, found the ideal spot in a curve of the Snake. It had everything—water, grazing, and trees, as well as bountiful hunting and fishing, isolation, and exceptional views. They named it the Bar B (Burt) C (Carncross). They quickly readied "a small town in the wilderness, complete and self-sustaining in every detail" for their first dudes.

By 1922, the Bar BC had 45 buildings, including two dining rooms, a lodge, single and double cabins, and even a dance hall; it had become a small empire and the social center and main employer in the Hole. Felicia Gizycka remembered her arrival at the Bar BC in 1916 with her mother, "Cissy" Patterson, owner of the *Washington Times Herald*. It was late, they were drenched, and unbeknownst to them, the Burts were hosting a costume party. At their knock, Katherine Burt opened the door and said, "Hello, I'm a cave woman." Cissy was so mad she swore to leave next day, but stayed the summer.

Initially against park extension, Burt later became convinced that it was right and fiercely advocated establishment of Grand Teton National Park. You can take a 16-mile mountain bike ride in the area of the Bar BC and see why it's an important addition to the park. Ride past the ranch, along Baseline Flat road, which goes north through moose habitat by the Snake. Continue past Burned Ridge (W) and past the turnoff and approach to Deadman's Bar and overlook (E)—old cabin remains still are found on the bar (also see Trip 6d, Mile 8.4); and past the potholes (W). Turn west and go two miles along the RKO Road to join the park road at the South Landing turnoff (Trip 6a, Mile 4.3). It's more of a downhill trip from north to south.

The aforementioned moose habitat is that of the fascinating Shiras moose, most active in the early morning and late evening. When the first heavy snows arrive, these moose drift out of the Teton canyons and onto the valley floor. Of prehistoric origin, this species must have been scarce in the valley during the 1800s because the early explorers and fur trappers rarely mentioned it. Of the deer family, it is the heaviest and most ungainly but long forelegs give it an advantage in swamps and deep snow. The bull sheds its distinctive palmate antlers in February or March.

0.3 8.5 **Cottonwood Creek.** Called East Teton River by the 1872 Hayden Survey, this creek has good fishing in July. Cottonwood drains Glacier Gulch and Jenny and Bradley lakes, then flows into the Snake. The faint milky color of late summer is suspended rock flour, ground out by the Teton Glacier. Beaver ponds, downstream near its mouth, were the setting for Sally Carrighar's book, *One Day at Teton Marsh.* In 1964, Disney and his cameramen stayed at the Bar BC to film the Carrighar book.

0.2 8.7 **The original Elbo Ranch** (W). The boundaries of this now-defunct guest ranch to the west still are marked by buck and rail fences. Californian Chester Goss bought 115 acres from Jim Manges and built tourist cabins, plus a store, gas station, baseball diamond, and a large rodeo

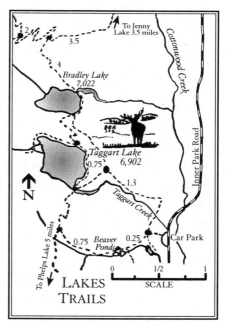

ground, complete with a racetrack, grandstands and refreshment stands. Goss and his partners named it the Elbo Ranch and erected a billboard proudly proclaiming it "The Home of the Hollywood Cowboy." In 1926, the billboard—Jackson Hole's first—was the last straw for "intense visual clutter." Horace Albright talked Goss into taking it down, but it helped stir Rockefeller to finance preservation of the park from such commercialism.

0.2 8.9 **Lakes Trail Parking Area** (see map). A number of loop trips begin here, including the 3.5 miles to Taggart Lake through a "ghost forest"—the result of the 1985 lightning-caused burn—and the 5.5 miles to the steeper Bradley Lake, with its over-the-moraine switchback stretches and stunning views of contrasting landscapes. The "ghost forest," with its saplings and luxuriant green cover, has become home to birds, elk and mule deer. To understand what you are seeing on this hike, pick up the interpretive trail guide at the Moose Visitor Center.

Beaver ponds can be seen on the south loop trail, 0.25 miles from this parking area. At three quarters of a mile, you will come across a grassed-over beaver pond. Beavers did too good a job—the enclosed water killed the trees, and old dams, discernible as low ridges, have silted in and grassed over. If you want to get off the beaten track, at the junction north of Taggart Lake, take the unofficial Avalanche Canyon trail west along the north side of the creek into rough moose habitat.

In addition to hiking opportunities, Bradley and Taggart lakes—named by and for members of the 1872 Hayden Survey—have good fly-fishing during the first three weeks of July. Taggart Creek, north of the parking area, is the major drainage for Avalanche Canyon and Taggart Lake. There, you'll find good fishing holes west of the road, in the dense brush below the moraine.

Interestingly enough, according to geologist Frank H. Bradley's 1872 report, Bradley Lake originally was named Taggart's Lake by the Hayden Survey. That summer W.R. Taggart, Bradley's assistant, explored the area. "The more northern of the two, which we have called Taggart's Lake, is surrounded by five concentric moraines, the elevations of which above the old riverchannel, which passes just outside of them, were taken by Mr. Taggart, as follows: The outer one, 162 1/2 feet; ...fifth 422 feet."

0.5 9.4 **Beaver Creek**. The creation of Grand Teton National Park in 1929 consisted of transferring Forest Service lands over to the NPS. The original USFS headquarters were located on Beaver Creek in a building called the Stewart Ranger Station. With establishment of the park in 1929, it became the first superintendent's office and remained so until 1959. Built in about 1910, the original, almost-square building was a fine log structure, its inside walls neatly hewn from eaves to floor with "tennant" corners. In about 1935, the walls were covered with modern plasterboard; later, "wings" were added. The station and Stewart Draw west of here were named for early rancher Henry Stewart of the JY Ranch.

Chapel of the Transfiguration

0.7 10.1 **Windy Point scenic turnout**. This uplifted fault block that tilts west attracts deep winter snowdrifts. West across the valley, you can see Death Canyon, the U-shaped gash in the Tetons. Its name refers to the rumored disappearance down this canyon of a member of the 1903 Bannon Survey.

Buck Mountain (el. 11,938), the southernmost of the crystalline peaks, looks like the Grand Teton in miniature. On old maps, it was known as "Alpenglow" because its sheer north face holds the last lingering red wash of the sun slipping over the Idaho plains.

Topographer Thomas M. Bannon and his recorder, George A. Buck, made the first ascent of Buck Mountain on Aug. 21, 1898; it now is climbed by 17 routes. From the top, Bannon and Buck reported seeing William Owen's flag on the Grand's summit, where it was placed 10 days earlier. Stone artifacts found at its high lakes indicate prehistoric visitors.

1.0 11.1 Turn off to the Chapel of the Transfiguration, Menor's (pronounced "mee-nors") Ferry, and Maude Noble Cabin. This turnoff leads east to these must-see historic buildings; parking is available at 0.3 mile.

MOOSE VILLAGE AND PARK HEADQUARTERS

Chapel of the Transfiguration. In 1920, Frank Williams, who operated the Double Diamond dude ranch—now the site of the Climbers' Ranch—was driving Mrs. George Woodward of Pennsylvania back from church services in Jackson. As they neared Moose in Williams' buckboard, Mrs. Woodward must have decided that she'd had enough of the bumpy sagebrush and dust on the 25-mile trip to her summer camp on Leigh Lake.

"Frank, wouldn't it be nice if we had a little church here at Moose," she said. Williams answered: "It would save a lot of travel, all right, Mrs. Woodward. Why don't you build one?" She thought a minute and said, "You know, maybe I'll do that."

After Mrs. Woodward discussed the idea with her old school chum, Maude Noble, to whom she had loaned $12,000 to buy the Menor's Ferry property. Miss Noble donated an acre of land and, in 1925, the building was completed, mostly through contributions and with logs from Timbered Island. The great plate-glass window above the altar frames the grandeur of the Tetons. It's been a favorite for weddings since Jack Dornan and Ellen M. Jones started the tradition with the first formal wedding here on Oct. 11, 1927.

Menor's Ferry. Thin, long-boned Bill (W.D.) Menor, the first man to settle west of the Snake, came to the Hole in 1882. He built a low, whitewashed cabin, started farming, opened a store that stocked fish hooks, tin pans, groceries and the vital Bull Durhams, and then built the ferry that was to be the Snake's most important crossing for 35 years. He charged $1 for a team or a car, 35 cents for a packhorse, 50 cents for "horsebackers." When a man on foot— possibly ranger Fryxell, who walked everywhere—once took the ferry, Bill told him, "You don't owe me a damn cent. Any fellow who can't afford a saddle horse can't afford a ferry!" Menor also had huckleberry rates for berry pickers. His home brew—he called it wine but never gave it time to mature—called for anything handy, like prunes, beets or raisins, but mostly he chose ever-lovin' huck berries to give it the "perfect tech (touch)."

Bill's younger brother, Holiday (H.H.) Menor, joined his brother in 1905. They took to arguing so much that, one day, Holiday stomped out of Bill's house and took up land on the opposite bank. For several years, they glared silently at each other across the river. When the Jackson Lake Dam broke in 1910, Allen Budge galloped south to warn Holiday. Reluctant to break the silence first, Holiday finally let better judgment win and warned his brother.

Storming and cussing—"You betcha Jesus"—through life, Holiday Menor was noted for manufacturing lime from deposits at Blacktail Butte; the lime was used mostly for whitewash. Though better-natured than his even harder-cussin' brother, this task made

Holiday as alkaline as the product, and friends shied away during limemaking season.

Each fall, as the freezing began and crippled the ferry for six months, everybody pitched in to build a "winter bridge" a quarter mile downstream. Even ferry passengers, protesting loudly, were drafted, and the bridge usually went in on schedule. Spring dismantling, however, was a different story. The river was open, the ferry in full swing. No one needed the bridge. But it had to be dismantled so the material wouldn't be carried out by the spring floods.

Hazards such as shifting gravel bars and tree snags caused further problems. With the river "in spate," Menor refused to operate the ferry after a huge tree snag hit it, broke the ropes, and caused the ferry to sweep downstream and hang up on a gravel bar. Neighbors gathered to consider the problem of Menor, while the ferry operator violently cussed his would-be rescuers.

In 1918, Bill sold out—tired of "high water and low water" and "fog, rain, wind, snow and sunshine on the Snake"—and moved to California. His brother followed him several years later. Maude Noble then acquired Bill's property, ran the ferry, and opened a teahouse.

In 1927, the immense dust clouds raised by the continuous procession of tourist cars blotted out all but the very tops of the Tetons. As soon as a steel truss bridge was built across the Snake, Maude Noble abandoned the ferry in 1927. Another era had passed.

Rockefeller's "Snakes" purchased the Menor property in 1933, and company president Harold Fabian preserved the old ferry boat; in 1949, Laurence Rockefeller financed its restoration. Today, you can take a free ride on the ferry—when conditions allow it to operate. The ferry boat is fastened to a cable stretched tightly across the river, and the swift currents power the pontoon boat on a diagonal course.

The National Park Story

Maude Noble Cabin. Built by Miss Noble in about 1921, this cabin had only a bedroom and living room; the kitchen and dining facilities were in Menor's cabin, to the north.

On July 26, 1923, the cabin was the site of an historic meeting—

and so begins the Grand Teton National Park story. Earlier that spring, a small group had been gathering at Joe Jones' store on Jackson Square, just north of Crabtree Corner. Under the dim light of kerosene lamps and seated on up-ended apple boxes amid the clutter of pickle barrels, wooden cracker boxes, canned goods and fruit jars, they discussed a plan for the future of Jackson's Hole— a National Recreational Area.

Advocates had been struggling to preserve wildlife and scenery since 1898. Efforts had intensified in 1918 and 1919 with introduction in Congress of bills to extend Yellowstone Park boundaries to include Jackson's Hole. During the summer of 1923, the Jackson Hole group invited Horace M. Albright, superintendent of Yellowstone Park and an advocate of park extension, to meet with them at the "Ferry Ranch." Miss Noble offered use of her cabin.

Albright recalled that meeting: "In 1923, when it seemed that development might get out of hand, and alarmed by the increasing travel, refreshment stands, gas stations and roadside structures, a group of Jackson Hole people invited me to join them at Menor's Ferry to discuss ways and means of 'saving the country.' When I arrived at the Ferry—late as I recall, I was a very busy superintendent of a great park—I found... Joe Jones, Dick Winger, Jack Eynon, Dr. Horace Carncross and his partner, Struthers Burt, of the Bar BC. My secretary Joe Joffe was with me."

At that meeting, the group came up with the "Jackson Hole Plan." Its primary element was to seek private funds to buy private lands and preserve them from commercialism. To that end, they decided to raise travel money to send two men east to solicit funds. The plan also called for creating a "museum on the hoof" to preserve the Old West character of the valley. It also aimed to keep out hotels, except at Jackson and Moran, to let dude ranches take care of visitors, to reintroduce native wildlife— such as pronghorn antelope—protect their ranges and, lastly, to do something about the elk.

Jack Eynon described why the elk were a problem: "[E]very day, all winter, there is a battle with them gettin' into haystacks and feed.... The millin' and drivin' of those panic-stricken animals is to blame for more death loss than starvation. We haven't had much luck in getting the government and the state to buy enough land. The elk ranches should be run by the biological survey. But legal hunting in the hills should be allowed." Everyone agreed.

When John D. Rockefeller brought his family to Yellowstone three years later, in July of 1926, Albright brought them to Jackson's Hole. The spectacular Tetons thrusting skyward made a profound impression on Rockefeller. "We spent the night of July 13 at old Jackson Lake Lodge," Albright recalled. "Next day was superb. As we drove along the road to the Bar BC Ranch, I let Mr. Rockefeller see things for himself... the devastation threatening the country... a telephone line being strung along the mountain side of the road. He asked me to send him data, a map and values of the private holdings. From the Bar BC, we drove to the JY Ranch, then owned by Henry Stewart, and had lunch."

"The scenery excels anything I have ever seen," Rockefeller said, "but the commercial exploitation developing along the highway is ruining it."

Returning that afternoon, they stopped on a little hill overlooking the Snake River on the old road north of the Bar BC. Albright described the scene: "The long pointed shadows of the Tetons were already racing across the river bottoms.... The hills were still bathed in sunshine.... As we stood on the little rise, I told Mr. and Mrs. Rockefeller of the meeting at Miss Noble's cabin three years earlier."

That winter, Albright sent Rockefeller a report and a map of the proposal; Rockefeller requested more data about the ideal proposal discussed that afternoon in 1923.

Rockefeller decided to restore the landscape and acquire lands for preservation of the wildlife. His representatives incorporated as Snake River Land Co.—the "Snakes," as they were called—on Aug. 25, 1927, and banker Robert Miller was hired to begin buying the land. Before he was finished, Rockefeller financed the purchase and relinquishment of some 35,310 acres at a cost of more than $1.4 million, paying an average of $40 per acre. The government withdrew unappropriated public lands from further settlement.

On Feb. 26, 1929, an act of Congress created Grand Teton National Park. The law provided for no roads or hotels within park boundaries, but the boundaries included only the Tetons and lakes at their bases, and so required only transferring Forest Service land to Park Service ownership. The boundaries did not encompass the Rockefeller-purchased lands and heeded little of the original Jackson Hole plan.

The political storms that swept Jackson's Hole during the next 20 years were more severe than her worst winter blizzards; it was a conservation battle unequalled in American history. The National Park Service worked to extend the park's boundaries, while Rockefeller insisted upon it—he had started the project with approval of Wyoming's governor and representatives in Congress. Smaller ranchers sold out, caught in the squeeze of Depression days: foreclosed mortgages, bankruptcies, frequent tax sales, property carrying more indebtedness than it was worth, and homesteads being abandoned. Selling gave them a way out.

Some of the more prosperous ranchers, however, opposed any park plan. Most Jackson Holers were undecided, including local officials who wanted to know how to run the county if most of it was tax-free and federally owned. Cattleman Robert D. Carey, governor and later senator, was a tough enemy of the park, while another governor, Leslie Miller, was its friend. The Western livestock growers opposed the government cutting off any rangelands. Their bitterness against federal control originated from earlier land-use regulations and conflicted with homestead settlement and the coming of barbed wire.

Other government entities also had problems with the park. The Forest Service, already administering the high timber country, was determined to hold the wooded areas. The U.S. Reclamation Service was jealous of its rights to Jackson Lake and had eyes on other waters in the valley. And the Wyoming Game and Fish Department was concerned about losing management of the game. Politics flamed into a furor.

Being forced to operate his properties put Rockefeller into business. His lodge, hotel and dude ranches came in conflict with local interests and increased the opposition. In November of 1942, Rockefeller delivered an ultimatum to Secretary of the Interior Ickes: Either establish the national park boundaries to take in the 35,000 acres he had purchased or he would sell the land on the open market. On March 16, 1943, Jackson Holers awoke stunned at the news of President Roosevelt's proclamation establishing 221,000 acres east of Teton Park boundaries as The Jackson Hole National Monument. Only the president could proclaim such a monument; on the other hand, national park boundaries required an act of Congress. The people of Wyoming had been deprived of a legislative hearing.

Wyoming Rep. Barrett and Sen. O'Mahoney persuaded Congress to pass a bill abolishing the monument. Roosevelt killed it with a memo of disapproval in December, 1944. The State of Wyoming sued the park superintendent and lost. Hearings, investigations, denunciations on national, state, and local political levels followed; more Barrett bills failed.

Then, on Dec. 6, 1949—22 years after his first Jackson Hole purchase—Rockefeller deeded 33,562 acres as a gift to the federal government. The following September, Congress established the current Grand Teton National Park, which encompassed Rockefeller lands and the monument. At the same time, it compromised and settled the claims of the Forest Service, the Reclamation people, and grazing interests; it established the boundaries of the National Elk Refuge under the U.S. Wildlife Service; it set up cooperation with the Wyoming Game and Fish Department; and it reimbursed Teton County for 25 years worth of taxes.

The 1950 act stated, flatly, that no national park boundary could be extended nor a national monument established in Wyoming without congressional action. It also abolished the ban against roads and hotels in the park. Within a few years, the areas around Jackson Lake Lodge and Colter Bay were turned from natural wilderness into deluxe vacation resorts, operated by Grand Teton Lodge Company, a Rockefeller business interest.

Undoubtedly, today's national park is not what that 1923 group in Maude Noble's cabin planned, but it is a heritage for which Americans will always be grateful.

Continue South on Park Road.

0.4 11.5 **Check-in Station**. Permits or fees are required. Pick up park maps and other Park Service literature, which gives campground information, park services, and locations and times of the park's interpretive programs—including campfire talks, slide shows, guided hikes, and museum tours.

0.2 11.7 Moose-Wilson Road (SW) (see Trip 11). The **Moose Post Office**, gas station, and store are located next to this turnoff road.

0.1 11.8 **Park Service Headquarters, Grand Teton National Park**. The Visitor Center has information, restrooms and an amazing supply of books, maps and pamphlets; get your camping and boating permits here as well.

0.02 11.8 **Snake River boat launching** and parking area; turnoff north. The scenic stretch of the Snake River ends here. The Snake River was called Yam-pah-pa, a kind of root, by the Indians; the first white explorers probably named it for the Shoshonean, or Snake, Indians.

A longtime favorite fishing stream, the Snake has a variety of fishing spots. Your luck will be best in the fall but early spring, mid-July and August can be fine as well, if the water is low and clear. While the variety of trout—cutthroat, mackinaw, brown, brook, rainbow and hybrid—like this river's rocky bottom, you also will find whitefish.

Leave Moose Village.

0.2 12.0 **Snake River Bridge**. Lt. Doane's winter-exploration party camped here Dec. 1, 1876, on its 52nd day out. By then, the men, weak from hunger and diarrhea, had grown desperate. "Warren and White followed a herd of elk till dark but did not get one...." They ate the last bite of food, beans, and then went to view the Tetons. Doane wrote: "The moonlight view was one of unspeakable grandeur. There are 22 summits in the line, all of them mighty mountains, with the gleaming spire of Mount Hayden [Grand Teton] rising in a pinnacle above all. The whole range is of naked rocks, in vast glittering masses, mostly coarse granites."

Doane's group stayed another day to hunt, but "the animals were too weak to carry us far uphill." They ate "16 magnificent trout" that Warren caught, and then "...shot Warren's horse for food." According to Doane, "We boned a quarter of the old horse and boiled the meat nearly all night, cracking the bones... endeavoring to extract a show of grease... to upholster a delicious and winsome gravy.... The gravy sauce was a dead failure. Horse meat may be very fine eating when smothered with French sauces, but the worn-out U.S. Cavalry plug was never intended for food. The flesh tastes exactly as the perspiration of the animal smells.... We ate it ravenously, stopping occasionally to rest our weary jaws.... It did not taste good."

0.2 12.2 **Dornan's** (N). The turnoff north leads to gas, stores, liquor/wine store, bar, guest cabins and, during July and August, the famous Chuck Wagon Tepees. At the Chuck Wagon—which is very popular with hungry mountain climbers down from the high country—enjoy all the cowboy grub you can eat.

Jack Dornan first came from Philadelphia to Jackson's Hole with his mother in 1918, and kept returning until he and his mother homesteaded 20 acres of land below Menor's Ferry and north of "Windy" Harrison. He lived in the old three-sided blacksmith's cabin with Holiday Menor, who helped the "dude boy from Philly" through that first winter. He worked for the U.S. Forest Service to build the first trails up Death Canyon. He became a skilled crafts-man and builder of log cabins. In the 1930s, he started his Spur Ranch—cabins, gas stations, snack bar and grocery store, with a beer parlor upstairs. He had just laid the ridge logs on the Spur Ranch Bar when Pearl Harbor happened. After the war, he returned in 1946 and, with his family, started all over again to rebuild a tourist business. The Chuck Wagon became an unqualified suc-cess; its big "Eat Here" sign on the barn and revolving yellow light on the bar's roof became valley landmarks. However, the yellow light flashed into the park superintendent's bedroom and drove him wild. At the taxpayer's expense, a new bridge was built to by-pass the settlement, with hopes of putting Dornan's out of busi-ness. But it was able to survive and now specializes in wines, hosts hootenannies, runs a chuck wagon restaurant and provides other amenities.

0.2 12.4   Moose Junction. Park Road joins U.S. 26-89-191. Turn left (N) to Moran (Trip 6d), or right (S) to Jackson (Trip 7).

Trip 6d

MOOSE JUNCTION NORTH TO MORAN JUNCTION
(18 miles)

0.0 0.0 Moose Junction. The Park Road joins Jackson Hole Highway (US 89-191-26) north to Moran and Dubois, or south to Jackson. Turn north.

0.9 0.9 Blacktail Butte practice rocks (E). Parking is east of the highway for those who want to scale these vertical walls of Madison limestone. Once famous as the source of Menor's whitewash, the walls are better known today for the 20 or so difficult, top-roped face climbs, rated from 5.9 to 5.12c. Fun, if you're a tiger.

0.3 1.2 Ditch Creek and Antelope Flats Road (E) (see Trip 13). The Jackson Hole highway now parallels the six-mile-long **Antelope Flats**, where thousands of pronghorn once roamed during the years they migrated between the lower Green River and this higher valley. The flats have been called the dustiest, driest, hottest area in the Hole, and may be the kind of country that only pronghorn can love. In March of 1906, big pronghorn herds, driven by storms, stampeded to a crossing of the Green near Pinedale; 10,000 reportedly drowned. It was the last of the big-herd migrations. Coupled with uncontrolled slaughter by hunters, extinction became a possibility for this animal. But tough regulations rebuilt the pronghorn population from an estimated 2,000 in 1906 to 100,000 in 1952. Nobody believed the cowboy who saw the first one in the area; then 21 were seen in 1958. The pronghorn antelope had returned to Antelope Flats!

the NATURALIST'S NOOK
Pronghorn Antelope

THE WHITE HAIRS ON THE ANTELOPE'S RUMP PATCHES STAND ERECT WHEN HE IS ALARMED. THESE ROSETTES REFLECT AN ASTONISHING AMOUNT OF LIGHT AND CAN BE SEEN FOR MILES.

THE PRONGHORN ANTELOPE CAN RUN FASTER THAN ANY OTHER AMERICAN ANIMAL. SPEEDS OF 60 MPH ARE BELIEVED POSSIBLE FOR SHORT DISTANCES

THE ANTELOPES EYES, LARGE & SET WELL TO THE SIDES OF HIS FACE, COVER A WIDE FIELD OF VISION WITHOUT MOVEMENT OF THE HEAD. THEIR "BINOCULAR" QUALITIES ARE AMAZING AND THEY CAN DISTINGUISH A MOVEMENT FOR MILES.

THE PRONGHORN IS ALSO A GOOD BROAD JUMPER. LEAPS OF 27 FEET LONG HAVE BEEN RECORDED & 14-FOOT LEAPS ARE COMMON AT HIGH SPEED.

BABY ANTELOPE DEVELOP RAPIDLY. WHEN ONLY 3 OR 4 DAYS OLD THEY CAN RUN 20 MPH. HOWEVER, FOR PROTECTION THEY RELY MOSTLY ON NATURAL CAMOUFLAGE. LYING QUIETLY, FLATTENED AGAINST THE GROUND, THEY CAN BE SEEN ONLY BY A CLOSE OBSERVER.

0.1 1.3   **Blacktail Ponds Overlook.** Watch for moose and beaver, as well as great photo possibilities. If you're looking for it, you can catch the unscheduled, but spectacular spring migration of elk. Hundreds of elk string out along the bottoms and head north to summer feeding grounds, one of the natural wonders of Jackson's Hole.

0.7 2.0   Cabins on the bench to the east are inholdings of longtime residents. The highway climbs Craighead Hill to the bench above.

1.5 3.5   **Glacier View Turnout.** You can appreciate the overall magnificence of the Teton Range best from this side of the valley. The highway has climbed from the Snake River terraces to the higher Antelope Flats. This vast outwash plain, primarily to the east, was formed by meltwater from Wisconsin-age ice. Looking southeast at Sheep Mountain (el. 11,239), you see the summit to the south and the livid scar of the Gros Ventre Slide to the north (see Trip 14, Mile 4.7). This marks the largest landslide in the United States, which occurred in 1925. In autumn, when hunting opens in the park, this section of highway is very popular. Grand Teton is the only national park to allow hunting, and hunters flock to the area each year to scan the Snake bottomlands for elk.

0.5 4.0 **Schwabacher Landing** (W). The westerly road will get you to raft and boat access, fishing and a picnic site. The Schwabachers sold to the Snake River Land Company and moved to the Daniel area.

1.4 5.4 **Teton Point Turnout** overlooking the Snake. The river's braided channels caused Lt. Doane's 1876 winter boat party much tribulation. The boat carried all of their goods because the animals were too weak. "The river is a fine broad stream but the current is... a mountain torrent and the channel divides so often that we counted over one hundred islands today...." Too often, they selected the wrong channel and ran their boat into shallow water. They sealed the boat by pouring water—which froze immediately—into the leaking seams. At that point, they were living on fish and boiled horse meat.

1.5 6.9 **Shane "townsite"** (E). In the summer of 1951, a small town sprang up a quarter mile east of the highway—the movie set of *Shane*. You can still locate a line of barish spots. Joe May was hired (for an astounding sum, he thought) to follow a sprinkler truck down the "main street" in his own truck. With the road thoroughly wet down, Joe drove back and forth, up and down, churning up ruts in the "road." The graveyard scene was filmed on Cemetery Hill, the little knoll 0.5 miles east of the highway; it's just south of the distant hill (Chip's Lookout) that has three or more distinct pines on its north side.

1.2 8.1 **Forest Service access road** and **Lost Creek Ranch** (E). This road crosses the north end of Antelope Flats. The left fork leads to Lost Creek Ranch (formerly Block S), where celebrities such as Danielle Steel, Ronald Reagan and his wife, Nancy, have stayed; the right fork continues south then forks east to climb over Shadow Mountain.

0.3 8.4 **Snake River Overlook.** This spot probably offers the most scenic of the Teton and Snake River panoramas; photographer Ansel Adams thought so and made it famous. Look northwest onto "Pothole" country (see Trip 6a, Mile 5.6). This overlook is on the great outwash plain, deposited by meltwater from the pre-Wisconsin ice that built up the moraine. Here, you are on the same level as the outwash plain south of the dark-timbered Burned Ridge moraine, across the river (WNW). The moraine was breached by the river's 285-foot-deep channel. The upper limit of that glacial ice reached above the highest timbered Teton slopes that are visible from this spot.

Deadman's Bar, the great timbered sand bar across the river, fills the "U" in the Snake below. The beautiful scene before you belies its position as the site of the Hole's goriest murder. According to the story told by Emile Wolff, the "Germans"—Henry Welter, an old schoolmate of Wolff's, T.H. Tiggerman, August Kellenberger and John Tonnar—came to the valley in May, 1886 looking for gold. They lived in tents on the bar below and built a cabin, the remains of which still are visible.

On July 19, Tonnar showed up at Wolff's Ranch north of here, asking for work. When Wolff questioned him, Tonnar said the others had gone hunting. For three weeks, he hayed for Wolff, until a posse picked him up. The posse told Wolff that a fisherman had discovered three decomposing bodies half hidden by rocks; they were identified as the Germans. Tonnar was taken to Evanston for trial, where he testified that the Germans had induced him to grubstake them, then beat him up badly, apparently so he would leave without his share. Instead, Tonnar nursed his bruises and tried to make friends. On the day of the murders, when the Germans told him he was no longer a partner, Tonnar got into an argument with Welter. As Tiggerman came up with a shovel, Tonnar jerked loose and ran for a gun. When the trio closed in with shovel and axe, Tonnar fired to kill. He carried the bodies by horse to a high bluff, threw them over head first, then covered them with rocks. Tonnar was acquitted by the jury because evidence was circumstantial; there were no eye witnesses! He left the country quickly. The Jackson Hole Museum has preserved the iron kettle used to boil the heads of the three victims so that the skulls could be used as evidence.

0.4 8.8   Turnoff (W) to **Deadmans Bar** and **Snake River access**. The highway curves down through the pine-covered **Burned Ridge moraine** into the Spread Creek drainage. The sharp turnoff goes west to the Deadman's Bar raft and boat access for the popular scenic run of the Snake.

1.3 10.1   **Glacial kettles**. Within the moraine, note the glacial kettles, or "potholes," some filled with small, swampy lakes. The largest, hard-to-spot Hedricks Lake, sits below the bare hill of Hedrick's Point, the site of the movie *Spencer's Mountain*.

You can see a huge beaver lodge in the lake. Years ago, Charlie Hedrick thought he could raise beaver in this area. It cost him so much to fence and raise them that it became a question as to whether they "skinned" him, or he them. Finally, he gave up and his beaver ended as fur pelts. A pair of trumpeter swans nested on Hedricks Lake until 1974, when they were shot; despite a reward, the scoundrels who shot them were not caught.

0.4 10.5   **Hedrick's Spring** (W). Hedrick built his homestead cabins west of here, near the spring, because of the excellent water. When he dug out the spring, he unearthed 12 buffalo heads. In 1889, Charlie, 15, had fought an enraged grizzly at Grand Lake, Colorado. Before the bear could kill him, a friend shot it. On the nightmarish trip to Denver, Hedrick almost died, but doctors wired his torn jaw back to his face. Terribly scarred and embarrassed, Charlie sought the remoteness of Jackson's Hole, shunning people until he could grow a beard. For many years, he carried the mail north of Jackson. After he sold his 427 acres to the Snake River Land Co. for $20,000, he worked for the Park Service, telling his favorite wild animal stories and playing his mouth organ at Jenny Lake campfires.

0.8 11.3   **Triangle X Ranch**. Started in 1927 by John S. "Dad" Turner, this dude ranch was sold to the "Snakes" for $20,000 in 1929 and then leased back to the family, which has run it as a "cattle ranch, farm and dude ranch" ever since. It's the only concessionaire-operated dude ranch in the national park system. "Dad" Turner's son, John, a former president of the Wyoming Senate, also served as director of the U.S. Fish and Wildlife Service in the Bush Administration. The ranch served as the location for two 1956 movies, *Jubal* and *Spencer's Mountain*.

0.9 12.2   **Cunningham Cabin Historic Site** (W). Turn north

Cunningham Cabin

at this junction, along a piece of the valley's old N-S settler road; it's 0.4 miles to the parking lot. Here, the small, dynamic J. Pierce Cunningham and his brother, Fred, started their ranches. They came to the Hole in 1885 and trapped for two years before filing for homesteads on adjoining tracts. In late 1892, Pierce wintered at John Cherry's Warm Spring Ranch. That same winter, young Mike Burnett, a top cowhand and good shot, arrived with burly George Spencer, trailing 50 horses with strange brands. Pierce let them winter over at his ranch and sold them hay.

The following spring, W. J. Anderson—who had helped catch Butch Cassidy the week before—plus Jack Williams, Bob Stevenson and Dave Stewart left Montana for Evanston, WY, and then headed for Jackson's Hole. They were pursuing horse thieves Spencer and Burnett, who considered themselves safe because of the valley's deep snow. At Teton Basin, the posse picked up a deputy sheriff and snowshoed over Teton Pass. In the Hole, they asked for help and were joined by valley residents Robert Miller, John Carnes, John Holland, Steve Leek, Josh Adams, Mose Giltner, and Frank Petersen.

Early on April 15, 1893, seven members of the posse took position at the Cunningham ranch, 150 yards northwest of the main cabin; the other five watched an adjoining cabin from the willows. Burnett, Spencer, and "Swede" Jackson, Cunningham's hired man were sleeping in the cabin. When a dog in the cabin started barking, Spencer, dressed and armed, came out to investigate. When he heard the command, "throw 'em up," he fired twice with lightning speed at the voice, barely missing a deputy sheriff. A volley answered him. Spencer kept firing until he collapsed and died with a cocked revolver in his hand.

At the first shot, Burnett, armed with a Winchester and a revolver, appeared on the opposite side of the cabin and fired off three shots with the revolver in his left hand. One shot drilled Williams' hat, creasing his scalp. The posse fired back and instantly killed Burnett. The posse found 53 horses stolen from Montana cattlemen Thomas Kent, John Chapman, and possibly Nelson Story.

The bodies, wrapped in a blanket, were buried in an unmarked grave, the approximate location of which the park has since marked. The posse never talked much about the affair but its members tried to justify their actions with their versions of the story. Some critics said the horse thieves died more bravely than the posse had acted. Some questioned the legal authority of Anderson's group, which stepped over into the Hole before realizing it was not lawfully authorized in this jurisdiction.

Nevertheless, the whole affair was all part of a greater plot. Just eight days before the Cunningham shootout, Butch Cassidy had been captured in nearby Star Valley for horse stealing. Members of the same posse were involved in both incidents. Wilson writer and history buff Doris Platt believes the posse first went after Butch Cassidy, then couldn't pass up the chance to catch the thieves in Jackson's Hole. Both events were part of a determined effort by Montana and Wyoming stockmen to rid the range of horse thieves.

A marker about 500 yards north of the Cunningham cabin locates the site of an old log fort that settlers built—with double walls—during the Indian scare of 1895 (see Trip 1, Mile 21.5). Fearing retaliation, settlers "forted up" and waited in fright. Nothing happened. The fort remained standing for years but was torn down shortly after Cunningham bought the place.

1.2 13.4 **Moosehead Ranch** (W). Fred and Eva Sanford Topping started this hunting lodge and dude ranch; Eva taught at the Elk school in 1927 and ran the Elk Post Office from 1932 to 1967.

0.4 13.8 **Spread Creek Bridge**. The creek drains Mt. Leidy Highlands to the east and is best fished after mid-July. A fault scarp starts 700 feet east of the bridge and extends east 0.75 miles, exposing gold-bearing quartzite conglomerates. The source of this quartzite has puzzled geologists, but Dr. Dave Love believes it is from the ancestral Targhee uplift, northwest of the Tetons. The fault created Spread Creek's delta-like mouth, which breaks into several channels before entering the Snake.

Of historic interest along Spread Creek are traces of Indian hunting camps and a mining ditch that later was enlarged for irrigating Ferrin's Elk Ranch to the north.

Directly north, note the prominent wedge-shaped uplift of Signal Mountain, an ice-carved butte of resistant rocks. The east-face cliffs are Huckleberry Ridge Tuff, which flowed south from a giant caldera in Yellowstone Park some 1.9 million years ago.

0.3 14.1 **Wolff Ranch** (E). Emile Wolff (1854-1928), one of the earliest homesteaders, was born in Luxembourg, immigrated to the United States and enlisted in the Army at age 16. While stationed at Ft. Hall, Idaho, his detachment was sent to find Lt. Doane's party on its 1876 winter trip through here. Wolff moved to the Hole in 1888. Three years later, he returned to Luxembourg, brought back a young wife, Marie, and took up this homestead. Life must have been strange to the meticulous new housekeeper. Emile had built a one-room cabin, filling the log chinks with mud in the usual manner. One day, he discovered that Marie had removed all the chinking, declaring she'd "not allow mud on the walls of my house." Only when winter came and strong winds drifted snow through the cracks onto the bed did Marie relent. By then, cow manure was the only available chinking material. Marie said: "I'll never be fussy again; I had to live with that cow manure all winter." Emile promised a better cabin, and built it in the spring.

2.0 16.1 **President Chester A. Arthur campsite**. On its way to Yellowstone Park in 1883, Arthur's presidential party stopped overnight on the Snake's east bank, 1.5 miles below the mouth of Buffalo Fork, at a spot they called Camp Hampton. The first of several presidents to visit Jackson Hole and Yellowstone, this was one of the most elaborate camping expeditions to hit the valley. President Arthur's soldier-escorted party left on horseback from Fort Washakie on Aug. 9, 1883 and came down the Gros Ventre River to Jackson's Hole.

This party of 300 attendants, including such notables as Secretary of War Robert T. Lincoln (son of President Lincoln), and Generals Sherman and Sheridan, marched north along the Snake—at the head of a retinue of 135 loaded packhorses—on an old trail that became known as the Yellowstone "Military Highway," locally called the "Bottle Trail." At each of their six valley campsites, small tent cities sprang up in minutes. Trout fishing was the chief entertainment. To keep the president in contact with

Bar BC Ranch (top).

On top of the Grand (right), 1924–L to R, Geraldine Lucas, Paul Petzoldt, Ike Powell, Allen Budge and Willie Crawford

Riding the old Skyline Trail (below, right).

Bill and Holiday Menor (below, left).

Menor's Old Ferry (bottom, left).

Maude Noble's Store, 1923 (bottom, right).

the outside world, military couriers were posted every 20 miles with fresh relays via Fort Washakie, Wyoming Territory, and Fort Ellis, Montana Territory.

0.7 16.8 **The Elk Ranch.** This was the extensive cattle domain of Josiah "Si" Ferrin, who came from Ogden's Hole and was an early game warden. Si first settled near the present Elk Refuge headquarters in Jackson before moving north, where he and his sons operated the largest cattle ranch in the valley, with nearly 4,000 head on 3,629 acres. Si fought a continuing battle to keep hungry elk from robbing his winter haystacks. High fences, dogs— nothing stopped the desperate animals. Then he erected a scarecrow and hung a lighted lantern on it to keep the elk away at night. "How did it work?," Si was asked. "Didn't," he replied. "Next morning, an elk came down to the house to get more oil for the lantern."

The Ferrins sold to Rockefeller in 1929 for $114,662.12 and trailed the last big herd over Ashton Road to Sugar City. When asked how many cattle were in the drive, Si quipped, "Dunno, ain't none of us can count. Must be 30 to 40 acres of 'em!" Dropping cattle prices and mis-ventures wiped out Si's fortune, and he died broke. After the Ferrins sold out, the Snake River Land Co. used the ranch to raise hay for "wild game" and livestock.

0.1 16.9 **Table Mountain** (el. 11,106). Look to the western horizon to see this mountain at the head of Cascade Canyon, the deepest gash north of the Grand. Table Mountain lies on the hydrographic divide of the range. As part of the 1872 Hayden Survey, photographer William H. Jackson climbed it from the west, horsepacking his heavy photo gear within 500 feet of the summit. Then he and his assistant set up near the top, and Jackson took his famous west-view shot of the Grand. Looking north from this stop, Whetstone Mountain is directly ahead.

0.6 17.5 **Buffalo Fork River.** This important Snake River tributary drains the remote Teton Wilderness, north, and enters the Snake west of here. Heavy beaver meadows and willow thickets make this lower section difficult to reach. Here, you can find good early-spring and fall fishing.

0.2 17.7 **Moran Junction.** U.S. 287-26 goes east over Togwotee Pass to Dubois (see Trip 4) and west to Moran and Yellowstone (see Trip 6e).

Trip 6e

MORAN JUNCTION WEST
TO JACKSON LAKE JUNCTION
(4 miles)

The Snake's early fordable possibilities along this stretch between Jackson Lake and the Buffalo Fork, long made it a main artery for early north-south travelers.

The "Military Highway" taken by President Arthur in 1883 (see Trip 6d, Mile 16.1) and the early Jackson-Moran stage route northward followed the Snake, fording the Buffalo Fork east of its present bridge and then continuing west along the Snake to the Oxbow. From the Oxbow, the highway—later the "main"road—cut northwest across the hills to Christian Pond and the Jackson Lake Lodge area, while the corduroyed old Allen freight road continued directly west (as does today's highway) to Doc Steele's saloon at Jackson Lake Junction. The Military Road was the main route connecting Jackson Hole with Yellowstone National Park and Montana. Many homesteaders located along the stage route, which the Reclamation Bureau improved in 1910 to haul coal from Lava Creek (E) to fire the boilers for steam power during construction of Jackson Lake Dam.

0.0 0.0 **Moran Jct.** U.S. 287 east to Togwotee Pass/Dubois (see Trip 4), or west to Jackson Lake/Yellowstone Park (via this trip and trip 5). U.S. 89-26-191 south to Jackson (see Trips 6d, 7).

0.2 0.2 Check-in Station. Fee required; pick up a park map and other Park Service literature.

0.2 0.4 **Three Rivers Ranch.** The road north leads to a gate and Struthers Burt's old summer retreat, Three Rivers Ranch, which he owned after easing out of the Bar BC management in 1929. It now is park land; the buildings have been removed.

0.3 0.7 Parking for raft/small boat access for a Snake River float trip. From here, a scenic boat meander with thrilling views of the ever-changing Tetons takes six hours to reach Moose and, for wildlife-watching purposes, is best done early in the day.

0.3 1.0 **Pacific Creek.** Late July brings spawning cutthroat temporarily into this creek.

In 1863, the valley's first prospectors, Walter DeLacy and 42 men, built a corral on Pacific Creek and held a miners' meeting. The group agreed that if a strike were made, each man would be considered a discoverer and entitled to five claims of 200 feet each. They panned the Pacific Creek-Buffalo Fork area looking for more than the few grains they saw. Eventually, they split up, with 15 men retracing their steps through Snake River Canyon and DeLacy and the others returning to Montana through Yellowstone. Had they found gold, the ensuing boom-and-bust scenario would have transformed this country into a different place than it is today.

Pacific Creek attracted trappers for more than a century. In about 1925, trapper Bill Rodenbush crossed the Snake here, pulled his traps, and headed for a nearby spruce tree to bury them. He found a hidden beaver trap (J.H. Museum); trappers 100 years apart had the same idea.

0.3 1.3 **Pacific Creek Road.** This north-angling road accesses Emma Matilda and Two Ocean lakes, as well as the **Teton Wilderness** and its network of trails into hunting, fishing and scenic country outside the southeast corner of Yellowstone Park. Most trails were made by the great herds of elk migrating from summer range on the Continental Divide to winter ranges in Jackson Hole.

Trappers, such as Jim Bridger and Osborne Russell, often used this route to the Yellowstone, hence names like Bridger Lake at the park's southeast corner. In 1835, Russell followed the Pacific Creek trail north to Two Ocean Pass, the heart of this wilderness. His journals give the first accurate description of this Continental Divide feature: "[W]e came to a smooth prairie... lying east and west.... On the South side, about midway of the prairie, stands a high snowy peak [Atlantic, el. 10,502] from whence issue a Stream of water which after entering the plain it divides equally one half running West and the other East... one bound for the Pacific and the other for the Atlantic ocean. Here a trout of 12 inches in length may cross the mountains [the Continental Divide] in safety."

In 1892, Theodore Roosevelt spent 10 days elk hunting at Two Ocean Pass. Of that trip he said: "[W]e came on the camp of a squaw-man, one Beaver Dick (see Trip 6b, Mile 1.6), an old mountain hunter, living in a skin tepee, where dwell his comely Indian wife and half-breed children. He had quite a herd of horses...." About wilderness, the president said: "Leave it as it is. You cannot improve on it. The ages have been at work and man can only mar it."

The oiled Pacific Creek road turns to gravel as it travels northeast for eight miles to a campground, hunting camps, corrals, the Teton Wilderness boundary, and the Pacific Creek trailhead. Fishing varies because of annual fluctuations in stream channels. At 1.4 miles along the oiled road lies the trailhead to Emma Matilda (0.5 miles) and Two Ocean (2.5 miles) lakes. In another 0.4 miles, you'll find the turnoff north on to the hilly road to Two Ocean Lake (2.2 miles), which is good for biking. While surveyor William Owen accurately named one lake for his wife, Two Ocean Lake is a misnomer because it only drains into Pacific Creek and thus the Pacific Ocean.

0.2 1.5 **Lozier Hill** (N). This was the site of Mrs. Roy Lozier's Wild Goose Inn (S), noted for its cakes and pies.

1.0 2.5 Parking (S). This old road wanders south through the homestead site of John Markham, superintendent of the Jackson Lake Dam from 1914-1932. His wife, Johanna, was the first registered nurse to practice in the valley and worked at the Reclamation Hospital.

In 1872, Hayden's Snake River division forded to the south bank of the Snake and split up: A small group headed south along the west bank of the Snake, while the main party headed southwest to the Tetons and camped near String Lake.

In 1895, Harris-Dunn & Co., alias Whetstone Mining Co., built the Conrad Ferry on the Snake one mile south of here. The company's placer concern, 10 miles north of here on Whetstone Creek—a branch of Pacific Creek—used the ferry to haul supplies being freighted from Idaho over Teton Pass. Captain Harris had interested Eastern capitalists in financing his "little" project.

The "town" and "Cemetery Hill" locations of Shane (top, right).

William. H. Jackson on Table Mountain (top, left), west of the Tetons, where he took his famous photo of the Grand Teton.

President Chester A. Arthur in Camp Hampton (above), on the Snake, near the Swallow Banks.

Mt. Moran and the Oxbow of the Snake (below).

The early Triangle X Dude Ranch (bottom).

The mining outfit built a road over swamps, streams and mountains, and packed in a sawmill, a ton of quicksilver, and a complete ferry boat and cable for the Snake crossing.

No region has ever tantalized gold prospectors like Jackson's Hole. Its elusive flour gold consistently disappears in the wash of gold pan and sluice box, and the mother lode has never been found. Pay-dirt streaks had been found near Gravel Mountain to the north, and Whetstone Mining figured it could recover it with mercury—as Uncle Jack Davis later did on the Snake. The sawmill cut four-inch planks for large, elaborate sluice boxes; two-inch pockets were bored into the planks. As river water flushed over the planks, gold was supposed to drop in and fill the pockets. Instead, pebbles filled the holes.

The only pockets filled to advantage were those of Captain Harris, who disappeared. Investors, trying to salvage something for their handsome paper certificates, sold the sawmill to Steve Leek. For years, the abandoned cabins served as poachers' hideouts, until irked law enforcers burned them. The sluice planks, cannibalized by settlers, found their way into many a valley outbuilding. Today, the same area's Harebell formation is being mined by museum people for plant fossils and dinosaur tracks found in the same quartzite conglomerates.

Disabled war veteran James M. Conrad ran the ferry—a square barge with no side rails—with winch and current. Two years later, when the company closed, Conrad continued with the ferry. That same year, cattle caused considerable damage when they stampeded and upset the ferry.

0.3 2.8 **Oxbow Bend** and scenic turnout. This spot has outstanding Teton reflections and wildlife viewing spots. Oxbow Bend did not always have a slow moving current; it was shaped as an oxbow as seen by the 1872 Hayden Survey, but in 1919 when the Jackson Lake Dam was enlarged, the narrow spit of land separating the river channels was dredged, creating the shortcut channel across the oxbow and allowing the current to bypass the U-shaped bend. The work created several islands. The largest, Crane Island on an Old Research Station map, became Heron Island when a rookery of herons took over. But the rookery moved downriver when the dam repairs of the 1980s disrupted the area.

A meeting in 1946 gave birth to the almost-forgotten Jackson

Hole Wildlife Park—1,500 acres of varied habitat along the Snake, between Old Moran and Pacific Creek. This land lease from Rockefeller's Jackson Hole Preserve, Inc.—intended to publicize the Jackson Hole National Monument with a live exhibit and the study of game animals—led to establishment of a biological field station north of Old Moran. Under director O.H. Paris, beginning in 1973, the research station focused on solving environmental problems in the park. The buffalo in the wildlife exhibit became the nub of today's park herd.

0.2 3.0   Trailhead (N) connects to **Emma Matilda Lake** trail.

0.5 3.5   **Cattleman's Bridge** and Allen homestead (S). This road takes off south through the old Allen homestead west of the Oxbow and ends up at Cattleman's Bridge over the Snake. The bridge was built in the early 1950s to move cattle from the "Potholes" to the Pilgrim Creek area. When grazing was removed to the Elk Ranch in 1957, cattle use was discontinued. The bridge was used for a St. Louis scene in the movie *Far Horizons*, as well as for a location in RKO's *Big Sky* (1952). The late Boots Allen, then new in Jackson Hole, took the part of the Indian princess during a boat-capsizing scene. A trail on the south side of the bridge goes south 1.5 miles to the east cliffs of Signal Mountain and an excellent exposure of Huckleberry Ridge Tuff. This second and largest of three major explosive eruptions of rhyolite welded tuff in central Yellowstone Park, engulfed the northern end of the Teton Range and flowed down both sides—at least 25 miles on the east side and 45 miles on the west. The trail continues southwest to join the Signal Mountain Trail near the base of Signal's south gully, a dim junction. The trail follows the west side of the drainage four miles to Jackson Point Overlook.

0.2 3.7   The road crosses the Charles J. Allen homestead on the west bank of the Oxbow. "The Bay" or "Allens Bay," now called the Oxbow, was the center of many community activities. The Allens settled in the area in 1897 and built the Elk Horn Hotel, a two-story hotel/roadhouse/store. Maria Allen, a midwife, operated a Moran post office from 1902-1907; she named it after artist Thomas Moran. On the hill above, north of this road, you can see the Allen (Moran) Cemetery (To reach it, see Trip 5, Mile 22). Some of the family names here include Budge, Wolff, Lozier, Nelson, Whiteman and Germann.

0.1 3.8   Site of the **Old Research Station** (S). In 1948, the first wildlife research program in this area was established as part of the Jackson Hole Wildlife Park. In 1950, the Jackson Hole Research Station became the first such facility in a national park; and in 1953, the New York Zoological Society and the University of Wyoming sponsored the renamed Jackson Hole Biological Research Station. In 1971, the Yellowstone Environmental Research Center program was established jointly by the University of Wyoming and the National Park Service. In 1977, that program merged with the Research Station to form the Research Center (see Trip 5, Mile 16.3).

The area, during the Research Station days, was used for movie locations such as *Big Sky* and *Wide Horizons.* Once an authentic Indian village was built west of the Oxbow, and used for several movies (also see Trip 6a, Mile 0.0).

0.1 3.9   **Jackson Lake Junction**. Doc Steele's Saloon, near here, initially catered to the thirsty crowd building the dam from 1910-15. He also was into mining and opened Jackson's first drugstore. Trip 5 goes north to Yellowstone; Trip 6a is Teton Park Road south to Jenny Lake and Moose.

Trip 7

MOOSE JUNCTION TO JACKSON
(12 miles)

0.0 0.0   Moose Junction. The Park Road joins the Jackson Hole Highway (U.S. 26-89-191). Turn south. **Blacktail Butte** (el. 7,688, 2.75 miles long) bounds the highway (E). It was named for blacktail (mule) deer that were plentiful here. You can ascend the butte from the south or southeast for great photos of the Tetons.

Hayden's 1872 survey party named the butte North Gros Ventre Butte, and geologist Frank H. Bradley reported: "Near the butte, large areas of sage had been burned off, and the grasses had grown up densely, forming fine pasturage; and on these, we again encountered antelope.... During the winter... they live upon the sage itself."

2.0 2.0   Before the park was established, much of the valley was patterned by grain and hayfields. By 1900, cattle raising was the chief industry, reaching a peak of 15,000 head in 1925. After the ranches sold out to the park interests, the land returned to sage and flowers. Spring fields of scarlet gilia, balsam root and the blue lupine blanket of June and July provide a colorful foreground to the Tetons.

0.8 2.8   Turnout (E). Just east of the turnout is the south end of **Blacktail Butte**. This is a complex fault block that has been scoured, faceted, and overridden by very early south-moving glaciers. The plateau that tails off the butte's south end was the site of prehistoric campsites, less than 5,000 years old. It provided a good overview of the valley. Drainage lines coming from the plateau suggest that flood water from a landslide dam breaking on the Gros Ventre River (E) 5,000 years ago, washed across the plateau. Note also the prominent north-south fault scarp along the base of the plateau.

Still looking east, the rugged **Gros Ventre Range and Wilderness Area** on the east skyline, summer range of bighorn sheep, elk, and a lot of cattle is dominated by **Sheep Mountain** (el. 11,239), alias the Sleeping Indian (as seen from Jackson). **Jackson Peak** (SE 10,741), in the wilderness area, is a very popular climb in the summer, as well as for winter ski trips. Due south is **East Gros Ventre Butte**, with **Snow King Mountain** and its ski runs in the background. The straight line of lights on the chairlift shows up at night for miles. **West Gros Ventre Butte** is SSW.

Looking northwest of this turnout, you can see the massive glacier-carved, U-shaped **Death Canyon** and its upper hanging canyon walls. The Teton normal fault forms the break in slope at the mountain's base. A few folks used to use the isolated and impractical Death Canyon route over Fox Creek Pass into Idaho—often for questionable reasons. A small tunnel and cabin foundations have been found in Upper Death Canyon, perhaps the work of John Condit and Andrew Davis, who were listed as gold miners in the 1900 Census.

Directly west is **Granite Canyon**, the most southern of the large Teton Canyons, where a trail leads to beautiful Marion Lake. At the canyon's head looms **Housetop Mountain** (el. 10,537). Between Granite and Death canyons are **Mt. Hunt** (el. 10,783), named for Wilson Price Hunt, leader of the westbound Astorian party, and **Prospectors Mountain** (el. 11,241), the highest and sharpest of the sedimentaries and a hangout for bighorns and goats. These are the **"Gabled Peaks,"** cemented sediments laid down in water in the distant geologic past.

Immediately to the north and following the rising skyline, the "Gabled Peaks" make way for the crystalline peaks, which begin with Buck Mountain. These are formed of molten rock, which later was twisted and shaped like plastic under earth pressures. While the jagged, crystalline summits attract climbers from throughout the world, the less-visited sedimentaries provide for wild and attractive travel.

1.0 3.8 **Jackson Municipal Airport** (W). The only airport located in a national park, this operation continues to stir controversy as it expands, overpowers and demeans its prime scenic location.

1.8 5.6 **Gros Ventre Junction.** Turnoff east to Kelly (see Trip 13, Mile 13.9) and Gros Ventre Campground. Turnoff west (see Trip 3a) to Jackson Hole Golf and Tennis Club, subdivision, and restaurant.

0.4 6.0 **Gros Ventre River.** The main channel flows between high levees, intended to control flooding. Upstream is good fishing very early or very late in the season, but downstream, former blue-ribbon fishing waters have disappeared with irrigation use.

The name "Gros Ventre," for the river and the range, is French for an Indian tribe now on the Fort Belknap Reserve in Montana; pronounced "Grow Vont," the term means "Big Belly." The Gros Ventres were part of the Blackfeet federation, the most powerful military force on the plains in the 19th century. Their love of warfare was constant, bloody and ferocious. Returning home after a visit of several years with their Arapahoe cousins in Colorado, about half of the tribe, including some 400 fighting men, passed through here in 1832. They encountered and fought with trappers going and coming from the rendezvous in Pierre's Hole (see Trip 3, Mile 0.0).

The Gros Ventre River has not been an easy river to control. In 1927, a flood rampaged toward this bridge (see Trip 13, Mile 7.0). When Forest Supervisor A.C. McCain rushed down from Kelly to warn onlookers who were standing on the bridge, his was the last vehicle to cross before the waters ripped the 75-ton steel structure from its concrete piers and carried it a quarter mile downstream; it was twisted beyond salvage.

0.9 6.9 Elk Refuge access (E); permission required. Beyond the locked gate, the 0.7 miles follows an old ranch road; park and hike east to an overlook of "Boyle's Ditch," called an "aquaduct" on maps. This huge ditch fulfills a geologist's dream, exposing some interesting glacial geology; small earthquakes have had their epicenters here. Undoubtedly, it is the most photographed "ditch" in the valley.

The geology would not have been revealed, if not for early ranchers diverting irrigation water from the higher Gros Ventre

River (N) into the lower Flat Creek meadows to the south. They had dug the usual shallow ditch and then opened it up. After three summers, they realized the ditch was gouging out a huge canyon. If they had not boxed it off and put in a pipe, the entire Gros Ventre River would have been diverted through the town of Jackson.

0.3 7.2 **Marysvale Post Office.** A quarter mile east of here, Fred E. White established the valley's first post office on his "Swamp" Ranch, on March 25, 1892; he called it "Marysvale," after his wife. To establish this post office and mail route, however, residents had to petition the postal department and carry the mail themselves for a year to prove the route feasible.

The mail-carrier petitioners who took their turns had the tough part, with little pay. According to postman Steve Leek, the marathon winter mail run demanded that he travel on homemade skis, with provisions, elk tallow for ski wax, and the outgoing mail on his back. To ford the icy Snake, carriers stripped from the waist down and waded through the river loaded with packs, ski equipment, and a clothes bundle. In February of 1896, one mail carrier lost his boat, toboggan, and snowshoes but saved his life and the mail.

Once across the Snake, the mail carrier dried, dressed, and headed for Teton Pass; for traction on the climb, Leek would twist rope around his skis. He once was caught in a pass avalanche but lived to describe the horror (see Trip 3, Mile 12.1).

The mail carrier's six-day trip to Rexburg, Idaho required one snow camp in the pass "igloo" and four nights with homesteaders along the way. He would return to Jackson Hole with 100 or more letters. In 1894, the official post office was moved to Maggie Simpson's home on Cache Creek, east of town, and renamed the Jackson Post Office.

0.4 7.6 South boundary of **Grand Teton National Park.** After 20 years of controversy, the park boundaries were extended in 1950 and now encompass 484 square miles. From this turnout, which sits on the Warm Spring fault, you can get a great view of the Tetons rising abruptly from the flats. Almost directly west across the valley, you can see the tram hut on the summit of Rendezvous Mountain, and the Jackson Hole Ski Area runs on the east slopes. Flat Creek once flowed west into the Gros Ventre River, but tectonism has diverted it south through Jackson.

0.3 7.9 **Warm Springs Road** and site of John Cherry's Warm Springs (later Neckell Springs) Ranch. The 80-degree Fahrenheit spring at the base of the hill—a half mile west of the highway—produced 500,000 gallons of soft water a day and once filled a swimming pool here. The spring emerges along the Warm Spring fault, which runs from west to northeast. Residents gauged cold winter days by the amount of steam in the air. North of the spring stood John Cherry's cabin (see Trip 3a, Mile 5.1); the foundation and well remain.

0.2 8.1 **Elk View Road** turnoff (W) to homesites. The parking east of the highway is for elk observation. In the days of wagon travel, teamsters called the uphill pull here "Botcher Hill;" in reality, it is the 150-foot fault scarp that created Flat Creek flats. The highway follows the trace of this fault for the next four miles, hugging East Gros Ventre Butte. Botcher was an early-day rancher and justice of the peace. As you drive south down Botchers Hill, notice the skyline directly ahead—it is an old rock landslide that the road cut through.

0.5 8.6 **National Fish Hatchery** (E). The turnoff east takes you to the hatchery, which is opened certain hours for visitors to watch the cutthroat, brook and lake trout propagated from fingerlings to creel size for Wyoming and Idaho waters. From the parking lot, the "Sleeping Indian," or Sheep Mountain (el. 11,239), forms the eastern skyline; it is the highest peak in the western Gros Ventre Range. The fluted terrain due east was caused by ice flows that scoured giant grooves as it moved south. Here, as elsewhere in the valley, the ice was as much as 2,000 feet thick and extended up bare slopes to treeline.

Of historical note: In the process of enlarging the parking lot, a campsite used by prehistoric, Sheepeater, and white people was unearthed. The Sheepeaters, skilled hide workers, were a Shoshone tribe that made fine antler and bone arrows, and piled wood and stone into "driveways" for herding bighorn sheep to slaughter.

0.3 8.9 **National Elk Refuge** (E). Stop at the parking area to view the immense wintering ground (E) of the wapiti, commonly called elk, which utilize this area beginning with the first heavy snowfall, usually in late November, until the snow begins to recede. One of the largest living species of the deer family, the wapiti ranks among the most majestic animals in North America. Those

W.C. "Slim" Lawrence (above) with his collection of elk tusks.

This was one of the photos (right) used in the early campaign to feed and save the elk herd.

Feeding the Elk (below). Miller Butte in background.

are antlers on their heads, not horns; they fall off each March and April. The size of the antlers and the number of branches on them determine an animal's age: 1- to 2-year-olds have short unbranched spikes; 3-year-olds have four points, and older bulls have five to six points.

Herds of wapiti once ranged the continent from coast to coast and as far north as 57 degrees, until relentless hunters all but destroyed them. In the 1880s, early homesteaders estimated that 25,000 elk made up the Jackson Hole herd. Mrs. Mae Tuttle recalled the waste: "There was so much game wasted in those days... it makes me shudder to think of the times we have shot down a fat elk and taken only the hams and the loins and left the rest to the coyotes." On the high summer ranges, elk remain alert and wary, seldom giving even the skilled hunter a shot. Come fall migration and the rutting season, they act like cattle. With little instinct for self-preservation, they become easy shots. On feedgrounds, they appear almost tame.

The elk traditionally trailed through Jackson Hole each fall on their way to winter forage in the Green River Basin and the Red Desert but their migration routes became blocked as settlement increased in the 1880s. Several severe winters decimated their numbers. In 1887, the Gros Ventre herd of 7,000 elk starved to death. Ten years later, more than 15,000 of the 35,000 elk in the Jackson herd died because they couldn't break the deep, crusty snow for forage. Many Jackson ranchers, with more sympathy than economic judgment, fed the starving animals.

Preservation of the Jackson Hole elk, the largest wild animal herd in the world, was an epic undertaking. The Jackson people fought encroachments of civilization, winter starvation and freezing, Indians, poachers, big-game slaughterers, tusk hunters, and politics to save the wapiti from extinction.

After Wyoming became a state in 1890, protection began in earnest, via state law. In 1895 Jackson lawmen, using armed force against the Indians, and the State of Wyoming—by decision of the U.S. Supreme Court—established that Wyoming law held jurisdiction over wild game. State game wardens were appointed, and the first hunting license system started in 1899. In 1904, D.C. Nowlin, the new warden, began a strong enforcement policy and, the following year, 500,000 acres were set aside as a Teton Game Preserve.

The epoch when more elk than beef was sold in the meat markets of Montana and Idaho was ending but tusk hunters continued taking their toll. They were not the only ones, because one pair of ivory elk tusks, the canine teeth of the elk, could bring from $10-$20, even $100, when used as charms and emblems of the Benevolent and Protective Order of Elks (BPOE). In a 1902 letter to *Outdoor Life*, Harvey Glidden wrote: "Elk teeth are the coin of the realm all over Jackson's Valley and vicinity for the purchase of supplies of all kinds, particularly whiskey."

One notorious gang, headed by Bill Binkley, Charlie Purdy and Charlie Isabel, slaughtered hundreds of elk, leaving the carcasses and selling the teeth. Efforts to catch and convict the gang frustrated law enforcers, though the whole valley knew who the culprits were. The Binkley gang used tricks to continue their trade: They decoyed wardens to a distant range, drove elk into secluded valleys, and used gun silencers, superior equipment, earth-covered hideouts and stilts made with elk feet that left no human prints.

A citizen's committee decided to take matters into its own hands. One night in 1906, an open meeting was called at the Clubhouse, and 20-35 well armed, prominent ranchers attended. Cool heads prevented an immediate rush to execute the tuskers. An unarmed delegation of three—Bill Seebohm, Charles Harvey and Holiday Menor—approached the Binkley homestead, the present-day Teton Valley Ranch. They confronted Binkley and Purdy and gave them 24 hours to "git." Binkley raged and threatened to shoot, but in the end, the tuskers agreed to leave the valley within 48 hours. A few hours later, Binkley's wife stopped him from gunning down some of the committee. Then, tusker-inspired rumors of a gun battle at the north end of the valley drew the posse there.

That gave Binkley's gang time to load elk heads and teeth and flee the country. But they were caught with the loot in Los Angeles, California. The case was prosecuted in federal court and, on Sept. 12, 1907, Judge "Grand Old Man" Meldrum sentenced Binkley and Purdy to three months in the Fort Yellowstone guardhouse for taking an elk in Yellowstone Park. Binkley escaped, Purdy served his term, and Isabel never was apprehended. Wholesale tusking was ended, although the last posse member living told how he later learned to bulldog wild elk and extract their tusks with forceps, without harming them. The BPOE finally discontinued using elk tusks as emblems.

Still, the elk starved and froze. In the severe winter of 1908-09, when about 20,000 elk were starving, a man could have walked on the carcasses for 15 miles. Valley folks raised $1,000 to buy hay, and the state began buying hay in 1909, to the tune of $5,000. At the appeal of the state game warden, the U.S. Biological Survey helped feed the big herds through the next year. Congress appropriated $20,000 in 1911 and more in 1912, to purchase feeding grounds. In 1925, the Izaac Walton League bought 1,760 additional acres. And U.S. allotments brought the refuge to its current size of 23,754 acres, which include wetlands, meadows and foothills that extend northeast from Jackson for 10 miles.

The Flat Creek drainage, once settled by hay ranchers, now provides winter feeding for at least 5,000 elk. The elk of the Jackson Unit descend from high summer ranges in Yellowstone and Teton Wilderness soon after the first snowfall in October or November. The migration is as unpredictable as the weather and cannot be determined more than a day or two in advance. Thaws can halt it; snows give it impetus. The refuge's high-wire fences prevent elk from moving west over the butte or south into Jackson. There is free movement to the east and north.

Although hay was used to feed the elk for many years, they now eat high-protein alfalfa pellets. To help pay for the feed, the Boy Scouts gather the shed antlers and auction them each year: 80 percent of the take goes to the refuge. The auction is held annually, usually the third weekend in May. The 4,900 pounds picked up in 1970 sold for $3,580.62, with Koreans being the heavy bidders. By 1994, nearly 7,600 pounds were collected and sold for $81,850, or an average of $10.76 per pound.

Refuge pastures can only support a limited number of elk, so hunting is allowed in both the refuge and the Grand Teton Park, the only national park that allows hunting within its bounds.

0.8 9.7 **The National Wildlife Art Museum** (W). More of a private art gallery, this wildlife art museum, dedicated in 1994, overlooks the National Elk Refuge. Visitors can sit in the sculpture garden and observe wildlife in its natural habitat and through the eyes of artists, at the same time. Built at a cost of $8 million and with 437 tons of stone, this Southwestern style gallery is a leader in wildlife art, the arts and environmental-education programs. Its collections range from local to worldwide artists, art and habitat. A gallery winner is the Habitat for Young People, where computers and viewer-activated audiovisual aids combine with a hands-on approach to art to explore the world of creativity, wildlife, biology and cultural history. Other amenities are an on-site reference library of art books and archival storage for collections. Besides an auditorium and cafe, the large lobby has a shop for gifts and books.

Affiliated with the museum during the winter months—mid-December until late March—is the **National Elk Refuge Sleigh Ride Center**. In a symbiotic relationship, the refuge shares such facilities as the lobby exhibit room, the auditorium for cooperative programs and an information center and ticket office, where you can buy tickets for the museum galleries and the winter sleigh rides on the refuge. There is parking for the refuge sleigh ride visitors at the museum as well.

Across the road from the museum is the 2.5-acre loading site for sleigh-rides. This site includes a shed, a shelter and platform—including a wheelchair ramp—for visitors waiting to board a sleigh or bus. A shuttle connects the museum area to the sleigh-ride area. It's a rare experience to ride the sleds into the heart of the elk herd, where 5,000 animals make excellent photographic subjects. Tamed by winter, the great elk paw the snow and munch on alfalfa pellets, fed to them each morning. They watch you curiously, drawing back when you approach, and bunching up. They radiate royalty.

Just to the south of the the sleigh-ride loading area are two cottonwood trees planted by Willis Winegar when he homesteaded that piece of land in 1909, after having visited Jackson Hole in 1879. He was the second Mormon bishop in the county, the first presiding elder and the biggest cattle rancher in the southern end of the valley.

0.9 10.6 Wilcox Gallery. Of geological note above the gallery is the U-shaped saddle, known as the "Gap," in East Gros Ventre Butte; it was cut by ancient ice flows. The brown andesite north of the saddle is one of eight distinct young volcanic sequences in the East and West Gros Ventre buttes. East Gros Ventre Butte, like the other buttes, is a fault-block remnant of the foundered ancestral Gros Ventre-Teton uplift.

The first all-white family came to Jackson Hole in 1888, when Martin Nelson, his wife, Bertha, and 4-year-old daughter, Cora, crossed Teton Pass on July 3. Nelson first built a house on the hillside to the west in 1891. When William Owen surveyed the homestead in 1897, Nelson learned that his house lay outside the property lines and so moved it into the swamp to the east, thereby gaining the unusual nickname of "Slough Grass" Nelson. One of the Nelsons' children drowned and initially was buried beside the butte above the highway. The remains were exhumed later and reburied in the town cemetery. Cora Nelson Barber lived in Jackson at the corner of King and Kelly streets until 1965.

1.2 11.8 **Waterfowl viewing**. Park here and enjoy hundreds of resident and migrating birds, protected by the U.S. Fish and Wildlife Service. Trumpeter swans, sandhill cranes, mallards, pintails, and teals are some that raise their broods on the refuge, while as many as 400 Canada geese ignore their migrating cousins and stay year-round.

You can usually see several pair of the rare trumpeter swan at this spot. Once nearly extinct, the last census found 735 of these birds in the United States. At the base of Miller Butte, northeast across Flat Creek, a series of large, slightly warm springs provide a year-round haven for the trumpeters.

Mose Giltner, who succeeded Nelson as the swamp owner, helped create the bird haven you see. In 1916, Giltner, who came to the Hole in 1889, drained the Flat Creek swamplands. With a floating dredge, he dug the channel six feet deeper, converted the terrain to hayland and eliminated the "disease-bearing swamp." Later, he moved to the mouth of Phillips Canyon.

Look south at **Snow King Mountain**, marked by obvious ski runs. Ice from the Buffalo Glaciation coalesced from the Yellowstone, Teton, Gros Ventre, and Absaroka areas, and moved south through Jackson Hole. The ice river overrode Snow King, scouring it and leaving the skyline notches. Subsequent tectonic events wiped out the glaciation evidence.

The townsite of **Jackson** has an interesting geologic history. First, it is built on a large alluvial fan formed by Cache Creek, east of Snow King. Second, it overlies vertical shale and sandstone, which creates problems for the town's water supply. Third, the town sits at the crossroads of the Jackson and Cache Creek thrust faults.

And, finally, it was the center of the big crunch when the rooted Gros Ventre Range, north of Cache Creek, met head-on with the rootless Overthrust Mountains (Hoback and Wyoming ranges) of the southwest; the impact on the Jackson area could be likened to a tiny VW being crushed between two semis.

0.2 12.0   **Flat Creek bridge**. Private property downstream, but upstream you can fish in August and September. Kids can fish off the bridge. Flat Creek drains the great Refuge meadow. Incredibly it is Wyoming's only catch-and-release stream. Its easily spooked Snake River finespot cutthroat *(Salmo clarki lewisi)* give serious fly casters some highly technical fishing and a few lessons in humility. The townhouses just north of the bridge were built into a cut in the butte and lie in an avalanche path.

Enter Jackson.

Trip 8

VISITING JACKSON

For many, the town of Jackson (el. 6,209) symbolizes the Old West. But how much of old Jackson remains? Buildings and malls have squeezed out the log buildings around the Square. But a few boardwalks still rumble under the click of cowboy boots, and jeans are still the favorite dress. Behind today's false-fronted stores, the charm of this old Western town survives in its people. A few of today's motel owners and shopkeepers are descendants of original homesteaders who sold out to park interests, moved into Jackson, and established businesses. But they may be an endangered species as new interests continue to take over.

A ride through the residential sections reveals log homes built early in the century. Their hand-hewn logs, carted in from the mountain forests by horse teams, tell the story of hardy pioneers determined to make this valley livable year-round, The lovely cottonwoods are also remnants of the pioneers. The saplings were freighted over Teton Pass by Roy Van Vleck, to give away to townfolks who wanted to plant them. The trees were stored on his property in Cache Creek overnight. By the next morning, many of the trees' roots had been eaten by hungry beavers, but the survivors of "the night of the beaver" can be seen along Broadway to this day.

The Jackson Hole Museum's great little **Tour of Historic Jackson** tells it like it was. As other towns in the valley have all but disappeared, Jackson has grown. Because it caters to the valley's lodges, ranches, hunting areas and Grand Teton National Park, Jackson's summer population surges with visitors—and the cooks, waitresses, clerks, guides, cowboys, and students needed to serve them. The population used to shrink drastically in winter but that no longer is the case. The fascinating Fall Arts Festival and a famous hunting season link summer to winter's booming ski season, and the town stays fairly full most of the year. Jackson services have expanded to answer the demand.

Not so long ago, there were only a handful of eating places, a couple of doctors and lawyers, a small hospital, an inconspicuous airport, and you could count the realtors on one hand. Now that the valley has been "rediscovered," however, it seems that everyone is conspiring to turn it into a rich-man's paradise, with the help of an unleashed airport, a highly active chamber of commerce, uncontrolled realtors and developers, who encourage the rich-valley idea but who won't touch affordable housing. The money guys cause higher taxes, which only they can afford, and big-city problems, which our town and county fathers can't control. Doctors, lawyers, merchants and chefs are Big Business, and a simpler way of life has gone the way of the pioneers. It has been said that if Hollywood wanted to capture the emotional center of Western history, its movies would be about land, and its villains would be realtors, surveyors, speculators and lawyers.

Boardwalk strolling, window shopping, and people watching are always absorbing pastimes in Jackson, with galleries and stores displaying alluring wares for visitors from throughout the world. Gambling has had its stormy ups and downs, with the Vegas-like elements out at the moment. But as gambling and lotteries flourish elsewhere in the nation, who knows how long before it returns?

The principal bars, booming with loud music and heavy summer trade, have become more elegant, losing much of their old-timey atmosphere. Gone are the backrooms and pine floors and the lusty, exciting mix-'em-up dances that attracted crowds from miles around. They have been replaced with urgent neon signs, soft lights, dime-sized dance floors, leather chairs, carpets, and trendy trios. If you really hanker after that old-timey flavor, though, check out the Coach at Wilson on a Sunday evening.

But let's talk about things that haven't changed too much. Linked closely with the region's history are relics stored and displayed in the **Jackson Hole Museum,** at the corner of Glenwood and Deloney streets, just north of the Wort Hotel. Privately started in 1958, through the dedicated efforts of W.C. "Slim" Lawrence (see Trip 5, Mile 16.3) and Homer Richards, it's a wonderful place to lose yourself for a summer afternoon. Here, the living history of Jackson Hole is revealed in various exhibits. The Native American room houses priceless exhibits of clothing, beads, and artifacts, covering the last 10,000 years. The trapper and mountain-man story unfolds in the exciting Fur Trade room, with items such as hand-forged beaver traps, and guns—from an 1824 horse pistol to the Sharps guns used to exterminate the buffalo. Among its history trove, you will find collections from the Bar BC Ranch and Deadman's Bar, branding irons left by horse thieves on the run and a prize collection of settler photographs. Other noteworthies are the Boone & Crockett record-sized heads of elk, mule deer and a grizzly skull (25 $\frac{1}{16}$ points). The elk was killed in about 1890 in the Bighorn Range. The mule deer was shot in Hoback Canyon, date unknown, and hung around for years before it was measured and pronounced the largest, at 217 points. The record Shiras moose head (205 $\frac{4}{8}$ points) was killed in 1952 at Green River Lakes in the Wind River Range. In a valley famous for its peaks and exciting stories, the museum offers a contrasting peek into the life of the Hole for a reasonable fee and a lot of fun.

The **Teton County Historical Center** is two blocks north, at the corner of Glenwood and Mercill streets. It usually has several exhibits on display at any given time. Its growing historical reference library, based on the Slim Lawrence collection, has become outstanding as well. These records include valley history, early newspapers and early census reports. The center has a friendly, capable and cooperative staff and is open weekdays; admission is free.

Jackson's nightlife starts off with a bang at the **Town Square Shootout**—a mock stage holdup, gun battle, and a hanging of the town desperado. It's great camera color. Or, before the sun sets, catch the next stagecoach for an Old West ride around Jackson.

The **Wort Hotel** (pronounced Wurt) and the **Cowboy Bar** have long been staples of Jackson nightlife. Charles J. Wort bought four Jackson lots in 1915 but it wasn't until 1941 that his sons, John and Jess, made their dad's dream of a Swiss chalet-type luxury hotel come true. Folks called them crazy but their crystal ball said "go ahead" and, for $90,000, they did. In 1950, they added the famous Silver Dollar Bar and, although gambling was illegal in Wyoming, it was tolerated in resort hotels, such as the Wort. All that ended with a big gambling cleanup in the mid-1950s. The old Wort burned in 1980 and was rebuilt along original lines. It still displays its long, curving Silver Dollar Bar, with 2,032 uncirculated 1921 gleaming bucks embedded in tenacious plastic and under glass.

Well-worn saddle seats, painted murals and weird knotty pine shapes—caused by parasites—decorate the Cowboy Bar's interior. The Cowboy started as a two-bit hamburger joint, the JR (Joe Ruby) Saloon, which served beer but was notorious for its gambling, fights, and gun-slinging incidents, where bullets would blow holes through the walls. Eventually, Ruby was given 24 hours "to git;" but before he left, he sold the place to Ben Goe, who renamed and redecorated the old watering hole, and added (illegal) gambling. The Feds never could prove a case against Goe, who had cohorts on Teton Pass using mirror signals to warn of the law's presence.

Artists must have been painting the Tetons since prehistoric days. Today, more than ever, the arts have flourished into an artists' colony, complete with handcrafters, art shows, and galleries that focus on everything from painting, photography and sculpture to jewelry and Indian art. And there is always the Mountain Artists Rendezvous, held two weekends each summer, to help you really appreciate what the valley has to offer.

The performing arts haven't been left out of the picture, outdoing themselves with symphony and chamber music, musical revues and stage plays, art films, and concerts by a variety of well-known musicians and singers from here and elsewhere. Excellent family entertainment of old-time drama at its villainous best, or professional musicals can be seen nightly at the Lighthouse (formerly the Pink Garter), Jackson Hole Playhouse and Dirty Jack's theatres.

The arts season—both visual and performing—climaxes with the September Fall Arts Festival. But if you run out of ideas, check in at the Chamber of Commerce's Visitor Center. Count on a picnic at North Park to watch the wildlife, take in the great view of the Gros Ventres, ponder Marjorie Torry's splendid sculpture of two trumpeters, and take the nature walk along Flat Creek to the large recreation center, built in 1994-95.

The ski hill that is six blocks south of the Town Square is called

Snow King Mountain. The double chairlift will sweep you over treetops to the summit and a perfect viewing spot from the glass-walled shelter, complete with snack bar. Winter or summer, the Jackson Hole panorama is spectacular. On the west skyline, you can see Teton Pass, Mt. Glory and its avalanche bowl, and the town of Wilson. To the northwest are the southern Teton sedimentaries with the glittering Snake River twisting at their feet, while the West and East Gros Ventre buttes dominate the foreground. To the north are the granite towers of the main Teton massif, while the sharp point of Jackson Peak (el. 10,741) and the Sleeping Indian (el. 11,239) are profiled on the northeast skyline. If you want some exercise, try walking up or down the service road (walk up with a free ride down) that switchbacks across Snow King's face. And once you're down, the Alpine Slide and miniature golf course next to the Snow King Resort provide fun for all ages.

Cemeteries always hold a bit of history. Between the chairlift and the slide is the **Aspen Hill Cemetery**, where many of the people who provided stories throughout this guide now rest. The oldest grave belongs to Jim Goe, whose funeral service was in Pap Deloney's store. Two of the most mysterious residents are John Cherry and the first Mrs. John Sargent, Adelaide Crane Sargent.

For more than a half century, Jackson Hole has hosted a rodeo. But what began as informal ranchhand contests has grown into a summer-long professional event. Cash purses, judged and timed events, and several skill categories—from calf roping to bronc riding—all are part of the wild and woolly proceedings in the lighted arena. Check with the Chamber of Commerce for rodeo nights, and take coats and blankets when you go. There is an admission fee.

EARLY JACKSON

When the John Simpson family came to the Hole in 1894, it homesteaded the current site of Jackson, and Maggie Simpson took over postal operations, calling the post office near Cache Creek, "Jackson." Before the Simpsons left the valley in 1900, Mrs. Robert Miller bought 80 acres of their land; she already had laid out the town of Jackson in her mind. She didn't have much to work with, if you believe Charlie Hedrick—who described "Jackson" as rocks, sagebrush, jackrabbits and mosquitoes, mixed in with a few fall hunters.

Nonetheless, Grace Miller's dream became reality on July 8, 1901, when the town was plotted. By 1903, it was a ragtag collection of six buildings, including Foster's saloon, Anderson's post office and hotel, Jimmy Simpson's building, and W.C. "Pap" Deloney's log store.

Pap Deloney's store, the first in the new community, was built on Deloney Street, across from St. John's Church, in 1899. Pap sold everything from hairpins to horsecollars, mixed with a liberal supply of goodwill and the latest news. As Cal Carrington put it: "Pap never refused the settlers anything. He had to accommodate me many times." When the cattle were sold, residents paid up their yearly debt and, because there was no bank, they left the remaining money with Pap for safeguarding. If Pap decided to go fishing, he would just up and go, leaving the store unlocked. Any trapper, rancher, guide, or cowboy coming in would wait on himself and leave his money and a note. Pronghorn antelope used to migrate right through town. Pap Deloney told of thousands of migrating animals that would take several days to pass his store. After 1906, though, that sight was a thing of the past. Pap blamed domestic sheep in Green River valley, but the wholesale slaughter of thousands of pronghorn probably had a lot more to do with their near extinction. Pap's old store eventually gave way to progress.

The **Clubhouse**, one of Jackson's six original buildings, started as the Gun Club in 1896 and remained the center of activity for many years. It still stands on the east side of the Town Square, with wide steps leading down to the street. At first, it was nothing more than a two-story log cabin used as a men's smoker-dancehall-courtroom. Although it was framed in 1905, the original logs are still inside the walls.

At various times, the lower level of the Clubhouse housed the Van Vleck Mercantile, a barber shop, butcher shop, drugstore and post office. But its best memories must stem from when the community hall was upstairs. Bunk-like benches around the walls accommodated sleepy children, while their parents danced the night away. Reels and polkas, livened by Pete Karns' fiddle, were favorites, and lunch was served at midnight. The first trials, mostly for game-law violations, also were here. When the Clubhouse began serving as a school in 1903, its opening was a gala occasion. As a makeshift band led the grand procession of 17 boys and eight girls

Jackson and the Tetons From Snow King Mountain (top.left).

Women Skiing at Moran, 1910.

Jumper John Curtis (left).

The young and vivacious Cissy Patterson (below, right).

Cissy Patterson, the hunter (below, left).

Young Cal Carrington, right, last of the Jackson Hole horsethieves.

to the new school, someone suddenly remembered there wasn't a desk in the school. Consternation reigned until Pap Deloney ordered the procession to halt before his store. After a hasty rearrangement of the dry goods and groceries, the children resumed their march to the Clubhouse, each with a small and large packing case, enough to suffice as chair and desk.

After a log school was built in 1905, the Clubhouse served other needs. In 1912, the new school was replaced by a two-story brick building that burned in 1915. School was held in churches until another was erected in 1916. High school was taught upstairs at the Clubhouse until 1929, when a new building took over.

Another building of historical note was the Reed Hotel. In 1903, Dr. Palmer built a four-room, two-story building, which he called an "insanitorium," and which "Ma" Reed bought in 1908. As the Reed Hotel, it was Jackson's only eating place. Ma allowed no smoking, swearing or fighting, and had brass knuckles to back up her rules. One day, she and her husband, Pat, up to their necks in debt, took a little vacation and never returned. Their employees, Rose and Henry Crabtree, paid off the debts and took over. The **Crabtree Hotel** became famous for its table, guests and practical jokes. Like the day, as the story goes, two strangers made the mistake of wearing white tie and tails to dinner. Outraged at this breach of frontier decorum, Si Ferrin stormed across the room, whipped out his knife, and slashed off a pair of the offending coat tails. "There, that's better," he said as he stepped back, satisfied. He looked around for the other stranger, who, by this time, was long gone. The original building—at Crabtree Corner, on the southwest corner of King and Broadway—was torn down in 1993; the replica has attempted to remain true to the original hotel and includes a "widow's walk" around the roof.

The oft-unnoticed **American Legion Hall**, at the corner of Cache and Gill—across from St. John's Church—hasn't changed since it was built with coped log corners in 1929. A scene of many functions, its moment in the sun came in 1933 at John D. Rockefeller's "trial by proxy." The fuss began three years earlier when *The Courier* burst forth with news that rocked the Hole: The man behind the "Jackson Hole Plan" to enlarge Grand Teton National Park and save it from commercialism was none other than Rockefeller (see Trip 6c, Mile 11.1). NPS Director Horace Albright had quietly brought in Rockefeller, who had quietly bought up 35,000 acres of valley land through the "Snakes," his Snake River Land Co., for a park and wildlife area to be added to the existing Grand Teton National Park.

With the *Courier*'s headlines, the opposition sprang alive and fought like wildcats. By the summer of 1933, tension and frayed tempers in the valley had reached boiling point and the lid was about to blow off. On the day of the hearing, the walls of the Legion Hall shivered with the ensuing hearing. Everybody had turned up, and almost everybody had something to say about the dirty tricks in the opposite camp. It was a free-for-all throughout the four days of bellyaching that August, when the subcommittee of the Senate Public Lands Committee sat in the American Legion Hall trying to unravel charges of collusion, conflict of interest, misrepresentation and unconscionable bargaining between Rockefeller and the Park Service. When it was all over, the subcommittee found that Rockefeller wasn't making any money from the project—a frivolous charge. How could he make money off land he was going to give away and on which he now was paying taxes? In the end, a disgusted *Denver Post* article concluded that the controversy was "...not even a tempest in a teapot."

In 1910, there still was no Town Square—just a water-filled gully, sagebrush, and a wagon road diagonalling across it. In 1914, Dick Winger secured seven lots for a park. Three years later, Mayor Winger graded the first street around the park; he cut low in front of the Clubhouse, which made a considerable step from sidewalk to street. As buildings went up around the Square, their foundation dirt helped fill the gully. The American Legion hauled in topsoil and seeded grass. When the landscaping was finished, John Colter's monument was erected. Finally, the impressive archways of shed elk antlers grew from one corner to a four-corner attraction. Although numerous buildings once stood on the park square, now only the "ancient" stage station—built in 1957—remains.

Jackson was incorporated in 1914, and Harry Wagner was its first mayor. The town made national headlines in 1920 when it elected an all-women council, the only city governed entirely by women at that time. Under Mayor Grace Miller, the enthusiastic corps of officials went on to a second term.

On the spiritual side, Jackson people always have contributed willingly to their churches. The Mormons built their first brick church in 1905. The Episcopal Church completed its rest home in 1912, started its hospital in 1915, and St. John's Church in 1916. In 1911, the Rev. T.H. Baxter began promoting the Baptist Church.

WINTER SPORTS

People have been skiing in Wyoming ever since Ed Creighton's Scandinavian linemen used skis to maintain the first transcontinental telegraph line in the 1860s. In Jackson Hole, the first skis were made of the native material at hand. Big John Emery of Flat Creek reportedly made the best skis out of "red (Douglas) fir." His technique included soaking the cured wood in water and lye to shape it.

Early skiing may have not made a pretty picture but it got people where they needed to go on the snow. Betty Woolsey (see Trip 3, Mile 16.5) described the early Jackson Hole skiing style: "The Hoback Boys... skied with a big long pole to steer with and... long homemade skis. Instead of bindings, they had... housings.... Boots were nailed to their skis.... [They wore knee-high mukluks] to keep them in the housings." They were the first hotdoggers.

Meanwhile, up on the Gros Ventre River, Butch Robinson was teaching his brother, Eddie, to ski on an extra-wide pair of boards and on a steep, snowy hill with just one tree in sight. Butch's instructions stressed riding the pole to control speed. Eddie took off, gained a little too much speed, and was out of control immediately, heading for the lone tree. "Ride your pole," Butch screamed, meaning for his brother to straddle the pole and squat on it. But Eddie crashed into the tree and knocked himself out. Later, Butch asked the obvious question but the still-stunned Ed replied, "I *was* riding my pole but the rear end was on top of one of the skis!"

The 1920s brought a big change when Mike O'Neil of the Forest Service brought in store-made skis and invented his own strap bindings. He also built the first ski jump. Early ski buff Neil Rafferty said that, in the winters of the 1930s, skiers did one of three things: They climbed to the top of the "town hill"—Snow King—and pointed down; built a ski jump and flew; or rode an elk skin for a sleigh.

As the sport of skiing took off, it became obvious that the terrain had to be improved. The town hill was covered with second growth because of the great 1879 fire that burned the entire Cache Creek ridge. In 1935, the Forest Service had the CCC build a horse/hiking/ski trail to the top and a small summit shelter. Jackson's first ski meet drew 20 competitors for a tough, twisting downhill course from Old Man Flat. Johnny Waldron was among those skiers and sported the first metal-edged boards. Because the skiers couldn't turn a tricky switchback, they were forced to stop and redirect. Despite complaints, the Forest Service supervisor was reluctant to allow more tree cutting, so secret night forays accomplished the job (shades of Bill Briggs' forays in the 1970s and 1980s for the same purpose). Really good snow was needed to cover the eight- to 10-inch stumps. As it turned out, however, the unwanted trees were on city property anyway.

By 1939, the Jackson Hole Ski Club was calling for bids for a lift. One of three bidders, Neil Rafferty got the lease, based on constructing a tow lift similar to one he had seen near Salt Lake City. That same winter, for the cost of a $500 cable turned by an old tractor, he had the lift going; Boots Allen was its first operator. For 10 cents an hour, Boots would "crank and crank and crank that damned Ford tractor til it'd nearly break your arm off." To folks accustomed to the luxury of a chair, the tow lift probably would seem primitive. The rider would hold a stick at the rope's end, which he dropped off on top. Then Rafferty would ride a dog sled up, collect the sticks, and coast down. Also in 1939, a log ski shelter was started but it collapsed that same winter: It then was rebuilt on a basement.

With establishment of a ski area and club, it made sense to organize some ski races. So began the annual tri-state meet of Wyoming, Idaho and Utah skiers. Because they were snowed in for days, the out-of-state skiers thought coming to a race in Jackson was like going to the North Pole. And those first races had their problems: The log jump landing was covered with hay, which elk ate up the night before the meet, and local favorite Ben Yokel broke his leg. Probably one of the benefits of the tri-state meet was that some of the out-of-state competitors, such as Ted Major and Jim and Virginia Huidekoper, eventually moved to Jackson's Hole.

It was the Huidekopers who prodded Rafferty into getting a chairlift. In 1945 the Jackson Hole Winter Sports Association was organized to get the chairlift, and townspeople invested $47,800 in the corporation to build a single-seater. A Colorado ore tramway, The Lilly, was bought and installed, and Rafferty took the first ride on Jan. 7, 1949. By that time, he was working full-time for the homegrown corporation.

Things didn't always go smoothly for the infant ski business on Snow King. One month and 10 days after its opening, the chair fasteners began slipping. Sightseer Lester May was riding down in a chair behind his wife when his chair slipped and banged into hers; all the fasteners had to be replaced. For years, Snow King had the best ski races and jump competitions in the United States, and it still turns out top competitors. Chuck Helm, Sun Valley's former orchestra leader, started the first ski school on the Town Hill.

Snow King continues to be the "Town Hill." With the baby rope tow, the beginners' Rafferty Lift—where night skiing is offered—the mid-lift and the main chair lift accessing 1,500 feet in vertical runs, it has been the place for Jacksonites to hone their skiing skills, be it through moguls or powder, as a racer or snowboarder. You can be sure there will be no lift lines at Snow King and if you need to learn to turn, try Bill Brigg's Great American Ski School. The ski club's log warming hut has been replaced by the Snow King Center, complete with a full-sized ice rink.

If the "Town Hill" isn't enough, try "The Big One"—the Jackson Hole Ski Area at Teton Village. Dramatic bowls, chutes, ridges, and glades drop 4,139 vertical feet from the summit of 10,450-foot Rendezvous Mountain to the base at Teton Village. In operation since 1966, Teton Village's numerous chairlifts (double, triple and quads) move crowds up to beginner, intermediate and expert slopes. Or take the 63-passenger aerial tram 2.5 miles to the summit in 12 minutes, barring high winds. Facilities at the area include a ski school, alpine and cross-country gear rentals and a complex of lodges, restaurants, condos, cabins, and shops circling the clock tower.

Although it is on the other side of the Tetons and so technically not in Jackson's Hole, Teton County has a third ski area—Grand Targhee Ski Resort. Located 45 miles from Jackson, Grand Targhee boasts powder skiing early and late in the season, when most resorts are praying for snow. Its services and facilities are comparable to Snow King and the Jackson Hole Ski Area.

Trip 9

Granite Creek Road
(10 miles)

This trip peeks into the Gros Ventre Range to the edge of its wilderness trailheads, where rugged scenery, a popular national forest campground, a hot water pool, fishing, and recreation all await you.

0.0 0.0   From Hoback Trip 1, Mile 23.0, turn north at the sign "**Granite Creek Recreation Area**," 11.8 miles east of Hoback Junction.

0.1 0.1   Put-in for Hoback kayaking.

0.2 0.3   East is **Battle Mountain** of nugget sandstone (see Trip 1, Mile 21.5). Wagons used to tip over when crossing Granite Creek at the ford here.

1.1 1.4   Hummocks. East of Granite Creek, south-moving ice from Granite and Little Granite creeks carried glacial debris to this spot, creating the topography.

0.1 1.5   Junction of **Granite** and **Little Granite creeks**. The main fork of the road continues over the bridge. The kayak put-in for the lower Granite Creek run is above the bridge. Before oil companies thoroughly explored this area, miners were digging for coal; the turnoff left (N) dead-ends in two miles at an old coal mine. From there, the Granite Highline Trail continues northwest along the Gros Ventre backbone to Cache Creek road and Jackson.

3.2 4.7   Terminal moraine cut through by Granite Creek (E).

217

1.2 5.9   Morainal debris. Note the large erratic boulders on the western skyline and the Precambrian dark rocks ahead on skyline.

1.2 7.1   Granite Creek Ranch Turnoff. Ahead, you can see the mouth of Granite Creek Canyon. Although it doesn't have the climbing granites of the nearby Tetons, the Gros Ventre Wilderness's colorful sedimentaries offer beautiful hiking and horseback riding. You are bound to see bighorn-sheep trails criss-crossing the high, sharp ridges.

1.0 8.1   Trailheads. The Highline Trail goes west and the Swift Creek Trail goes east to Swift Creek Falls, a fork of which leads to Dr. McLeod's lake.

0.9 9.0   **Granite Creek Campground** (E).

0.3 9.3   **Granite Creek Falls**. Parking for the trail is northeast. The falls were used in the lyrical movie, *A River Runs Through It* (1992). Local river guide Breck O'Neil was coordinator of river stunts for the film.

0.4 9.7   **Granite Hot Spring** (N). The road ends at the parking lot with a trail and bridge leading to the pool and changing house; it's open summer and winter. The spring emerges from the Cache Creek fault at the rate of some 300 gallons per minute and a temperature of 106 degrees Fahrenheit.

To the east, the awesome cliffs of **The Open Door Peak** (el. 9,204) tower 2,200 feet above the hot-spring pool. Open Door's smooth walls have succumbed to climbers; it's a nice climb to contemplate from a floating position.

If you have a more adventurous soul, try the Jackson-Granite Creek Trail, which starts between the pool and bathhouse and heads north and west up Granite Creek, past Turquoise Lake and Gros Peak (el. 11,180), for 14 miles before reaching Cache Creek Road and Jackson. Alternate destinations include Jackson Peak and Goodwin Lake.

Trip 10
WILSON-FALL CREEK ROAD
(17 miles)

This road seeks natural grades as it wanders through the foothills of the Snake River Range (W), the floodplains of lower Fish Creek and the Snake River, and overlooks the river where trappers forded braided channels en route to Mosquito Creek Pass. This trip starts at Wilson and ends at Snake River Canyon.

0.0 0.0 **Wilson** (el. 6,207) (see Trip 3, Mile 17.8), near the Stagecoach Bar. Turn south at the Fall Creek Road sign. Astonishingly, the houses to the east for the next five miles lie in the Fish Creek and Snake River floodplains.

0.6 0.6 Indian encampments. Early hunters used obsidian found here.

0.4 1.0 Indian Paintbrush subdivision and **Black Canyon** (W). When a well was drilled here, ancient ice was found in an obsidian layer 180 to 200 feet down. The ice probably was frozen during a glacier period more than 10,000 years ago and remained after the glacier melted.

0.9 1.9 Crescent H Ranch (W). When Lt. Doane and his party made their winter exploration of Snake River by boat, the only person they found living in the valley was John Pierce, a friend of Beaver Dick Leigh. Pierce had a cabin in this area, at the base of the range. This "gigantic raw-boned and grisled old volunteer" soldier could hardly believe that Doane's party was boating the

219

Snake in winter or that it had gotten through with animals. Pierce restocked their dwindling supplies with elk meat, salt and flour, in return for clothing and rifle shells. He was trapping furs (not beaver) and had told Beaver Dick earlier that he was heading elsewhere. He was pretty nervous about the Doane party's motives.

1.9 3.8 **Mosquito Creek Road** (W) into the Snake River Range. Ed Blair helped Steve Leek set up the valley's first water-powered mill on Mill Creek, about four miles west of here. The mill was brought over Teton Pass from Market Lake, Idaho, in 1893. The road followed the old trapper and Indian trail over Mosquito Creek Pass and was used sometimes instead of Teton Pass; traces of early Indian camps can be found along the creek.

Mosquito Creek was used early on by sheepherders wanting to graze their animals in Jackson's Hole. One outfit attempted to bring a herd over this pass in 1901 but armed men stopped them, killing some of the sheep and so badly scaring the herder that he galloped out of the country, leaving the scattered remnants of his herd. Early Jackson Hole settlers had been crowded out by sheep elsewhere and were determined not to let it happen here. They believed the valley too small for both sheep and cattle, and they thought that sheep would run wild game out. Those who wanted sheep kept them fenced on their own land. Sheep were limited so successfully that when a little woolly lamb was exhibited at one July Fourth celebration in the valley, the children had no idea what it was. Old-timers joked that they weren't even permitted to wear wool socks.

0.2 4.0 Pavement ends. At this point, the Snake River (E) is divided into many channels, which makes for easier crossing by horses, so this was one of the preferred early fords. The ford linked the Hoback trail (see Trip 1, Mile 40.6) with either Mosquito Creek or Teton pass. In 1834, Osborne Russell and his party, confronted with an eastward crossing, made a bull boat of a green elk hide stretched over a basket frame of willows. Part of their gear reached safety in this conveyance, but it sank on the return trip. Next, they attempted an unwieldy driftwood raft, which they loaded with men and remaining baggage; it also sank. Russell, who didn't know how to swim, learned remarkably fast when he noticed the rest of the party was too busy to save him. Gloomily, the party huddled on the east bank in a downpour on the Fourth of July, "not knowing at what minute we might be aroused by the shrill cry of the hostile savages with which the country was infested, while not an article for defense, excepting our butcher knives, remained in our possession." The next day, however, they found their raft lodged on a gravel bar below; they dried out their clothes and continued east.

2.5 6.5 **Munger Mountain** (el. 8,383) ahead. Pre-Wisconsin ice overrode all but Munger's highest summit.

1.8 8.3   Butler Creek subdivision (W). The Fall Creek road climbs out of the Snake floodplains to circle west of Munger Mountain.

1.9 10.2 **Red Top Meadows** and top of pass. Turnoff (W) to Trails End Ranch and the North Fork and South Fork Fall Creek trailheads to the Snake River Range divide, nine miles.

0.2 10.4 Red Top Meadows Residential Treatment Center (W), a boys ranch. The main road twists south.

1.5 11.9 The vast colorful willow bottoms of Fall Creek.

2.1 14.0 Fall Creek. Here begins the climb to Pritchard Pass.

3.0 17.0   Cottonwood Park Center (E); elk feeding grounds and marshes (W). Note the old irrigation ditch on the hillside (W).

0.1 17.1 Junction with Snake River Canyon Road, U.S. 26-89 (see Trip 2).

Trip 11
MOOSE-WILSON ROAD
(15 miles)

With country-lane charm, this winding, narrow road explores the aspened base of the Tetons. Its route still follows the early track, as it meanders past dude ranches that made Jackson Hole famous.

0.0 0.0   Moose Post Office; turn west from Park Road (Trip 6c, Mile 11.7). The Murie Ranch (SW) was the old STS Ranch. In 1927, the *Jackson Hole Courier* announced the arrival of a young biologist-naturalist named Olaus Murie, out of Alaska. The Biological Survey, for whom he worked, instructed Murie "to make a complete study of the famous elk herd in Jackson Hole." His wife, Margaret, and two babies followed him into the valley. His experiences in Alaska and Jackson Hole changed him into a conservationist. In the late 1940s, unhappy with the Biological Survey, which had loaned him to the National Park Service, Murie accepted the post as director of the Wilderness Society, working half time at half salary and directing the society's affairs from his ranch in Moose. The Muries had pooled their resources with his brother, Adolph, and Mardy's sister, Louise, to buy the STS dude ranch. For 17 years, Olaus Murie directed activities of the Wilderness Society and was an important spokesman for the modern conservation movement. He and his wife co-authored books about life in the wilderness with young children and the study of elk and nature. After her husband's death in 1963, Mardy Murie continued with the environmental causes.

2.0 2.0   Sawmill ponds (S). Good viewing site for moose and birds. Sawmill Ponds, originally called Huckleberry Springs, is the source of Reserve Creek and the chain of small ponds which parallel this trip. The ponds provide excellent wildlife habitat for moose, beaver, otter, mink muskrat, and nesting waterfowl. The ponds were smaller until beaver moved in and enlarged them. Al Young's sawmill operated here from 1920-29. After that the STS Dude Ranch used the area for horseback riding.

1.0 3.0   Death Canyon Trailhead. Turnoff (W) goes to a fork; the left fork goes to the park patrol cabin and parking for the Valley and Death Canyon trails; the right fork goes to the abandoned White Grass Ranch. Started in 1913 by Harold Hammond and Tucker Bispham, the White Grass became one of the largest spreads in the area. From 1919, Hammond and Bispham wrangled dudes, ran a fox farm and a boys' camp, and operated the only ranch with a concrete-lined swimming pool. The death of the last owner, Frank Galey, in 1985—and a fire that burned the main lodge—killed off the longest operating dude ranch in the valley.

0.7 3.7   R Lazy S Ranch. Once owned by Owen Wister as a private retreat, the R Lazy S's first furniture included cots and packing crates. Wister, told to go west because of his health, first visited Jackson Hole in 1887 on a big-game hunting trip, the start of his love affair with the West. *The Virginian* first came out in *Harpers Magazine*, starting as short stories in 1894. Teton Basin, Jackson's Hole and Wind River Valley provided the setting and many of the characters for Wister's 1902 novel, *The Virginian* (see Trip 12, Mile 2.4). In 1911, he returned with his family and bought these 151 acres. Wister, his wife and five children, a governess and handyman lived here for only two months each summer. When Mrs. Wister died in 1912, Wister never returned to the Hole, and the house stood empty for several years until he sold it in 1920. It narrowly escaped being torched for Park Service firemen's practice; instead the two-story cabin was dismantled, stored for years, and then moved to the main street (U.S. 87-30) of Medicine Bow, where scenes from *The Virginian* also were set.

1.3 5.0   The JY (Joy-Young) **Ranch.** The first of the famous dude ranches, the JY is at the south end of Phelps Lake. The lake was named by the 1872 Hayden Survey for the hunter who discovered it. W.R. Taggart found it was hemmed in by three moraines.

The ranch was started in 1908 by Louis H. Joy. Owen Wister and his family were among its earliest guests. Fannie Kemble Wister described the cuisine and their visit of 1911: The scanty food was "driven over the mountains… from Idaho…. [Meat consisted of elk and] dried, smoked, salted bear meat like dark brown leather." At breakfast, she often found dead flies plastered between the flapjacks, like so many winged raisins. The roustabout who brought hot water to the Wisters every morning had, they thought, "something permanently wrong with his jaw." The lumpy jaw turned out to be a wad of tobacco.

Henry Stewart bought the JY Ranch in 1920 and expanded it until, by 1927, it was the valley's largest. That year, he sold the JY to Rockefeller's "Snakes," and it became a Rockefeller retreat. In 1983, the park acquired 1,221 acres of the JY Ranch east of this road.

1.0 6.0 **Granite Canyon Trailhead** and parking (W); see trails at the end of the chapter.

2.3 8.3 **Teton Village** (W). Started in 1906 as a tiny post office, Teton Village now is the valley's largest ski resort. Here you'll find hotels, shops, condos, restaurants, a post office, medical clinic, and a concert hall. The aerial tram to the summit of Rendezvous Mountain is open winters and summers. The Grand Teton Festival Orchestra entertains with a summer schedule of musical activities.

South of Teton Village, the road becomes WY 390. The Snake River Ranch (E), is the Stanley Resor domain. He made his fortune as president of the J. Walter Thompson ad agency and, in the 1920s-1930s, bought up ranches north of Wilson, establishing himself as owner of one of the valley's largest ranches.

3.1 11.4 Hay ranches give way slowly to the still-growing and highly developed strip along Teton Village Road. The "Wilderness Acres" subdivision in the Snake's rocky river bottom was homesteaded by bachelor and valley eccentric, John Lockwood Dodge, one of the valley's three remittance men. Living on a monthly retainer sent by his sister, Carrie, John had his own ideas of how things should be done, like poking a lodgepole pine through his cabin window and into the stove to save him the chore of chopping firewood. As the wood burned, he pushed the log farther into the stove. John loved poetry, a hangover from New England col-

the NATURALIST'S NOOK
the MOOSE

WE THINK HE IS THE LARGEST ANTLERED MAMMAL THAT EVER LIVED ON EARTH. LIKE DEER, BULL MOOSE SHED THEIR ANTLERS ANNUALLY & GROW NEW SETS. THEY GROW BROADER & HEAVIER EACH YEAR UNTIL THE BULLS ARE SEVERAL YEARS OLD.

DESPITE THEIR ENORMOUS SIZE, MOOSE CAN RUN SWIFTLY WITH SCARCELY A SOUND.

MOOSE LIKE WATER PLANTS AND DUCK THEIR HEADS UNDER WATER ... SOMETIMES FOR AS LONG AS A MINUTE ... TO GET THEIR FAVORITE DELICACIES. WILLOW IS AN IMPORTANT WINTER FOOD IN SOME AREAS.

TO AVOID FLYS IN SUMMER, A MOOSE COW & CALF MAY SPEND A LOT OF TIME NEARLY SUBMERGED IN WATER. IF THE CALF TIRES IT RESTS ITS NECK ON THE MOTHER'S WITHERS OR THROWS A FRONT LEG OVER HER NECK. SHE THEN TOWS IT ALONG HER SHOULDERS. MOOSE ARE STRONG SWIMMERS.

lege days. Come spring, he would sit on his plow pulled by his two mules, Hobo and Bobo. When the mules got going, he would drop the reins, open his poetry book and spend the morning reading aloud. The mules wandered where they pleased, leaving figure-eight trails and modernistic patterns; but John didn't care. "The whole field has got to be plowed anyway!" he would say.

Dodge and friend John Dudley Sargent had the most complete libraries in the valley.

When his sister visited him, she realized that his log cabin in the wilderness was not the grand mansion he had written about and she insisted that he come home. "What do you see in this Godforsaken place?" she asked. John's arm swept up toward the Tetons, "Ye gods, Carrie, what more does a man want when he has all that?"

1.2 12.6   Developments to the south include Jackson Hole

Raquet and Tennis Club at the Aspens(W), which has a choice restaurant, and farther along is the billion-dollar extravaganza called Teton Pines (W). Built around the golf course, Teton Pines is the extreme manifestation of the new Jackson Hole—the millionaire's paradise. Then, it's back to regular businesses, restaurants and homes to the junction.

2.3 14.9 **Snake River Access**. Turn east and drive 0.5 miles to this major access point to the Snake. This gravel-pit area in the floodplains of the Snake provides good bird-watching habitat. WY 22 provides more access to the Snake at the Snake River bridge, 0.1 miles below.

0.1 15.00   WY 22 Junction (Trip 3). Turn west 0.3 miles to Wilson; turn east 6.7 miles to Jackson.

TRAILS

Death Canyon Trail. From Trip 11, at the Death Canyon Trailhead sign, turn west and drive 1.5 miles to trailhead parking. Walk 100 yards west to Valley Trail, take it left (W) two miles to Phelps Lake Overlook and junction. Here you take a right (W) for Death Canyon or take a left (S) for the Valley Trail.

Open-Granite Canyon Trail. From Phelps Lake Overlook (see above) take left fork, Valley Trail, south a mile to junction. Right fork goes west into Open Canyon, climbs south over Mt. Hunt Divide and drops into and joins North Fork Granite Canyon Trail.

Granite Canyon Trail. From Mile 6 parking lot, above, hike west two miles to Valley Trail. Take it right (N), then left (W) up Granite Canyon to Teton Crest Trail. Right (N) 0.5 miles to Marion Lake.

Rendezvous Mountain Trail. From Teton Village, climb the maintenance road to the tram summit (el. 10,450, free ride down). By taking the tram up, you can enjoy high-country scenery, snow in July, nature trails or, for those whose knees can take it, a 12-mile hike and 4,139-foot descent of Granite Canyon to Teton Village, as follows. From the tram, the trail west goes to and down the south fork of Granite Creek to the junction with Granite Canyon Trail (Marion Lake W). Descend Granite Creek east to Valley Trail; go south to Teton Village, then south and east to Granite Creek parking lot.

Trip 12
FLAT CREEK ROAD
(14 miles)

In 1892, the road to Kelly and northern Jackson Hole followed the Flat Creek Road, passing east of Miller Butte and skirting the present-day National Elk Refuge meadows on the east. From there, it prowled along sites of early outlaw skirmishes and hideouts, rambling past the homesteads of the first settlers. When the Gros Ventre flooded in 1927, it washed out the road. Then Cache Creek Drive (U.S. 191) north out of Jackson became the main route.

0.0 0.0   **Jackson Square**. From its southeast corner, take Broadway east, passing three historic buildings—Billy Mercill's General Merchandise (on the Square, corner of Center and Broadway), the Van Vleck Cottage at 135 E. Broadway, and the Miller Town House, north on Willow Street.

0.6 0.6   The second **St. John's Hospital**, built in 1960, has been converted to doctors' offices. The new hospital next door (E) was completed in 1992. In pioneer times, neighbors' wives helped bring babies into the world and take care of the sick, though doctors of varying abilities came and went. In 1915, the Men's Club built a church and a log hospital. The next year, young Dr. C. W. Huff, three years out of medical school, brought the valley the year-round medical attention it sorely needed. Led by Dr. Huff and the Rev. Royal Balcolm—an Episcopal minister—the crusading Jackson people built their church and a log hospital on the current site

227

the NATURALIST'S NOOK

the Elk

THE ELK, OR WAPITI IS A LARGE DEER. HE GOT THE NAME ELK FROM THE ENGLISH WHO CAME TO VIRGINIA & PROCLAIMED HIM TO BE AN ELK... *Which is the name given to the European moose!*

Hi Piker!

A BULL CAN HAVE AS MANY AS 60 MATES IN ONE SEASON.

AFTER THE MATING SEASON THE HERD IS USUALLY LED BY A WISE OLD COW

NATURE HELPS TO PROTECT THE NEW BORN ELK BY GIVING HIM A PERFECT CAMOUFLAGE SUIT AND VERY LITTLE SCENT.

of St. John's Episcopal Church. For many years, Miss Kiddy and her nurses assisted Dr. Huff. The building has since been sliced up, one section used as a private home on the north end of East Gros Ventre Butte.

For the Cache Creek bike ride, turn right (S) on Redmond, then left on Cache Creek Drive, which turns into a dirt road. The trail is four miles to the wilderness boundary.

0.2 0.8 **National Elk Refuge Headquarters**. Interestingly enough, this first land to be taken from its wildlife occupants by settlement has become the elk's last winter refuge. Now 23,754 acres, the refuge began with the purchase of Robert Miller's ranch in 1914; the addition of the Guy Germaine property followed a year later. Presidential orders set aside public lands and, in 1927, the

Izaac Walton League gave 1,760 acres. Congressman Winter's bill provided 12,000 additional privately owned acres, and Rockefeller added land south of the Gros Ventre River and east of the highway in 1950.

0.2 1.0   Flat Creek Road (N). At this junction, take the left road north through the National Elk Refuge. (The right fork leads to Cache Creek Canyon road and trails, Jackson's favorite "back-yard" outing for biking, skiing, hiking or walking the dog. Five miles from this junction, up Cache Creek, several trails take off into the Gros Ventres. For the Cache-Game loop, watch for the Game Creek sign after you pass the barrier. Push up the trail, a steep rise, to the ridge. Ride to the saddle east of Snow King Mountain and follow the main trail down to Game Creek's dirt road. Turn left down to U.S. 89 and Jackson. Right is Leeks Canyon.)

0.7 1.7   **Robert E. Miller homestead,** a historical site. Two-hundred pound trapper Miller (1863-1934) built his empire by loaning money at 12-percent interest. The 19-year-old came in to trap and hunt in the valley in 1882 and returned to live here in 1885, which made him the first permanent resident. This fine log house contrasts strikingly with the one-room outlaw cabin in which he initially homesteaded. Miller told oldtimers that he "bought" the homestead from the outlaw Teton Jackson or his lieutenant Thompson. The Land Office, however, records Miller as the first owner. Certainly, outlaws had no desire to record their hide-out with the U.S. government, and Miller no doubt made a good bargain. Logs from the original Outlaw Cabin have gone into other buildings now on the refuge.

Miller's Illinois bride, Grace Green Miller (1863-1948), arrived in 1893 to find the first cabin stripped of its flooring. While the owner was absent on his wedding trip, an enterprising neighbor had taken it to build a flume. So Grace Miller's housekeeping began on a dirt floor. Astute Mrs. Miller was the first to file a desert claim and the first woman mayor in the United States.

Usually one jump ahead of everyone, Robert Miller had a knack for acquiring land and livestock. When Teton National Forest was established in 1905, he became the first supervisor and served as such for 16 years. To a man resourceful enough to live off the country, Miller's salary as forest supervisor was pure gravy. Years later, he boasted that he still had the first dollar he made.

Few others in the valley had such cash flow, and Miller thus became the financier of the community. He was called "Old 12 Percent" because his interest rate was high. If he didn't get paid back in cash, he'd collect in kind—like the time he received one and a half tons of hay from the Mormons during their first struggling winter. In 1914, Miller organized the Jackson State Bank on Crabtree Corner, with most of the $10,000 capital subscribed by local citizens. When Rockefeller decided to buy the lands for the national park, Miller was employed. Nearly everyone was mortgaged to Miller at one time or another, so he pressured many to close a deal. "Now is the time to pay off," he explained. "I want to count all my money."

0.7 2.4 **Miller Butte** (W) with Miller Springs at the south end. Early People left tepee rings on the butte's 1.5-mile-long ridge (permission required). "Outlaws Ledge" or "Ft. Standoff," at the butte's south end, was dynamited to build the former road on solid ground. A scar of fresher rock remains. Strategically, **"Outlaws Ledge"** commanded the only practical entrance to upper Flat Creek and the outlaw hangouts because swamplands blocked all other routes.

In Owen Wister's book, *The Virginian*, Steve tells about lying on the ledge to report the movements of the posse. After hearing the early outlaw stories firsthand, Wister novelized them, but protected individuals by changing names. In Chapter 33, he describes the Jackson Hole setting: "Somewhere at the eastern base of the Tetons… those hoofprints disappear into a mountain sanctuary where many crooked paths have led. He that took another man's possessions or… life could always run here if the law or popular justice were too hot at his heels. Steep ranges and forests walled him in from the world on all four sides, almost without a break; and every entrance lay through intricate solitudes… among whose thousand hiding places it was easy to be lost.

"Down in the bottom was a spread of level land, broad and beautiful, with the blue and silver Tetons rising from its chain of lakes… and in and out of this hollow square of mountains, where… game and natural pasture abounded, there skulked a nomadic and distrustful population. This in due time built cabins, took wives, begot children, and came to speak of itself as 'the honest settlers of Jackson's Hole.' It is a commodious title, and doubtless today more accurate than it once was."

The valley has kept the myths of the outlaws alive. When asked by visitors where the outlaws were, one old-timer replied with an ironic twinkle in his eye: "Take a good look at us; we're all still here."

A newspaper item dated Oct. 12, 1886, headlined "MOUN-TAIN OUTLAWS... Teton Jackson... The Haunts of Bandits and Horse Thieves," sheds further light on the valley's reputation in the early days: "Teton Jackson has lately escaped from the Boise City penitentiary in which he was incarcerated last August to serve... 14 years for horse stealing.... From his fastness in Jackson's Hole, Teton led his reckless band of outlaws on their wild forays, until not a ranch within a... hundred miles had escaped visitations or herds failed to pay tribute.... The stolen stock was received... the brands blotched or changed, and the animals incorporated with those already on his ranges.... When the suitable time came, the stock were driven in small bunches to... surrounding settlements where it could be most easily disposed of....

"In May 1886, Teton accompanied by... Blackie Marks, made a raid from Jackson's hole into Idaho and drove off 39 head of mares and colts belonging to... Hines & Stout, ranchmen [near] Blackfoot.... A posse, tracing them into Wyoming... lost the trail in the foothills of the Wind [River] mountains.... At this juncture, W.F. Hosford... Wyoming stock detective... telegraphed Sheriff Canton of Johnson county to keep a lookout for the thieves and stolen stock.... In a day or two... Canton was on their trail through the Big Horn basin... came upon the stolen stock grazing on the range and by nightfall had located a cabin 'nearby.'

"Hosford got his prisoner to Blackfoot and he was duly tried.... Teton told Hosford... the band had numbered as high as 10 men. Their hold was a strongly built log house in the center of a morass (swamp) in Jackson's hole which could be held against almost anything but artillery. They obtained their supplies from two men resident of the hole, named Holland and Carnes. These men were married to squaws, and had hay ranches... made annual fall trips to Green River City for winter supplies for themselves and the robber band.

"Both Holland and Carnes have a bunch of good blooded horses. The nucleus of these herds... from the ranges of Mr. Harkness in Bingham county, Idaho....

"While Hosford was… after Teton, a posse started out from Blackfoot for Jackson's hole. They… encountered a portion of Teton's band under the efficient… Bill Thompson, Teton's lieutenant…. After a sharp fight in the open ground the robbers retreated to their log castle in the morass, and the posse let them stay there. They recovered, however, seven [additional] head of the Hines & Stout horses… making the entire number stolen….

"The gang is still there yet, and it is to them that Teton will at once make his way…." Sheriff Canton described Teton Jackson: "He was not a pleasant companion…. He was about 45, over six feet in height, weight 190, stubby beard, raw-boned, coarse features, flaming red hair, red face, and eyes as black as a snake's."

Teton Jackson was only part of the larger picture. During the 1890s, horse thieves were working as traders in the several states around Wyoming. They would steal from one area, winter the stock in a hideout like Jackson Hole, change or remove the brands via a red-hot frying pan—allowing time to heal—then head the other direction to "market" in the spring (see Trip 6d, Mile 12.2). Now and then, posses would organize and go after the thieves, with or without authorization.

Before the outlaws used Miller's Butte, the site was visited by earlier nomadic inhabitants, whose tepee rings and tools, cave shelters, and obsidian flakes from toolmaking have been found.

1.0 3.4 **Sheep Mountain**, aka the **Sleeping Indian**. Its name is obvious when you see the head and feathered headdress profiled by the south summit, with the chest as the north summit.

1.0 4.4 Road Junction. Take the left (N) fork over Nowlin Creek, which drains Curtis Canyon. Dan C. Nowlin initiated the official census of 1900, counting 638 men, women and children living in the valley in June of 1900. Listed as a farmer, Nowlin also was a game warden. The Curtis brothers ranched at the mouth of the canyon about one mile ESE. Called "Slow-up" and "Flare-up," both Curtises were powerful men. Jim Chambers once saw Slow-up hold a kicking cow forcibly with one hand and milk her with the other. Flare-up would fly off the handle and fight in a minute. Slow-up, on the other hand, "was eeeezzy goin', slow talkin'," as Jim Chambers tells it. "One day, his neighbor, Si Ferrin, came over and said, 'Slow-up, if you don't pen your pigs up I'll kill them and I'll beat hell outta you.' Slow-up, easy-like drawls, 'Okay Si.' Two,

the NATURALIST'S NOOK

BIG HORN SHEEP

THEY USUALLY LIVE IN HIGH ROCKY COUNTRY. THE ADULT BIGHORN IS A MAJESTIC ANIMAL WEIGHING AS MUCH AS 350 LBS.

THEY'RE EXTREMELY SURE-FOOTED. THE BOTTOM OF EACH FOOT IS CONCAVE. THIS ENABLES THEM TO WALK & RUN OVER ROCKS EASILY.

LAMBS GROW RAPIDLY. WHEN FIRST BORN THEY CAN WALK UNDER A STANDING EWE. WITHIN A MONTH THEY MUST FREQUENTLY KNEEL TO NURSE.

BIGHORN LAMBS ARE VERY PLAYFUL. THEY PLAY GAMES OF TAG & FOLLOW-THE-LEADER, JUMPING OVER ROCKS & RUNNING AROUND PINNACLES.

three days later, he came up to Si's place. 'Well, Si, I penned my pigs up… but Si, y' know, I've been thinkin'… you said you'd beat hell outta me and I just don't think you can do it.' Si had to talk like the devil to change his mind."

0.1 4.5 **John Holland's homestead.** The first in the valley, John Holland's homestead was located about a quarter mile east. Holland trapped in Jackson's Hole in the 1870s, but returned in 1884 with his friend, John Carnes. The pair dragged the first wagons up from Green River, over Bacon Creek, and down the Gros Ventre River trail. Holland built his cabin, put in the first garden, and obtained one of the few territorial water rights. After the turn of the century, he moved to Salem, Oregon, where he died at 65 from a leg infected by a glass cut.

According to Cal Carrington, "The first trial to come up in Jackson was under John Holland right out on his ranch. There was no courthouse. He had a little log cabin, 10 by 12. A man by the name of John West comes in down the Hoback with his family, some cows, a horse or two, and he had a mowing machine. Dick Turpin was living right close to Jackson and was out hunting; and while he wasn't home West dragged in his mowing machine and started mowing that property Dick claimed.

"Turpin came back, walked up behind. West had a six-shooter hanging on the seat of the machine and Dick grabbed the six-shooter with one hand and the reins with the other, and hit West over the head with the six-shooter. West had him arrested. Holland was appointed Justice of the Peace by Rathbun. But the court turned Turpin loose and ordered West out of the country. They all belonged to the brotherhood so he had no chance and he went out." (Justice of the Peace records show a warrant was served by Robert E. Miller, the trial set for July 31, 1892, with the case of "intent to commit murder" dismissed.)

0.9 5.4 Junction. We will go left, but the **Curtis Canyon Road** corkscrews east and right, past an overlook that offers an impressive view, and up to the Curtis Canyon campground. The road continues up the ridge to another fork. The left fork goes to Sheep Creek Trail and the ski hut, while the right one deteriorates into a jeep and logging road for 4.5 miles to the Goodwin Lake trailhead and parking area three miles from the lake. The trail gets you into the **Gros Ventre Wilderness**, to Goodwin Lake (brookies), to climbing rocks above the lake, and to the start of the Jackson Peak climb up the northeast ridge.

Back at the junction, take the left fork. Settler **John Carnes' homestead**, a three-room cabin, was about 0.5 miles west. Mustered out of the Union Army in July 1866, Carnes re-enlisted for Indian fighting, which he survived, only to become very ill later on a construction project. A Bannock Indian, Millie Sorelle, nursed him and they married, living together until her death in 1923. She was the first female resident in the valley. When Carnes and Holland moved into the valley in 1884, they horsepacked in dismantled farm machinery piece-by-piece. Carnes and Holland were with the posse in 1892 at the Cunningham ranch (see Trip 6d, mile 12.2). Holland was the nucleus of the bachelor society in the 1890s; its residents were described by Tom Crawford as a "homeless, reckless straight-shooting and hard-drinking set." Nevertheless, their hospitality was very appreciated by the early families. After the Indian trouble of 1895, Carnes moved to the Fort Hall Indian Reservation, where he died in July of 1931.

0.1 5.5 **Junction.** Take the right fork northeast to a good view of **Jackson Peak** (el. 10,741) to the southeast.

2.4 7.9 **Flat Creek crossing**. Note the "closed to fishing" sign, except during August and September, when you can go after cutthroat, brook, rainbow, hybrid, and whitefish.

At the junction north of the creek, take a right. Here, you will find the site of **Roy McBride's homestead**. He and his wife came to the Hole in 1896 and floored their cabin with wide rough-sawn boards. The roof was made of poles, thatched with straw, and then covered with dirt and planted with grass. Mrs. McBride ordered white sheeting from Montgomery Ward and tacked it over the ceiling to keep dust from sifting down; the sheeting was taken down once a year and washed. She also papered the inside log walls with the *Congressional Record*, matching the pattern so it looked like wallpaper.

On the less-domestic side, McBride was an expert rifleman and wolf hunter. Once, he fired six shots and killed six wolves, reportedly the scourge of Wyoming stockmen. Excessive numbers of wolves once ranged the Gros Ventre hills, according to the stockmen. In 1914, Jackson Hole cattlemen paid private bounties as much as $62 for a single adult wolf and $22 for a pup. The next year, $500,000 was spent in Wyoming to reduce the wolf population. There seems to be much confusion about the demise of the wolf in the state. According to the July 25, 1946 *Courier*, the last wolf was killed in 1927. But that turned out to be false and, by 1928, the Wyoming Game and Fish Department had declared that five wolves remained within the state, two of them in Jackson Hole. That also may be false, however, because other reports indicate they had disappeared by about 1916.

2.0 9.9 Junction. The left fork is the old road north to Kelly.

0.1 10.00 Old power plant site and **trailhead for Sheep Mountain**. Without electricity until the 1920s, the valley's first power plant was built on Cache Creek and then moved to this site. A dam and sluice system generated the power, but you could get electricity only from dark to midnight; eventually, it became available on certain days for washing machines and electric irons. Rural Electric Association (REA) later took over.

Jim May Homestead (above) and Grovont Post Office, 1910.

Joe Pfeifer, the last Days of the Homestead Era (right).

The Flying V Ranch (now the Teton Science School) of Dollie and Jack Woodman, pre-1935 (below).

To climb Sheep Mountain (el. 11,239), follow its long western spur, just north of the road, for two miles to the summit plateau, then head south and to the west side of summit mass. From there, you can scramble to the summit.

From the power plant, a jeep road continues four more miles. At 0.5 miles east, there is a USFS sign and the locked gate of Flat Creek Ranch. A trail bypasses the ranch on the left (N) and follows Flat Creek south into the Gros Ventre Wilderness, where it joins Granite Creek and Cache Creek trails.

Flat Creek Ranch is "The Countess's Place," nestled near a blue, trout-filled lake. This mysterious place has been almost inaccessible since buckboard wagon days. A careful search today probably would reveal the old stone blinds where Indians hunted, or traces of corrals where outlaws hid stolen horses. Cal (California) Carrington—a cowboy, cattle driver, Bar BC hand and one-time crony of John Holland and other early settlers—homesteaded Flat Creek Ranch. He sold it to his lifelong friend, Eleanor "Cissy" Patterson, who once was married to the flamboyant, womanizing Count Gizycki.*

The way Cissy's daughter—Felicia Gizycka*—tells the story, Carrington, a former horse thief, attached himself to her mother, becoming her guide and the manager of Flat Creek Ranch. Cissy Patterson was one of the most powerful and influential women of the 20th century; she was an outrageously outspoken and incredibly wealthy and passionate woman who dominated Washington society and revolutionized American journalism before her death in 1948. In Wyoming, she and Felicia were dudes at the Bar BC, where Cal Carrington—tall, powerful, rangy, and ruggedly handsome—was the foreman.

He had drifted into the Hole in 1897 and belonged to a gang of six rustlers, identified by the red squaw bandanas they wore. They specialized in stealing horses, rebranding them, and then selling them across the state line. Of the group, only Carrington was never caught and jailed. Born in Sweden, his real name was Enoch Julin.

After the Bar BC stay, "the Countess" wanted her own place, and so rented the White Grass Ranch for a summer and hired

---

* *The different name suffixes relate to the gender of the person.*

Carrington. Her Eastern life was in such turmoil that she could only find peace in the Hole and, in 1923, finally talked Carrington into selling his place to her for $5,000. She added more buildings, including the lodge and had wagons haul in furniture, including a piano, antiques, and rugs. She loved sitting on the porch and watching animals feed near the lake. Her dearest, closest friend in the Hole was Rose Crabtree.

Carrington outlived an era, dying in a comfortable hospital bed in Driggs, Idaho on Dec. 22, 1959. His tight lips about himself and early Jackson characters left much of the story untold. He did, however, reveal a little: "When I came to Jackson's Hole I didn't have nothin' but a long rope and an old buckskin horse. I lived with Dick Turpin, I lived with Holland, I was around Miller some. They were the old-timers. Turpin built his first cabin on Chimney Creek and trapped there for a living, and then it run along quite a while… and then the cattle race picked up. It was T.H. and a bunch of them, and they picked up cattle off the Green River trail and drove them back up here for a start. Course they'd some horses and whenever they got a stray I think they pushed him in here."

Of the old-timers, Carrington recalled: "You see they formed a brotherhood, and they dug up $90 between them. Bob Miller was secretary and whatever they wanted to do they all went in together, see! They all had a red squaw bandana for a badge. If you saw a man in the country and he was riding around without a red bandana you knew he was a stranger. They all had that when I hit Jackson (1897) but the next year they quit wearing them.

Carrington told about his "pre-Countess days" living up Flat Creek: "I lived up in the canyon where the horse thieves [Cal & his buddies] took the horses up. All I had to do was to put up two pair of boards and that shut the whole canyon off, and there was a meadow above there…. The horses stayed in there, and the horse thieves had everything on their side."

According to Charlie Petersen, Carrington said Holland built the corrals. "Up above the old cabin on Flat Creek there's a kinduva fortification of the Indians. There's two there. Rock walls with holes in it along the game trail between the creek and a ledge. They'd go there and bunk up and when the game came along they'd shoot them with an arrow. When I first went up there, there was sticks across where they'd had skins or something over them for shade."

Jackson attorney E.N. Moody looked after "the Countess's Place" in his cowboy days. "When I first went up there," he said, "the road Carrington used had been cut through the fallen-down timber, the logs sawed so wagon wheels barely cleared between, with only half an inch left on each side. It was slow and difficult." As an intruder's wheels clipped the standing trees, the noise telegraphed a warning to the outlaws. After all his partners had been put in jail, Cal joined the Bar BC "because it was time to get respectable and go into dudin'."

Trip 13

ANTELOPE FLATS ROAD, MORMON ROW, AND KELLY ROAD

(14 miles)

Until 1906, the year of the last migration of pronghorn antelope from Green River Basin, the flats to the north were the range-
land of thousands of pronghorn antelope (see Trip 6d, Mile 1.2).
Locally, this once heavily ranched country, officially called Grovont
for the post office, was named Mormon Row. It was one of several
settings for the Western classic movie, *Shane*, and is known to park
hunters as the "Hayfields."

0.0 0.0   Junction of U.S. 191-26-89 (Trip 6d) and Antelope
Flats Road, which crosses the south end of Antelope Flats, passes
north of Blacktail Butte (S). Within the butte's habitat, a small elk
herd summers, as do several other shy-type animals.

0.3 0.3   **Paintbrush Point** (S). The turnoff south leads to the
later home of the Harrison Crandall family. A Kansas farm boy,
Crandall worked for the U.S. Biological Service at Boise, Idaho,
long enough to buy a Model T. In 1922, he loaded it with his 3A
Special Eastman camera, his worldly possessions, and his bride,
Hildegard, and took off for the Tetons, where he spent the summer camping by String Lake. Encouraged by Moran fur trader and
storekeeper Charlie Fesler, Crandall began selling postcard-sized
pictures that he and Hilda printed by sunlight, developed in a tent,
and washed in the lake.

In 1923, Crandall homesteaded a quarter section east of String Lake, built a tent dance hall, and played the slide trombone, while Hilda beat out the melody on the piano. Those Saturday night dollars paid for a photo studio and equipment. Crandall prowled the mountains and backcountry, recording vistas never before photographed. When the park was established in 1929, he was ready with his prolific files to meet the demand; through his Crandall Studios at Jenny Lake, thousands of visitors were able to take the Tetons home with them. Many a college student paid for his tuition working summers for Crandall. When the old log studio, now the Jenny Lake Visitor Center/Museum, was turned into a gift store for some years, it had bats in the belfry, which forced the clerks to cover the art and counters at night.

0.5 0.8   Turnoff (N) to several homes: the bear-studying Craighead families, and Indian dancers and authors, Gladys and Reginald Laubin, among others.

0.9 1.7   **Mormon Row Junction**. In 1908, when President Teddy Roosevelt issued an executive order abolishing Yellowstone National Forest and expanding Teton National Forest, he opened new lands to homesteading. John and T. Alma Moulton were the first to homestead along this road. The pink ranch house to the north, built in 1934, belonged to John (1887-1989) and Bartha Moulton, but for the first years of the homestead they lived in the little cabin nearby. While proving up his homestead, he worked on other ranches and trapped beaver and coyotes. Although the Moultons sold this land to the park in 1953, they had a lifetime lease. His house was used for scenes in *Spencer's Mountain*.

Today, Mormon Row dead-ends north in about 0.5 miles, above the next homestead, which is the old Heniger place. An old track continues north, once the main route from the town of Jackson to north Jackson's Hole.

As early as 1890, the thrifty hardworking Mormons saw great possibilities in this rich hayland. They concentrated their houses companionably along this road. The Mays arrived first and were followed by the Moultons, Budges, Chambers, and others. With pronghorn antelope herds close at hand, the ranchers could pick off one or two for meat easily; as fences built up, however, the animals disappeared.

Turn south to check out the memories of Mormon Row.

0.5 The buildings with the picturesque barn (W) belonged to the T. Alma Moulton homestead. When Thomas and Sarah Moulton immigrated from England to America with their children, including just-born Charles Alma, in 1856, they joined the Saints' trek to Salt Lake. Arriving late at the Iowa City rail terminal, their group learned that all covered wagons were gone and they'd have to use handcarts. Thus the 10 Moultons—three adults and seven children—joined the ill-fated Willie Handcart Company. After waiting for 250 carts of green, unseasoned wood to be built, the company started its 1,300-mile trek to Utah on July 15, with the Moultons pushing two handcarts that held all of their possessions. It was much too late to start such a trip and, by the time the company reached Fort Laramie at the end of September, freezes had set in and food was short. It's all a matter of record now how some 62 to 77 members of the company died en route. Miraculously, though, the entire Moulton family survived this historic tragedy.

Charles, the Moulton infant of the handcart trek, eventually married Rhoda Duke and moved to Teton Basin, Idaho. They had nine children, three of whom took out homesteads on Mormon Row. Thomas, Alma and John first rode into Jackson's Hole in 1907 and took out adjacent homesteads on Mormon Row. They hauled logs from Timbered Island for their cabins. In 1912, Alva brought his wife, Lucile, and baby, Clark, to live in the inadequate one-room cabin. Alma started building his barn in 1913, and this vital livestock shelter looked like a big box by the time he ran out of money, but it worked. Then he built the frame house for his growing family. It was 1928 before he and Clark added the barn's hayloft and a half-pitch roof; in 1934, it received a lean-to for the mail-run horses. In 1939, Clark and brother Harley added a hog barn on the north side and roofed it with tin. The family dairying used the original center section, and horses used the southside lean-to. It took decades to complete and part of a century before it became an American symbol, one of the most photographed landmarks in the valley. It also was used for location shots in *Spencer's Mountain*. The scene of Henry Fonda trying to milk the cows was unforgettable to these dairy farmers.

East across the road lived the Andy Chambers family. Andy acquired the last homestead on the Row—in 1912. Ida Belle Kneedy Chambers (1897-1988), born in the Ozarks, joined her father when he homesteaded the Antelope Springs Ranch north of Kelly, at the base of Shadow Mountain. Ida taught at the Grovont and Elk schools, and then married Andy Chambers in 1918. When he was called into the service in World War I, Ida found herself hauling water from nearby Ditch Creek, or melting snow. That July, after school closed, Ida plowed and cultivated 60 acres with Andy's two horses. For 27 years, she and Andy operated the ranch, ran the post office/store, and raised seven children, which prompted her to say: "The last diaper I wash is going to be raised on a pole and flown as a flag until it shreds." When they finally got a well, it was hand-dug by neighbor Joe Pfeifer, and it brought up colored clay water. Ida lost her parents, the Kneedys, and a foster brother in the Kelly Flood. When the Chambers moved to Jackson and sold the ranch to the park in the 1940s, they kept a lifetime lease for the children. "You have to live a long time to beat out a Rockefeller."

0.3 **Grovont**. Next (W) are the ruins of Joe Eggleson's old barn. Along the south boundary of Eggleson's 160 acres was the old east-west road (0.2), going west around Blacktail Butte to Menor's Ferry. Where it crossed with Mormon Row clustered the "village" of Grovont—the church (0.1) on the northeast corner, and the school (0.2) on the southeast corner (where the power line is), on land donated by Hans Harthoorn.

0.2 Hayfields hunting area. The large posts in the ground on both sides of the road mark the north boundary of the Hayfields hunting area.

0.1 The **Henrie May homestead** (W). Henrie's father, James May, settled on the 160 acres south of his son in 1896, then sold that to Henrie and moved across the road to his 160 acres there. George Riniker homesteaded east of Henrie May.

In 1894, James May came to Jackson's Hole searching for a homestead. He chose the land east of Blacktail Butte because the thick sagebrush meant rich productive soil and the nearby Gros Ventre River meant water. When he returned two years later with his family and the Charles Allen and Roy McBride families, he filed his homestead claim. The group wintered over with some of the valley's homesteaders, and the next summer, May built a cabin west of the road using logs from the butte behind. Then he bought a two-story pre-cut frame house, which was erected across (east of) the road by the crew that came with the house. A problem arose when Ann May insisted on a blue roof, with paint she had bought, and the crew had only yellow paint. In the end, the two paints were mixed, resulting in a bilious green for the roof, doors and cupboards.

The most urgent but time-consuming chore was hauling water from the Gros Ventre for the stock. It was only years later that the Mormon Rowers finally got wells, hand-dug by Joe Pfeifer. In 1916, James May became a justice of the peace. In 1896-97, he planted the old cottonwoods you see along the road (W).

During the Depression, families in Jackson's Hole were having a tough time making ends meet. When George Riniker decided to sell his sheep for $1.25 each, Chloe May told her husband, Joe, to buy them. Now Joe, a true cowman, hated sheep, but Chloe's arguments about the benefits of sheep—wool *and* meat—won out, and Joe bought them. Chloe said: "You don't have to like them." Joe and two other ranchers leased Blacktail Butte and kept the sheep there and on their own land; the sheep got them through the Depression. When Gladys May Kent was in fifth grade, the teacher proposed that the class draw names and each write a little rhyme about that person. Wilber Clark drew Gladys' name and wrote: "A freckled-face girl lives over the way./Her daddy's a sheep herder, and her last name's May." Everybody laughed but Gladys.

The Park Service dismantled the Henrie May house in 1960.

When Rockefeller and his Snake River Land Company were buying up land during the Depression, Mormon Row was not included because Gov. Emerson believed these lands were better used for farming. The schoolhouse shook with weighty discussions as those residents discussed being left out of the project. They finally petitioned Emerson to retract.

Rockefeller's representative, Harold Fabian, told them to agree on a fixed per-acre price. Dick Winger helped them determine the figure—$50 an acre. Complicated by objections from Sen. Carey, however, Rockefeller backed out. Later, the Park Service acquired these lands. Then, for years, 2,774 acres were leased to the Elk Refuge for hay production for winter feedings. When pellets became more practical, hay production stopped and the lands were left to nature. Irrigation ditches and a few pronghorn antelope are still seen but the "hayfields" are the focus of fall hunting in the park.

0.4 The **Jim Budge homestead** was south of the May property, at the base of the down-faulted spur of Blacktail Butte (building

The Kelly Bridge before the Flood (above). L to R–W.J. Kelly House, Barn, and Sawmill, built 1917-18.

The Kents' old timey Kelly Store (left) before the 1971 fire.

Swirling waters encircle a building on what is now the Teton Valley Ranch (below).

foundations are still visible). The Budges, who had come in with the Mays, also were the first homesteaders in the area. In 1897, the Budge cabin had one room, a sod-roof, a door and window. When mud and rain leaked through the roof, Nan Budge put the children under the oilcloth-covered kitchen table. By 1901, the Budge cabin had five rooms and stables.

Nan loved to fish in the Gros Ventre; from the back of her horse, she wielded her bamboo pole and trolled up and down the river.

South of the main Budge gate, another gate and parking area mark the start of a trail west: Either climb the southeast ridge of Blacktail Butte or hike along the old road that once cut west across the south base of the butte. A trail—formerly a wagon road—goes up the butte's large south-side central gully to the summit. The gully holds springs that prehistoric people used.

Return to Antelope Flat Road, mile 1.7. Continue east.

1.1 2.8 **Joe Pfeifer's homestead**. Gone are the rotting remnants of a past era, the Pfeifer homestead, demolished by an Aug. 28, 1994 lightning strike that torched the ranch and 3,200 acres east of it. The picturesque old buildings portrayed the time Pfeifer lived here, alone on a homestead he never got around to finishing; his battery radio was the only modern touch.

Each settler had his reason for coming to the Hole, and Joe's was the free land. When he was working in the Butte copper mines, he saw a map—on a saloon wall—of lands open for homesteading. He put his finger randomly on the map; he'd picked Jackson's Hole, so he headed south. In 1910, this land was part of the Forest Reserve, but if no timber was on the land, the forester could release it. When this tract was released, Joe had 60 days to file as a desert claim. He built his first cabin with a dirt roof and pole floor. In 1912, he built the cabin that survived until 1994, with a board floor, and door and openings facing east because weather came out of the west. (Other buildings that stood to the south before the fire were built by "Happy Hooligan" Ireton, who later left the valley.)

For a while, Pfeifer's spread and way of life were part of the Jackson school curriculum, in which you would find questions such as: "How did he make a living here?" Well, during winters, he often worked the Butte mines, but during summertime, hunting and fishing in the Hole was the life. He worked as a handyman on two of the Jackson Lake dams, and peeled tepee poles and logs. He also invented a "snomobile" from old wooden skis and a car that never worked. He had a garden, and his acreage produced enough feed for his three white horses. He once bought a cow that died before he got her home. He was famous for his huckleberry wine but when he took Gladys Kent to his secret huck patch on Shadow Mountain, his wandering trail so bamfoozled her that she never found it again. He also had two old wagons that he sold to the *Shane* film company for $25. "They seemed to like 'em," he said. "I couldn't use 'em anymore."

Joe, who had helped many Mormon Rowers dig their wells, worked on his own well in 1915. He did all the digging by hand. He'd first rig a wooden windlass over the well site and, with a short-handled shovel, dig the dirt out and pitch it aside. As he got deeper, however, big steel buckets strung on a rope through two strategically placed pullies and pulled by a horse lifted the dirt and rocks to the surface. As he got lower, he cribbed the walls with split logs to forestall any cave-ins. Most wells were about 100 feet deep. Ironically, on his own well, the deeper he went, the drier it became. At 104 feet, he had to use a sprinkler to keep the dust down, so he gave up and decided to use the hole for a vegetable cellar. He was still carrying water from Ditch Creek when he died in 1964. Pfeifer, born in West Virginia in 1879, sold his land to Roy Chambers, who sold it to the park after Joe's death.

Three things should be noted as you travel east of the Pfeifer place. First, there's the scorched earth of the 1994 Row Fire, which we can all watch evolve; second, the road begins to climb over the slow rise of the Ditch Creek alluvial fan, the largest such feature in Jackson Hole; and third, you can see the 1988 Hunter Burn at the south end of Shadow Mountain combined with the 1994 burn.

0.6 3.4 **Four-way junction**. Once called Mail Box Junction, this used to be marked by a string of post-office boxes. Turn right (S) to Kelly. The road east led to the old Hunter Hereford Ranch, now park land. The road left (N) goes to a junction: The right fork leads to Wyoming's premier impressionist painter Conrad Schwiering's (1916-1986) home and studio; the left fork contours the base of Shadow Mountain for half a mile to a second fork. The most traveled road at this fork goes right to enter the national forest, climbing to several great overlooks, past clearcuts and into

the NATURALIST'S NOOK

White-tail Deer

SEVERAL THOUSAND WHITE-TAIL DEER LIVE IN WYOMING, HOWEVER THE MULE DEER IS THE MOST COMMON.

WHITE-TAIL

MULE

WHITE-TAILS ARE SMALLER THAN MULE DEER & THEY DO NOT ORDINARILY RUN WITH A BOUNDING GAIT. THEIR TAILS APPEAR FLATTER AND BROADER - ARE PREDOMINANTLY WHITE. ANTLERS USUALLY TURN SHARPLY FORWARD & EARS ARE SMALLER

HERE I AM!

CONCEALMENT IS THE WHITE-TAIL FAWN'S ONLY DEFENSE DURING THE FIRST FEW WEEKS OF HIS LIFE. ITS PROTECTIVE COLORING, AS WELL AS LACK OF STRONG SCENT IS OF GREAT HELP.

WHITE-TAIL DOES HAVE BEEN KNOWN TO CATCH & EAT FISH IN THE SHALLOW WATER OF SMALL STREAMS. THEY DISABLE FISH BY STRIKING THEM WITH THEIR HOOVES.

THEY SEEM TO HAVE GREAT ANTIPATHY FOR SNAKES. THEY'VE BEEN SEEN PRANCING AROUND A SNAKE BREATHING HEAVILY AND SNORTING WITH EXCITEMENT. SOMETIMES A DEER WILL JUMP ON THE SNAKE WITH ALL FOUR FEET BUNCHED TOGETHER

huckleberry and fall hunting country. The left fork, the old pioneer road, continues north along the mountain base to the Triangle X and the Cunningham ranches.

0.8 4.2 **Ditch Creek**. It's hard to believe that a tiny stream could have deposited such an enormous alluvial fan. At the "Mining" Ditch, Hayden Surveyor Orestes St. John found prospect pits and the remains of a ditch here in 1878. He was told that gold prospectors dug the six-mile ditch—from the present-day Teton Science School to the Snake River—by hand in about 1870-71. When the water was diverted into the ditches, it ran about three miles before it sank into the gravel. The prospectors found "flour gold" but never in commercial amounts. The ditches, later surveyed by W.O. Owen, indicate the magnitude of the effort. USFS records show that Martin Henrie got the first permit to graze cattle and horses in the Teton Forest Reserve in the Ditch Creek area in 1902. The idea caught on with ranchers.

0.7 4.9 **Teton Science School** and Forest Service access road to upper Ditch Creek. The school, at the mouth of Ditch Creek, sponsors year-round natural-science programs and workshops for people 8 years old and older. The summer adult seminars, for people 18 and older, address various topics relating to the Greater Yellowstone Ecosystem, including endangered species, geology/archaeology of Jackson Hole, canoe trips, night skies, birding, river hydrology and fire ecology. The 1994 Row Fire burned extremely close to the school, and its students now study its effects on the country.

The Science School location has gone by various names— Flying V, Ramshorn, and Elbo—and owners, including mountaineers Paul Petzoldt, Gus and Theodore Koven who bought the Flying V from the Woodmans in 1935. As the Ramshorn, the small ranch aimed to become a profitable dude ranch, hunting outfit and climbing headquarters, but that partnership failed in 1937. In 1956, the park bought the property from A. Adams for $68,000 and, two years later, issued a concession permit to Katie Starratt, manager of the old (W side) Elbo; the Ramshorn became the new Elbo dude ranch. When Starratt died in 1974, the park issued a special-use permit to the Grand Teton Environmental Education Center to operate a school. The bare hills in the foreground (E) are chiefly glacial deposits left by ice flowing south from the Absarokas and west down the Gros Ventre River.

0.5 5.4 From this small hill at the top of the Ditch Creek fan, notice how the sage-covered slope of the fan tapers down to its south edge to merge with the hayfields at the bottom, creating a distinguishing line. During the Kelly flood of 1927, the most frightened of the Kelly people waited out the rampaging flood waters from this site.

0.5 5.9 Jct. Gros Ventre River Road (E, Trip 14). Continue south down "raptor alley," where hawks hunt the several "towns" of Unita ground squirrels. Straight ahead (S) looms pyramid-shaped Jackson Peak (el. 10,741), composed of Precambrian granite and located in the Gros Ventre Wilderness; the popular Goodwin Lake is below its north shoulder.

Because the Hayfields become the Kelly killing fields every fall, the elk have made some strategic changes in their habits; they move mostly at night from the park into the refuge and have shifted migration routes westward. Their old trails can still be seen across the hills to the east.

0.1 6.0 Gate (W). If you take this former county road 0.8 miles west (not during hunting season), then hike 0.3 miles to a point north of the big warm-water ditch, you'll be standing on Joe May's old horse pasture and the site of the Starrett homestead, where Alan Ladd, as the drifter Shane, came to the homesteaders' assistance in the timeless classic movie, *Shane*.

0.9 6.9 Gate to the long-running **Teton Valley Ranch** (E), which raises longhorn cattle on the 1,200-acre spread and has operated a summer youth camp since 1939, when Wendall "Weenie" and Mary Ellen Wilson came out West to establish their dream camp. The portion of the ranch south of the Gros Ventre River was the homestead of elk tusker Binkley. The Teton Valley gate stands on a bench above Kelly (S). On the same bench but opposite the gate and about 100 feet west of the road is a grassy area and three cottonwoods surrounded by sage. This is the site of the Helmar Bark house, which survived the Kelly flood and then became the Kelly Post Office.

0.1 7.0 **Kelly**. W.J. Kelly and his bride, Sophie, came to Jackson's Hole from Idaho in 1909 and were largely responsible for settlement and growth here. Politically competitive with Jackson, Kelly lost the county seat to Jackson in 1921, by only 22 votes.

In 1927, the year of the **Gros Ventre Flood**, Kelly boasted 80 inhabitants—35 families—plus a post office, church, dance hall, garage, hotel, two stores, and a sawmill. Two years before, the Gros Ventre slide (see Trip 14, Mile 4.7) caused great commotion in this community. The new dam created by the slide had worried downstream people, but unnecessarily so, according to state engineer Frank C. Emerson and surveyor W.O. Owen, who examined the 200-foot-high dam and proclaimed it "perfectly safe; it would never wash out." They were certain that when the new lake topped the dam, it would spill over and flow into the river bed.

Still, town folk like Anna Kent, and especially Mrs. Kneedy, were very nervous. Mrs. Kneedy and son, Joe, often slept on high ground, especially after the lake filled. After a year of apparent calm, worries eased, and life returned to normal along the Gros Ventre. At her husband's ridicule, Mrs. Kneedy and Joe moved back into the house.

Forest ranger Charlie Dibble moved to Kelly in 1925, when his Horsetail Creek ranger station was inundated by the newly created lake. But he kept a suspicious eye on the unengineered dam. He became uneasy in May of 1927, when heavy snows swelled the drainage into it. His journal noted that the Gros Ventre was "bank full and full of debris" the morning of May 18. While he and others poled away the heavy driftwood piling up at the Kelly bridge, he saw a sight that chilled him—a hayrack that had been floating in the middle of Slide Lake since 1925 was coming downstream. Instantly alerted, he and cowboy Jack Ellis drove Dibble's Model T upriver three and a half miles, where he met the flood's first wave, overflowing banks by five or six feet. Behind it was a 50-foot wall of water, filled with churning debris, "like a stampeding herd of elk with horns (trees) flying, and a roar of grinding, hissing and swishing water." Farther up, they found a large log house and barn rolled over on the Woodward Ranch on Turpin Creek. The men cut fences to free stock and floorboarded it back to Kelly, warning that the flood was 15 minutes behind them. There had been so many "wolf" cries since the slide had occurred that the ranger had difficulty convincing people that the flood was a great wall of water, not just water creeping up the banks. H.M. Kneedy begged neighbors to help him save his waterwheel, ignoring repeated warnings from the ranger. He and his family stayed in the house. At the two-room school, the teacher sent her 14 pupils home immediately.

Postmaster Raymond Kent was behind Dibble, loading office books into his truck; he sent 13-year-old Donald north to higher ground with the horses and then drove the truck north out of town, picking up people as he went. He tried to get "little Joe Kneedy" to come along, but Joe said he'd "go with Mama and Daddy."

Ethel Carlson (Jump) had been reminded to keep her car gassed up but had forgotten. When the warning came, she piled the car with goods and took off, only to get a few yards before running out of gas. She and the kids took off but she remembered something, ran back to the car, checked her husband's trousers, and found $10. That was all they would have to start a new life.

From the higher bench north of town, many eyes watched the town of Kelly dissolve in the mad swirling waters. They watched the water ricochet and lash back and forth. And they heard the "terrific unexplainable roar and grinding of hissing, swishing water" that

swept boulders, trees and buildings before it. They saw the buildings—hotel, mercantile, garage, stables, homes—wash away, one
by one. They saw the Kneedys in their two-story house by the river
climb out onto the roof and then disappear; some saw May Lovejoy
and her sister, Maude Smith, loading valuables into the wagon,
whipping the horses and turning their buckboard at a right angle
to the oncoming water, only to be bowled over by the rushing torrent.

Mr. and Mrs. Frank Almy, in their 60s, in their open car, were
swept into the flood and separated. Mrs. Almy was rolled and buffeted by flood waters for a mile, then climbed out—gasping and
nearly strangling—with her glasses and false teeth still in place.
Mr. Almy was caught in the fork of a cottonwood tree and saved.
When reunited, their grief gave way to anger over the way the other
had been too awed to move out of the flood's path. Four men saved
themselves by clinging to trees. Max Edick and a hired hand, Clint
Stevens, were trying to save some pigs and chickens when the flood
came. The two climbed onto the chicken house. When a hayrack
floated by, Stevens jumped on it; his body was found wedged in a
tree four miles below. By 11 a.m., only the Episcopal church, the
parsonage next door, and the school—now Yurtville's bathhouse—
had survived the flood.

Flood waters reached only to the bench and irrigation ditches
and, by late afternoon, the river was back within its banks. The
search for bodies began. Sisters May Lovejoy and Maude Smith
both drowned. Mrs. Lovejoy's body was never found. Although everyone had ample warning, six people died, and 35 families were
homeless—at a cost of $300,000. The Grovont church was turned
into a morgue; the Red Cross headquartered at James May's house.
Martha Marean described the desolation of Kelly: "...Nothing but
a rubble of boulders and rock, where once huge trees, lawns, bushes
and flowers had been." Not a piece of the Kelly bridge remained.
The rushing waters filled the irrigation ditches with boulders, dirt
and debris, ruined headgates, and washed away all the Kelly soil.
The Kelly family returned to Idaho, while others moved to Jackson or elsewhere in the valley.

Turn south across the cattle guard into Kelly; just east, you'll
see what's left of the old Trinity Church, built in 1911. After the
flood, Ray and Anna Kent bought up the land around to subdivide.

When the Kent family moved into the old church building some time after the flood, they turned it into the post office and an old-timey country store with a big old stove for chatting around and huge wheels of cheese to slice with an impressive knife. The building burned in 1971. The little parsonage to the south was added on to several times and is the home of Donald and Gladys Kent, Kelly's unofficial historians.

Kelly sometimes had been called "The Bridge" because the former timber bridge—upstream from today's main bridge and marked by old pilings—was part of the old Long Hollow road south to Jackson. The town's main claim to fame today is its post office, a tiny store with an interesting rock bin, two phone booths, a lyrical coyote community, modest cabins, placidly grazing longhorns awaiting sale, fascinating transient neighbors including buffalo, elk, moose, coyotes, and deer, a tightening web of unsightly power lines, an even more unsightly substation, the excellent Kelly school, and "Yurtville." The white-topped yurts, visible across Donald Kent's big field (W), are Kelly's unique answer to the low-cost housing crunch.

0.2 7.2 **Kelly Post Office** and Gros Ventre Slide Inn.

1.3 8.5 Between Kelly and Mormon Row, you often can see wildlife leaping the fence of the National Elk Refuge (S) as the animals move between the refuge and the park hayfields/Blacktail Butte (N). But every hunting season, this stretch of road near Mormon Row—the Kelly Kill Line—becomes the hangout of "hunters," sportsmen that is, lucky enough to draw a permit to hunt in Grand Teton National Park, the only national park that allows hunting. They sit along here in their pickups, waiting for the migrating elk to come off the butte and cross the hayfields and the road into the refuge. When the animals get close enough the "hunters" start firing their high-powered rifles that can shoot anything within two miles. Passers-by get to watch first hand the slaughter of the terrorized elk and watch as the "deputized Park Rangers" prevent the animals from crossing and escaping into the refuge—a dismal scene.

Hunting in the park was a compromise that the National Park Service was forced to make in 1949, in order to end the controversy brought on by the effort to add the Rockefeller land to Grand Teton Park. Although the NPS balked at continued hunting in the park—as demanded by the Wyoming Game and Fish Department—it made the compromise to keep peace. Under the agreement, the elk herd is administered jointly by Game and Fish and the NPS; hunters are deputized as temporary park rangers and allowed to kill surplus animals.

0.5 9.0   South end of **Mormon Row**. In March of 1985, another film crew showed up in the Hole to make a movie. This time, the set crew of *Rocky IV* (1985), featuring Sylvester Stallone, built some Russian-type cabin exteriors north of here. The weather didn't cooperate, though, producing sunny days for a wintry Siberian setting. One night, the crew sprayed water on Rocky's cabin in hopes of creating icicles as big as Drago's thighs; the next morning, the camera crew hustled to capture a glimpse of them before they dripped into oblivion. This road bends to follow the river but the old road cut directly west, across the south end of Blacktail Butte. This major curve has been deadly to some drivers.

0.2 9.2   **Gros Ventre Campground** (S): Tents and trailers, 14-day limit. Good fishing access here; muddlers and various small dry flies work well.

0.3 9.5   **Blacktail Butte** is a complex fault block in the middle of the valley. Scientists now know, however, that it has been scoured, faceted, and overridden by south-moving pre-Wisconsin ice that probably was 1,000 feet thick on top of the butte. It was split in half by the Flat Creek reverse fault, which you can trace from the prominent skyline notch, left, south down the central valley. Along the fault emerge several springs that attracted prehistoric Indians, who left evidence of campsites, quarries, and crude artifacts. The bare, fluted, southside slopes are slip-off glaciated marks scoured by the ice that overrode the butte.

2.1 11.6   Teewinot Formation. This road cut to the north is a vertebrate fossil site of the Teewinot Formation, representing the bottom deposits of Lake Teewinot, a great lake that covered the valley floor of the Hole. Fossilized fragments of beaver, mice, shrews, and insectivores have been found. Looking southeast across the river to the Elk Refuge, you can see a white scar. Although there is no salt here, elk love to lick the bed of white pumice. The east skyline is the Sleeping Indian (el. 11,239). A river of ice, 2,000 to 3,000 feet thick, passed over and shaped the rounded hills to the east and south.

2.3 13.9   **Gros Ventre Junction**, U.S. 191-26-189, (see Trip 7). Jackson is south; Moose, Moran and Dubois are north.

Trip 14
GROS VENTRE ROAD
(27 miles)

_____

For a study of earth movements, both ancient and recent, you can't surpass this trip, even by the standards of Montana's Hebgen Lake earthquake of 1959. The famous one, of course, was the 1925 Gros Ventre Slide, a mile-long mountain mass that slid 2,000 feet into the valley, as cowboys watched. Before that came the Upper Gros Ventre Slide (1908-1912), and hundreds of other mud flows and tumbled masses on creeks that show spectacular shifts in mountain sides. The Big One in landslides, however, happened 5,000 years ago. It created a giant prehistoric Slide Lake that touched off the granddaddy of all floods and left only obscure signs for the geologists to solve the mystery. The geology tells an exciting story. Other points of interest are a colorful canyon, plus old Indian camps, their trails and tepee rings scattered along the upper river and good fishing in lakes and streams, except during June high waters.

The Gros Ventre (pronounced "grow vont") was a major route into the valley for the Early People, Indians, trappers, and some settlers, who traveled from the Wind River via Union Pass and Green River valleys. The old wagon road could not be maintained on the moving mountain sides and finally was abandoned.

Osborne Russell, with Bridger's brigades in July 1835, told of the first of three trips through the canyon: "[We] followed… the 'Grosvent fork' in an East direction about 2 Mils…. In fording it we lost 2 Rifles.... We followed [it] thro the mountain east passing thro narrow defiles over rocky precipices and deep gulches" into Wind River country. President Chester Arthur's Yellowstone-bound cavalcade trooped from Fort Washakie over the Continental Divide via Sheridan Pass in 1883, packed down the Gros Ventre, and set up three camps on the banks.

In 1884, John Carnes and John Holland brought the first wagon over this route from Green River. Phil Smith, an early park ranger, laughingly told how he once took an old Model T over this road into Green River valley, with human muscle power pushing it the last 100 feet over the divide. They were mostly following migration routes.

0.0 0.0   Turn east at Mile 5.9, Trip 13, one mile north of Kelly.

0.3 0.3   Note the large irrigation ditch. Just north of the road, an earlier hot spring deposited this travertine ledge. Glacial debris formed the hill to the north. And ancient south-moving ice produced the upland swales—giant grooves cut in Paleozoic rock—that climb 500 to 1,000 feet up the hillsides (SE).

0.1 0.4   **Kelly** (Luke)**Warm Springs**. This is Kelly's social center on blue-sky days and a favorite place for swimming and kayak-roll practice; NBC news anchor Tom Brokaw, for one, started his kayaking career here, under the tutelage of Yvon Chouinard. The spring flows out of a fault at an estimated 5 million gallons per day and a maximum of 86 degrees Fahrenheit. Nitrogen bubbles keep the water agitated, and guppies, mollusks, some micro-organisms, and frogs hang out around the moss. In 1900, there was a constant roaring noise in these foothills, apparently from one of the many belching steam holes that later became inactive. After the Kelly flood, the quiescent springs started up again. The Mormon Row residents called it the miracle spring. For 20 years, they had hauled river water for their animals, but now a disaster brought the blessing of a warm spring that stayed open year-round. They dug the nearby irrigation ditch for their drylands.

0.7 1.1   *"Shane"* Cabins (N). Originally built by homesteader Johnny Erwin and occupied by Luther Taylor between 1923 and 1948, this became park land in 1956. It was one of several locations for the *Shane* movie. The scene here was the cattle stampede, which thundered right on through.

1.1 2.2   Cattle guard. It was near here that Ranger Dibble met the first floodwaters of the Gros Ventre River; the main wall came 15 minutes later with a terrific roar of grinding, hissing, swishing water, spiked with trees and rocks.

0.1 2.3   **Grand Teton National Park** and **Bridger-Teton National Forest boundary.** You can put in here for boating the lower Gros Ventre to the Kelly dam. A deep trout pool lies in the river curve, south, at the base of a Tensleep sandstone cliff, but beyond that awaits the white froth of the Cherry Popper Rapids.

North of the highway is bouldery glacial debris left by the south-flowing ice river through Jackson Hole; the river merged here with ice flowing down the Gros Ventre. The huge chunks of Huckleberry Ridge tuff came out of Yellowstone and mixed with granite erratics out of the Wind River Range, more than 50 miles southeast. The Jackson Hole ice dammed the valley here, forming a 30-mile-long lake behind it.

0.4 2.7   **Shifted River Channel.** At this point, the river and the road are very close, only because of the 1927 flood. Before the flood, the road was here but the river channel was farther south. That left room north of the channel for the Bill Woodward ranch, between the river and the road. When the flood struck the Woodward buildings here, waters rolled over the large log house and barn like small boxes. Nobody was home at the time but when they arrived, nothing was left, not even the land on which the ranch had stood. The river had been diverted northward by massive slide deposits across the old channel.

0.3 3.0   **Turpin Creek.** The 1901 Grand Teton Quadrangle shows the original Gros Ventre Road/Indian Trapper Trail going north up Turpin Creek for a mile or so, twisting eastward across the upper hills for three miles, then descending and coming out of the hills at Atherton Creek.

When Roy and Becky Chambers ran the friendly old Flying V dude ranch (S), Roy used to take his dudes up what he called the "Ohmygawd" trail. When asked why he called it that, he replied, "You'll see." When the riders crested the hills of upper Turpin Creek and confronted the stunning expanse of Jackson Hole and the Teton Range laid out before them, they invariably cried, "Oh my God!"

0.6 3.6   At the top of the hill, park for a view of the **Devils Elbow Slide,** directly across the river. This ancient slide, involving the same sandstones and shales as did the Lower Gros Ventre Slide

(E), slid across the river and up this side, probably damming the river up to the present road. Not as high as the 1925 slide, it was a mile wide, extending from the 1925 slide west as far as the near horizon. That ancient slide also impounded a huge lake. Observe landslide debris to the north. And while you're here, take a hike west of the parking lot to the **Marriage Tree**, one of the valley's more impressive scenic spots for weddings.

0.2 3.8   Turnout. The poisonous selenium indicator/converter two-grooved milk vetch *Astragalus bisulcatus* grows prolifically here. Cattle eating it are affected by chronic selenium poisoning.

0.6 4.4   Notice the landslide debris plastered against the red Chugwater formation.

0.2 4.6   Taylor Ranches (S). Above the bridge lies the put-in point for running the **Upper Gros Ventre River.** This run through the tricky landslide debris becomes Class VI during high water, making it the hardest run in the valley.

0.1 4.7   **Gros Ventre Slide Geological Area**. This turnout includes an exhibit, toilet, and self-guiding nature hike. Note how high the slide debris was thrown on the north side of the road. You can see the entire rock slide, a textbook example, from here. At 4:20 p.m. on June 23, 1925, on the site of older slides, the Gros Ventre Slide broke loose from Sheep Mountain, 2,000 feet above the river, roared down the mountain and swept across the river valley, its momentum carrying debris 350 feet up the north side—all within three minutes. It produced wind with a velocity of 200 mph, which stripped the upper trees. It created a 225-foot-high dam, half a mile wide, which blocked the river and formed a lake 200 feet deep and three miles long behind it. It was the largest such slide of historical record in the nation. It later was said that if earth had been moved as fast from the Panama Canal, it could have been built in less than an hour.

Several things contributed to the slide: the river cutting away its base, heavy rains soaking the soils on the mountain, and earthquake tremors shaking it. All of this brought the Tensleep sandstone—the large light-colored blocks—sliding down and buckling over the underlying, water-soaked, tipped slick shales, which are the red, pink, and purple beds visible in the debris. The pink Amsden shale overlain by the hard Tensleep sandstone are exposed left of the slide scar.

The Gros Ventre Slide and the dam that blocked the river (above).
The slide that blocked the Gros Ventre River, 1925 (below).
Guil Huff's House after the slide and before rising waters carried it away (bottom).

Billy Bierer first ranched the land that now lies under the lake. In 1920, he sold to Guil Huff, perhaps because he noticed the supersaturated soil and swampy pools with no outlets and had predicted that Sheep Mountain would slide if earthquake tremors hit when the mountain was most saturated. "Anywhere on that slope, if I lay my ear to the ground, I can hear water truckin' and runnin' underneath. It's running between strata.... There is a wet line running between stratas, and the time will come when the entire mountain will slip down into the canyon below. For instance... these earthquake tremors that are coming so often are going to hit at about the right time when the mountain is the wooziest, and down she'll come." All those factors came together in June, 1925. It was a rainy month and severe tremors were shaking Jackson Hole. Small slides began running off Sheep Mountain.

Guil and Violet Huff had put all their savings and work into the ranch and home. Their lovely log house was on a bench overlooking the river. On the afternoon of June 23, Violet looked out of a window and saw the top of the slide: "Trees started moving and tipping. Dust rose above them. I wondered for a minute, then I realized what it was." That same afternoon, Huff, whose ranch lay between the mountain and the river, stopped plowing his lower field and rode out to investigate the small slides. He watched a dust cloud and saw trees begin to move and lean. He was startled when the 30-foot cut bank at the mountain base suddenly rolled into the river. Then, with a roar like a dozen express trains, the north end of the peak peeled off, fanned out, and headed for him. Terrified, Huff whipped his horse upstream to his ranch. As he stopped to open the gate, the slide shot past him, only 30 feet away, taking the fence and all and burying his ranch completely; his new $7,500 house was untouched.

The sight of that slide scared the dickens out of a couple of cowboys, who never really could give a coherent account of what happened in the three minutes it took to cause such havoc. Farney Cole and 18-year-old Boyd Charter, up across the river, had been moving horses when they heard rocks rolling and looked up at a roaring sound to see strange dust spirals and a cloud of dirt. They watched, dumbfounded, as the mountainside moved and spread out, the slide heading for Huff's ranch. In seconds, Charter spurred his horse upriver toward the Horsetail Ranger Station. Cole watched in horror as Guil Huff tried to outrace a mass of granite, trees, and boulders; he headed toward the Huff place to help.

Up at the Horsetail Ranger Station, Charlie Dibble heard "a rumbling, grating noise" but didn't know the cause and went on working. He had just transferred from the Weiser National Forest in Idaho the week before, and everything was new to him. Then Charter came dashing up on a sweating cow pony and, cussing and stammering in his excitement, tried to describe what he and Cole had just witnessed. Dibble cranked up his Model T and the two rushed up the road toward the Huff ranch. All that night, they helped the Huffs haul their possessions from the house to the ranger station, upstream on higher ground, while small slides continued to run down the mountain. Others were evacuating the nearby Bill Card ranch (now part of Verland Taylor's ranch, across the river). The crews finished before dawn, and the Huffs fell into an exhausted sleep on a mattress on the floor of the station's office cabin.

When the Huffs returned to their home, it was already 18 inches under water. They watched it disappear under the new lake. Huff didn't wait for a new road to be built to the ranger station to retrieve his belongings. He and Henry Francis packed the goods over the mountain and away from the lake.

Dibble and his family stayed until June 29, when hard rain and terrible roars awakened them; fearing the worst, they raced up the hill in their night clothes and stayed until the roar quieted. They returned, put on dry clothes, then took the Model T and drove to a high spot, pitched a tent, and camped. In the morning, they saw that the mountain had settled, making large terraces. Water was lapping against the station foundation. They collected their belongings and left. Three days later, the station floated away on the lake.

The dam blocked the river, which poured in to create Lower Slide Lake; folks soon began calling it "Sudden Lake." For two weeks, the river was dry below the dam but began to flow again as water found its way through the porous debris. Seepage kept pace with inflow for two years. In 1927, heavy rain and melting snow caused the lake to rise rapidly. On May 18, the top 50 feet of the dam washed out and lowered the lake that much, causing the sudden and disastrous flood that wiped out Kelly four miles below (see Trip 13, Mile 7.0). The high water mark can still be seen south of the lake.

Though the most spectacular, this slide is only one of a series of such earth movements in the valley. They are the most important erosive force here. The lake is the valley's second largest , with average depth of 45 feet—complete with snags and good fishing.

0.7 5.4   The badly slumped road cut (N) has been a source of clues to the giant prehistoric Slide Lake. Along here was a delta 600 feet above the existing lake, where a stream dumped silt along an old lake shore. Contained in the layers of sediment was an ancient log, carbon dated at 5,000 years, as well as very old carbon trash, mollusks and bison bones. These deposits have collected at an elevation only slightly lower than the top of Devils Elbow Slide and now are considered evidence that the north edge of that earlier lake was impounded behind that slide. The lake was short-lived, geologically speaking. It emptied quickly, leaving little sediment and possibly creating the granddaddy flood of all northwest Wyoming history. The cataclysm left little record and wiped out all Indian artifacts. Maintaining the road ahead is hard because of the red/green Sundance shales, which like to slide.

0.6 6.0   **Atherton Creek Campground**. When 12 people turned up at a July 4 picnic at Jenny Lake in the 1880s, "Old Man Atherton" complained about too many people and moved from Flat Creek to this spot. If he was around today, he would have to move again. The boat ramp, gusty winds, stark tree snags and educated fish make this a place for windsurfers and fishermen to congregate. The next 1.5 miles cross the debris of a large slide out of Atherton Creek (N) that occurred before 1925.

0.1 6.1   The 1901 Grand Teton topo map shows that the old Gros Ventre Road/Indian Trapper Trail climbed north along the east side of Atherton Creek. You can still follow the tracks west over the hills into Turpin Creek. This was the route that the Arthur presidential party of 1883 took from Camp Arthur near Horsetail Creek (E). According to the official record: "We had climbed a long hill five miles from Camp Arthur, when there burst upon our view a scene as grand and majestic as we had ever witnessed" (*Following the Frontier with F. Jay Haynes* by Freeman Tilden). According to Tilden, "It was when the party got its full view of the mighty scarp of the Tetons that they began to experience the supreme scenic quality of this corner of Wyoming which in later years was preserved in its integrity by the National Park Service."

1.6 7.7 **Horsetail Creek**. This was the approximate site of Camp Arthur, the second Gros Ventre camp of the presidential party of 1883. On the east side, a trail climbs into the Mount Leidy Highlands. You can see the old post-slide road cut above.

Eight days after the 1925 slide, rising waters reached the ranger station, which was located here. After the slide, the Huff and Card furnishings were temporarily transferred to the ranger station. Rain during the night of June 30 caused Dibble and his family, still at the station, to expect another slide. At midnight, a loud roaring convinced them to move to higher ground, as the mountain settled and buckled into terraces, but still held. Three days later, their station floated away. The Dibbles moved to Kelly, where they experienced the 1927 flood disaster. The slow-moving **Red Slide** to the south, across the river, triggered when its toe was saturated by water from Lower Slide Lake; it is still moving and has almost pinched off the east end of the lake.

0.5 8.2 Trailhead and old ford. A boat will get you to the start of the trail up Redmond Creek (S), which, after a mile, forks east to Grizzly Lake (not visible).

1.0 9.2 Ahead is the spectacular panorama of the **Red Hills anticline**. An oil company drilled two dry holes, one to 1,231 feet, near the crest of the steep canyon (N). All it got out of the deal were oil stains.

Directly south across the river, the sharp ridge paralleling the water is part of an enormous landslide that skidded north. Grizzly Lake is impounded behind this barrier. Notice a conspicuous fault line in the hayfield ahead.

1.8 11.0 **Gros Ventre Bridge** and trailhead. Bighorn sheep hang out during the winters in the red cliffs (NE); expect to see them until June. From the bridge (west end), take the hiking or mountain-bike trail (skimpy in high water) that follows a bit of the washed-out Gros Ventre Road east across the **Lavender Slide** to Slate Creek. Former Gov. Cliff Hansen's property is south of the bridge.

0.4 11.4 **Parking and Trailhead**. The trail goes south a mile to join a major east-west trail. Turn west a mile to a junction. The right (W) fork goes to Grizzly Lake, while the left (E) fork goes to **Blue Miners Lake** (nine miles), in its lovely cirque; or keep going up the ridge to the summit of **Sheep Mountain** (11 miles).

0.2 11.6 **Red Hills Campground** (N).

the NATURALIST'S NOOK
Black Bear

THE "BLACK" BEAR MAY BE BLACK OR ANY SHADE OF BROWN FROM YELLOWISH TO SILVERY TO REDDISH CINNAMON. A VERY BLACK MOTHER MAY HAVE A BLOND, REDHEAD OR BRUNETTE IN THE SAME LITTER.

MOTHER BEARS ARE GOOD PARENTS. THEY READILY PLAY WITH THEIR OFFSPRING BUT WILL ALSO DISCIPLINE THEM WITH SHARP CUFFS WHEN NECESSARY.

AT TODAY'S PRICES YOU GOTTA WORK HARD!

I'M SURE HE WASN'T THERE WHEN I WENT TO SLEEP ????

BEARS EAT MANY KINDS OF WILD FRUIT & BERRIES, LARGE QUANTITIES OF GRASSES, TENDER SEDGES & CLOVER, THE INNER BARK OF SOME TREES AND NUTS

ORDINARILY HE IS AN INDEPENDENT CREATURE WHO WORKS HARD FOR A LIVING & MINDS HIS OWN BUSINESS.

CUBS ARE BORN DURING THE "WINTER SLEEP." THEY WEIGH ONLY 6 TO 8 OUNCES AT BIRTH & DO NOT OPEN THEIR EYES FOR ABOUT 40 DAYS.

0.4 12.0 **Crystal Creek Campground** (N).

0.7 12.7 **Crystal Creek bridge**. Because there is no Cretaceous shale in the Crystal Creek drainage, its water is clearer. Dick Turpin (1840-1919) eventually lived west of this creek. Turpin—a Civil War scout, Indian fighter, tie cutter and miner—came in 1888 with stolen mules. According to his service records, his real name was William A. Swalley, a teamster, born in 1840 in Alabama. After wintering in Turpin Meadows (see Trip 4a, Mile 4.0), he moved to Turpin Creek (1889) and then back to Jackson. Finally, when he thought the valley below was becoming too crowded, he located here, where he lived out his last days.

Some called Turpin mean and ornery. Although scrupulously

honest—well, up to a point—he had a fiery temper. His eyes would blaze out of his thick bushy beard. Turpin never talked of his past. It is said he thought he had knifed and killed a man and came here to hide; years later, he learned that the man had recovered. He feared no one. He once stared Tom Horn down in a threatened gun duel. Turpin and Swede Nelson whipsawed lumber—which John Carnes used to floor his cabin—on Turpin Creek. The story is told of Butch Robinson, a short, powerful man, going up to Turpin's door and pounding on it. Turpin's gruff voice, annoyed, growled, "By gawd partner, kick it down!" With a grizzly-like thrust, Robinson brought his heavy boot back and kicked the door. Down it went. Both men stood staring, surprised. "Well, that's what I told y' to do, didn't I," Turpin said. Suspicious at first of the phone that the forest rangers installed in his cabin, he soon saw its potential. "By gawd, partner, I can just holler down to Pap Deloney and he'll send it up!"

0.4 13.1   For a hike into the **Gros Ventre Wilderness**, turn (S) on the bumpy road that bypasses the Red Rock Ranch (W) to a primitive campsite on **Crystal Creek** (good fishing). The trail into the Gros Ventre Wilderness crosses icy Crystal Creek at least a dozen times—tennies are welcome for the sharp stones.

This 360-degree viewpoint on the Gros Ventre Road covers very interesting geology. North are the Mt. Leidy Highlands in the Bridger-Teton National Forest—first-rate grizzly habitat, but also an area of heavy clearcutting by the Forest Service. **Mt. Leidy** (el. 10,326), **Middle Leidy**, and **East Leidy** are the three prominent humps on the north skyline; they are composed of more than 1,000 feet of gold-bearing Pinyon Conglomerate from the Paleocene period. The Mt. Leidy Highlands are drained by Slate Creek (N). A huge shale landslide moved into this drainage from the west and shifted Slate Creek east against the gray hills (NE). You can detect recent movement by living trees, tilted in various directions. The huge **Lavender Slide** (NW) flowed out of the Lavender Hills down to the Gros Ventre River.

The young, lumpy Crystal Creek lateral moraine (SE at road level) butted up to the Lavender Slide in the river channel to dam the river and impound a lake. When meltwater from the ice in the Mt. Leidy area flushed gold-bearing quartzite gravel down Slate Creek and into the lake behind the moraine/landslide dam, gold was concentrated in the gravels. Many have attempted to retrieve the gold during the last 100 years. The latest (1965), by Westinghouse Corp., cost $1 million and involved building a two-story elaborate "mill." But it was not geared to recover the "flour gold" of micro-dandruff size, and it failed.

The death knell for wolves in Jackson Hole sounded in May of 1914, when the *Courier* reported 15 wolves had killed one of P. Redmond's cows and four yearlings near Crystal Creek. Redmond and Roy McBride collected their cattle and hired a night guard. In July, the Fish Creek Wolf Association was formed to wipe out the wolves. It hired Walter Dallas to hunt them, and bounties were set: $62 for females, $52 for males, $22 for pups, and $1.50 for coyotes. By the early 1920s, the wolves were gone.

Looking south up the glaciated valley of **Crystal Creek**, the canyon cliffs show evidence of prehistoric Indian shelters. Sites around Crystal Creek show bones of dinosaurs in rock and the only petroglyphs in the area. Old wickiups, tepee rings and other signs of Indians are up the Gros Ventre. *All* are illegal to disturb. "An arrowhead shoved into a shoebox is gone," says Professor Charlie Love of Western Wyoming College in Rock Springs. "Their value is gone because the context in which they are found can't be studied." Love promises to immortalize finders of such sites by naming the sites after them. Just call him collect.

Crystal Peak (10,967), on the far skyline at the head of the creek, is of Madison limestone, as are the other skyline peaks. West and in line with the road is a fan-shaped landslide that extends down to the Crystal Creek bridge. You can see the pull-away scar near the top of Red Butte. Still moving, it causes problems for road maintenance.

0.2 13.3 Another side trip turns off (N) on Slate Creek Road to a fork: Take a left to see the remains of the 1965 Westinghouse operation—debris, rock piles, and a vandalized orange dragline, which has been much used for target practice. Go right for the old ford across the river to the Slate Creek trails.

Continue east on the Gros Ventre Road, over Crystal's lateral moraine, with its fresh potholes that formed as buried glacial ice melted out underneath. One of these collapsed within recent times when a Hansen bull broke through the surface turf but was rescued intact.

2.3 15.6 **Alkali Creek** divides glacial moraine debris (W) from landslide debris (E). For the next 3.8 miles, the road parallels or crosses humpy landslides. These earth movements have crept slowly north during the last 50 years to dam the Gros Ventre River and form the Upper Slide Lake.

0.7 16.3 Dibble's Race Track, where Charlie Dibble's team of horses spooked and ran away with him. Looking south, note the front of mud flows.

0.9 17.2 View of **Upper Slide Lake** to the northeast and the actual **Upper Slide** to the south. In 1908, the peak to the south was called Slide Mountain (el. 9,200) locally, because its north end started to peel from the top and took two years to settle into the river. Bottomless cracks appeared, always changing; earth would settle around a portion of land and form a small peak. Trees were moved, their tops buried and their roots thrust in the air. Red brick soil turned the river a bloody color. It was impossible to establish any road or phone line for years because the slowly shifting earth created uncrossable crevices. The slide finally dammed off the river, forming a medium-sized lake, which still is being filled. Geologist Eliot Blackwelder called it an "earth flow." Two trumpeter swans hang out here, their broods always a worry to the local bird club. Notice the landslide debris to the south for the next two miles.

1.3 18.5 Turnoff (N) to Upper Slide Lake and put-in point for kayaking the Upper-Upper Gros Ventre; there's a classy little rapid just below. Fishing is good when the water clears.

0.7 19.2 Across the river, the scarred hills represent a failed Forest Service reseeding venture to offset overgrazing.

0.4 19.6 Across the river, you can see widespread coal beds. These are slightly exposed and 50 feet thick. In 1892, the Jackson Hole Coal Co. formed and located 52 coal claims of 160 acres each in this area. Assessment work was done by one 60-foot tunnel along a 15-foot coal vein that Dick Turpin dug on the south side of this coal ridge. The first load of coal was brought to Jackson in February, 1924 and was used by Harry Wagner, who had been Jackson's first mayor.

0.3 19.9 Road forks. Take a left across the river for **Dry Cottonwood Creek Road** (see below), a twisting, steep, dry-weather-only road to **Gunsight Pass** and a great view. Or, stay right, on the south side of the river, and continue past Goosewing Ranger Station (two miles). It's several more miles upriver to the mouth of Fish Creek.

Goosewing is a very old campsite, where traces of early Indians have been found. In 1883, President Arthur's party camped nearby, at its Camp Isham. Beyond the mouth of Fish Creek, the upper Gros Ventre River and the road along it both right-angle south. This upper road gives access to major trails into the Gros Ventre Wilderness and to the isolated Darwin Ranch.

DRY COTTONWOOD CREEK ROAD

0.2 20.1 Cross Gros Ventre bridge.

0.2 20.3 From this junction, three Forest Service roads/trails split off: One road goes north to an Upper Gros Ventre soil and water project; a trail goes northeast up Coal Mine Draw. (There's a spring in the gully east of here, near old coal-mining buildings.) Take the third, main (SE) road, FS 30410, which goes east past ranches (S).

2.0 22.3 Junction. Take a left up **Dry Cottonwood Creek Road** to **Gunsight Pass**, five miles. This switchbacking hard-pull road, on slumped sandstone, shale, conglomerate and coal, was built in 1953-54 by Placid Oil Co. to get to its Sohare test drill. Large slumps of material continue to fall off the escarpments.

5.0 27.3 Turn around at the test hole and return 0.8 miles to the fine overview. The Tetons are west. The **Upper Gros Ventre River** valley is south, and beyond it is the Gros Ventre Range and Wilderness Area. Northeast is Togwotee Pass, with the volcanic conglomerate of the Absaroka Range on the horizon. Basaltic Lava Mountain is the broad dome-shaped peak with dark west cliffs, south of Togwotee Pass. The heavily timbered Continental Divide is to its east. The tremendous Wind River Range, truncated in part by the summit peneplain, is visible far to the southeast, with the Bacon Ridge anticline in the foreground. Bacon Ridge, 14 crow miles southeast, is where the old Indian trail came in from the Green River valley. It followed the ancient migration route of the game animals, as evidenced by four- to five-foot-deep ruts. Return to Gros Ventre Junction and Trip 13. Left (S) to Kelly.

A Selected Bibliography

Albee, H.F., W.S.Langley, Jr., and J.D. Love. 1977. "Geology of the Snake River Range and Adjacent area": in Wyoming Geol. Assoc. 29th Ann. Field Conf. Guidebook.

American Alpine Club. *Accidents in North American Mountaineering*.

Bonney, Lorraine. *Wyoming Mountain Ranges*. 1987. Helena, MT: American Geographic Publishing.

Bonney, Orrin H. and Lorraine G. 1992. *The Grand Controversy*. American Alpine Club.

————. 1970. *Battle Drums & Geysers*, Vol. III. *Winter Exploration of the Snake River, 1876-77*. Chicago: Swallow Press.

————. 1985. *Field Book, The Teton and Gros Ventre Ranges*. Revised edition; Kelly, Wyoming: L.G. Bonney.

————. Oral history tapes.

Burt, Nathaniel. 1983. *Jackson Hole Journal*. Norman: University of Oklahoma Press.

Diem, Lenore L. 1989. *The Research Station's Place in History*. University of Wyoming-National Park Service.

Diem, Lenore L., Kenneth L. Diem, and W.C. Lawrence. 1986. *A Tale of Dough Gods, Bear Grease, Cantaloupe and Sucker Oil*. University of Wyoming-National Park Service.

Hayden, F. V. 1873. *Sixth Annual Report of the United States Geological Survey of the Territories Embracing Portions of Montana, Wyoming, Idaho, and Utah, 1872*. Washington, D.C.: GPO.

Love, J.D. and Jane. M. *Road Log, Jackson to Dinwoody and return*. Geol. Survey of Wyoming Public Information Circular 20.

Love, J.D. and Reed, John C., Jr. 1979. *Creation of a Teton Landscape*. Reprint. Moose, Wyoming: Grand Teton Natural History Association.

Love, J. David, leader. 1989. *Yellowstone and Grand Teton National Parks and the Middle Rocky Mountains.* American Geophysical Union.

Platts, Doris B. 1988. *The Pass.* Wilson, Wyoming: Published by the author.

———. 1989. *Wolftimes.* Wilson, Wyoming: Published by the author.

———. 1991. *John Cherry, His Lies, Life, and Legend.* Wilson, Wyoming: Published by the author.

Sanborn, Margaret. 1993. *The Grand Tetons: The Story of Taming the Western Wilderness.* Moose, Wyoming: Homestead Publishing.

Teton County Historical Society. *Tour of Historic Jackson.*

Thompson, Edith M. and William Leigh Thompson. 1982. *Beaver Dick: The Honor and the Heartbreak.* Laramie, Wyoming: Jelm Mountain Press.

Wister, Owen. 1902. *The Virginian.* New York: The Macmillan Company.

Periodicals

Downer, Gene, ed. *Teton Magazine.*

Jackson Hole Courier.

National Park Service: Grand Teton National Park. *Teewinot.*

Photographic Credits

Page 24
W.H. Jackson. The Three Tetons—the Grand, Middle and South Tetons.
Kent Fiske. Gneiss–taffy-like pegmatite, muscavite and quartz.
Wyoming Tourism. Boating on Jenny Lake.
Richard W. Emery. Climbing School with Glenn Exum.
Carl Schreier. Golden-mantled ground squirrel.

Page 47
Finis Mitchell. The Gros Ventre Range. Shoal Peak (center).
Teton County Historical Center. Al Austin, the "Cowboy Poet."
O.H. Bonney. The Old Swinging Bridge.
S. N. Leek. Photographing the Elk.
O.H. Bonney. First School.

Page 64
S.N. Leek. Placer Mining in Jackson Hole.
Montana Historical Society. N. P. Langford, first superintendent of Yellowstone National Park.
Western History Research Center. Victor-Jackson Passenger Stage, Teton Pass.

Page 71
Teton County Historical Center. The Snake River bridge during the 1925 Gros Ventre Flood.
Teton County Historical Center. Uncle Nick's Cabin on Fish Creek.
Teton County Historical Center. The winter hazards of Teton Pass.

Page 86
Teton County Historical Center. Early Holmes Cave explorers inside the Holland Chamber.
Courtesy Edith Thompson, her sister. Olga Mauger—What Happened to her?
Teton County Historical Center. John Cherry on his desert claim.

Page 96
Teton County Historical Center. Beaver Tooth Neil's Store.
Frank Wood. A Ned Frost party in the Teton Wilderness, below Yount's Peak.

Page 107
W.C. Lawrence. Slim Lawrence at Ed Sheffield's Snake River Station.
L.G. Bonney. Fire Ring campsites on the Pre-dam shoreline of Jackson Lake.
W.C. Lawrence. Tusker Cabin
Teton County Historical Center. Ed Harrington, alias Ed Trafton.
Teton County Historical Center. The building of Sheffield Lodge, of Moran.

Page 124
George Atteberry. 1951 Mt. Moran plane crash. The first visit after the winter rescue attempt.

Grand Teton Lodge Co. The lounge at Jackson Lake Lodge.
TCHC. Tusk hunter Charles Purdy, right, at a tusker headquarters at Loon Lake near Ashton, Idaho.
TCHC. The Freight Line. Roy Osborne drove the last freight outfit from Ashton to Moran.

Page 150
Courtesy Joe Pfeifer. Building Jackson Lake Dam, 1910.
Wm. H. Jackson, 1872. Courtesy Edith Thompson. Beaver Dick's First Family.
H.C. Crandall. Amphitheater Lake.
O.H. Bonney. St. John (I) and Rockchuck (J). R. Climbing Route.
H.C. Crandall. Crandall Studio at Jenny Lake, now the Jenny Lake Visitor Center/Museum.
Union Pacific Railroad. Tetons from Signal Mountain.

Page 157
L.G. Bonney. Theodore Teepe Memorial Stone.
O.H. Bonney. The Historic Belly Roll, Spaulding-Owen Route, Grand Teton.
Carl Schreier. Hidden Falls.
Teton County Historical Center. Camping at Lake Solitude.
O.H. Bonney. Schoolroom Glacier.
Finis Mitchell. Teton Range.

Page 184
Teton County Historical Center. Bar BC Ranch.
Allen Budge. On top of the Grand 1924.
Teton County Historical Center. Riding the old Skyline Trail.
Teton County Historical Center. Bill and Holiday Menor.
Western History Research Center. Menor's Old Ferry.
NPS, Yellowstone. Maude Noble's Store, 1923.

Page 189
Jackson Hole Film Commission. The "town" and "Cemetery Hill" locations in Shane.
TCHC. Wm. H. Jackson on Table Mountain, west of the Tetons.
F. Jay Haynes. President Chester A. Arthur in Camp Hampton, on the Snake.
Carl Schreier. Mt. Moran and the Oxbow of the Snake River.
Teton County Historical Center. The early Triangle X Dude Ranch.

Page 198
Roger LaVake. W.C. "Slim" Lawrence with his collection of elk tusks.
S.N. Leek. This was one of the photos used in the early campaign to save the elk herd.
S.N. Leek. Feeding the Elk. Miller Butte in background.

Page 211
Jackson Hole Chamber of Commerce. Jackson and the Tetons From Snow King Mountain
TCHC. Jumper John Curtis.
Floyd Bous Collection. Women Skiing at Moran, 1910.
TCHC. The young and vivacious Cissy Patterson.
TCHC. Cissy Patterson, the hunter.
TCHC. Young Cal Carrington, right, last of the Jackson Hole horsethieves.

Page 236
TCHC. Jim May homestead and Grovont Post Office, 1910.
O.H. Bonney. Joe Pfeifer, the last Days of the Homestead Era.
TCHC. The Flying V Ranch (Teton Science School) of Dollie and Jack Woodman, pre-1935.

Page 245
TCHC. The Kelly Bridge before the Flood.
TCHC. The Kents' old timey Kelly Store before the 1971 fire.
TCHC. Swirling waters encircle a building on what is now the Teton Valley Ranch.

Page 259
Robert Casebeer, U.S. Forest Service. The Gros Ventre Slide and the dam that blocked the river.
TCHC. The slide that blocked the Gros Ventre River, 1925.
TCHC. Guil Huff's House after the slide and before rising waters carried it away.

INDEX

Many items are listed in catchall general categories such as: battles, boating, bridges, cabins, campgrounds, faults, forts, glaciers, highways, Indians, junctions, museums, post offices, ranches, roads (back roads & jeep), schools, swimming, recreation areas, trails, waterfalls, wilderness areas.

A

Absaroka Range, 15, 82, 84, 87, 132
accidents; Cube Point, 144; Disappointment Pk, 162; first climbing, 155; Grand Teton, 155, 159-161; Ice Pt., 144; Middle Teton, 156; Mt. Moran, 134; Nez Perce, 155; Mt. Owen, 137; Storm Point, 143; Teewinot, 142
accommodations. See Chamber of Commerce, or campgrounds
airport, 79, 194, 206
Alaska Basin, 148
Albright, Horace, 130, 132, 141, 165, 170, 171, 212
Alkali Creek, 267
Allen, Boots, 215
Allen, Charles, 120, 191, 243
Almy, Frank & Mrs., 252
Alpine, 54, 55
American Legion Hall, 212
Amoretti chain, 119
Amoretti Lodge, 119, 120
Amphitheater Lake, 153, 162
Anderson, A.A., 41, 88
Anderson, Mary A., 44
Angle, Albert, 87
Angle Mtn., 85, 87
antelope, 22, 37, 49, 176, 177, 210, 240, 241
Antelope Flats, 176, 178, 240; Road, 240

Antelope Pass, 44, 74
Appalachian Mtn Club, 159
archeology, 105
Arizona Creek, 104, 106, 122
Arizona George, 102
Arizona Island, 105, 108
Arizona Lake, 109
arrowheads. See Indians
artifacts, 39, 42, 63, 103, 105, 108, 167, 180
arts, 206, 208, 224, 247
Arthur, Pres. Chester, 101, 122, 183, 186, 256, 262
campsites in JH, 79, 122, 183, 262, 263, 268
Ashton, ID, 103, 121, 125
Aspens, 226
Astor, John Jacob, 18
Astoria Hot Springs, 58, 59
Astorians, 18, 32, 39, 53, 55, 61, 115
Atherton Creek, 257, 262
Atlantic Creek, 94
Austin, Al, 38, 39, 41, 122
avalanches, 37, 139, 204; Bull of the Woods, 37; Mt. Glory, 44, 69
Avalanche Canyon, 147, 166

B

Bacon Ridge, 233, 268
Bailey Creek, 57
Baillie-Grohman, Wm. A., 80
Balcolm, Rev. R., 227

Baldy Mtn. L.O., 89
Bannon Survey, 167
Bannon, Thomas M., 167
Barber bros., 78
Barber, Cora, 78, 203
Barrett, Rep., 173
bars, 205; Bailey, 58, 59; Cowboy, 207, 208; Dornans, 175; JR, 208; Pine, 59; Silver Dollar, 207; Stagecoach, 70, 206, 219
Battle Mtn., 35, 36, 217
battles: 1895 Indian scare. See Indians; Pierre's Hole, 40, 62, 63
Baxter Pinnacle,
bear, 22, 133, 264; grizzly, 82, 85, 92, 94, 102, 103, 125, 265
beaver, 145, 165, 166, 180
Beaver Creek, 166
Beery, Wallace, 130
bentonite, 85
Berolzheimer, Alfred, 112
Berry Creek, 104, 105, 123
Beulah Lake, 101, 103
Bierer, Billy, 260
bighorn sheep. See sheep
biking, mtn., 23, 70, 89, 133, 140, 149, 164, 228, 229, 263
Binkley, Bill, 200, 250
Biological Research Center. See Research Center
Bircher Roadhouse, 66
birding, 26, 42, 50, 59, 74, 75, 120, 125, 203, 222, 226, 249
birds: herons, 190; pelicans, 42; prairie falcons, 41; trumpeter swans, 120, 125, 180, 203
Bitch Creek, 125
Bivouac Pk, 116, 134
Black Canyon, 68, 219
Black Rock Creek, 88
Black Rock Ranger Sta., 88
Blacktail Butte, 169, 176, 193, 240, 243, 244, 253, 254
Blacktail Ponds, 177
boating, 20, 135, 174, 217, 256; Colter Bay, 20, 113; Jackson Lake, 20, 109; Jenny Lake, 20, 146, 151, 152; Leigh Lake, 137; Lower Slide Lake, 262; Snake River, 54, 56, 119, 174, 187; String Lake, 20, 137
boats: bull skin, 51; canoe, 20; fold, 54; kayak, 20, 56; rafts, 119; sail, 113
Bondurant, 34
Bonneville, Capt. B.L.E., 40, 62
Bonneville Pass, 82
Bonney, O.H., 54, 70, 153

Bonney, Roger, 54
Botcher Hill, 196
Boyles Ditch, 194
Boyles Hill, 45, 50, 51, 73, 74
Bradley, F.H., 100, 166, 193
Bradley Lake, 166
Breccia Pk, 84, 85, 87
Bridger, James, 33, 35, 51, 62, 80, 187
Bridger Lake, 94, 187
Bridger-Teton National Forest. See national forests
bridges:; Cattleman's, 131, 191; CCC, 59; Flat Creek, 203; Gros Ventre, 263; Kelly, 252, 253; Snake River, 41, 51, 60, 73, 102, 128, 174; swinging, 41; Teton Pass, 70
Briggs, Bill, 153, 215, 216
Brooks, Gov. Bryant, 82
Brooks Lake, 81
Brooks Lake Falls, 83
Brooks Lake Lodge, 82
Brooks Lake Recreational Area. See recreational areas
Bryan Flat, 38
Bryan Flat Guard Station, 38
Buck, Geo. A., 167
Buck Mtn., 155, 167, 194
Buck Mtn. Pass, 148
Bucket Springs, 69
Budge, Allen & family, 167, 241, 244, buffalo, 191
Buffalo Fork, 87, 92, 94, 97, 99, 130, 185, 186
Buffalo Ice Age, 103, 109, 133, 203
Burned Ridge, 135, 164, 179, 180
Burro Hill, 97
Burt, Struthers, 164, 170, 187,
Burt, Katherine, 164

C

cabins: Arizona Creek, 106; Arizona Island, 108; Brinkerhoff, 130; Cherry, 196; Cunningham, 181, 234; elk tusker, 103, 108; Maude Noble, 167, 169, 171, 173; outlaw, 229; Wilson (Nick), 72; Wister (Owen) 223
Cache Creek, 15, 69, 203, 215, 217, 229, 235
Cache Creek Road, 25, 228
Campbell, Robert, 63
Camp Creek, 38, 42
campgrounds: Atherton Creek, 262; Box Creek, 95; Brooks Falls, 83; Brooks Lake, 82; Buffalo Fork, 95; Climbers, 152, 163; Colter Bay, 113, 116; Curtis Canyon, 234; East Table

Creek, 57; Elbow, 57; Flagg Ranch, 102; Four Mile Mdw Picnic, 88, 95; Granite Creek, 218; Grassy Lake Road, 122, 123; Gros Ventre, 254; Hatchet, 85, 89; Hoback, 38; Jenny Lake, 140, 151; Kozy, 36; Lizard Pt, 104; Mike Harris, 66; Moose Creek, 65; Pacific Creek, 188; Red Hills, 264; Sheffield Creek, 102; Signal Mtn, 131; Snake River Picnic, 103; Teton Canyon, 65, 158; Trail Creek, 66; Wind River Lake Picnic, 83
campsites, mtn., 153, 265
Canton, Frank, 231, 232
Carey, Sen. R.D., 172, 244
Carncross, Dr. H., 164, 170
Carnes, John, 43, 181, 231, 233, 234, 256
Carrington, Cal, 67, 210, 233, 237, 238
Cascade Canyon, 137, 140, 141, 143, 185
Cascade Creek, 122, 125
Cathedral Peaks, 136, 143
cattle, 258
CCC. See Civilian Conservation Corps
cemeteries: Allen, 120, 191; Aspen Hill, 77, 209; Elliott, 70; South Park (first), 46
chair lifts, 216, 224, 226
Chamber of Commerce, 31, 206, 208
Chambers, Andy, 241, 242
Chambers, Jim, 232
Chambers, Ida Belle Kneedy, 242
Chambers, Roy, 247, 257
Chapel of Sacred Heart, 130
Chapel of Transfiguration, 162, 167-8
Charter, Bert, 75
Charter, Boyd, 260
Cheney, Selar, 42, 45, 46
Cherry, John, 43, 49, 75, 76, 90, 142, 196, 209
Chouinard, Yvon, 143, 153
Christian Creek, 119, 120, 127
churches, 130, 214
Civilian Conservation Corps (CCC), 53, 59, 129, 152, 215
Clause Pk, 33
clearcutting, 82, 83, 85, 90, 234, 247
climbers' camp (old), 152
Climbers Ranch, 28
climbing, mtn.. See peaks by name
climbing schools. See schools
clothing, 29
Cloudveil Dome, 126
Clubhouse, 210, 212
Clyde, Norman, 134

coal & mines, 92, 217, 267, 268
Cole, Farney, 260
Colter Bay, 113, 127, 173
Colter, John, 18
Conant Creek, 117
Connor, Melissa, 105
Continental Divide, 82, 84, 94, 188, 256, 268
Cottonwood Creek, 165
Countess, The. See Eleanor Patterson
Count, John, 59
Crabtree Hotel, 212
Crabtree, Rose, 212, 238
Craighead bros., 177, 241
Crandall, H.H., 92, 151, 240
Crandall, Hilda, 92, 240
Crandall Studio, 151, 241
Crater Lake, 69
Crowe, Frank, 121
Crystal Creek, 264, 265, 266
Cube Point, 144
Cunningham Cabin. See cabins
Cunningham, J.P., 36, 181
Curtis bros., 232
Curtis Canyon, 232

D

Davis, Camp, 38
Davis, Eleanor, 156, 158, 162
Davis, Prof. J.B., 38
Davis, Uncle Jack, 58, 188
Deadman Pk, 33
Deadman's Bar, 164, 179, 180
Death Canyon, 17, 148, 167, 194
deer, 22; mule, 192; white-tail, 248
DeLacy, Capt. W.W., 39, 53, 75, 187
Deloney, Chas. (Pap), 44, 210
desert claims, 91, 229, 246
DeSmet, Father, 51, 62
Devils Elbow Slide, 257, 262
Deyo, Fred, 98
Dibble, Charlie, 250, 257, 261, 263, 267
Dike, Black, 133, 135, 158, 163
Dike Pinnacle, 158, 163
Dime Creek, 103, 122, 123
dinosaurs, 14, 88, 94, 103, 266
Disappointment Pk, 27, 153, 154, 162
Disney films, 54, 165
Ditch Creek, 176, 243, 247, 248
Doane, Lt. G.C., 19, 54, 55, 56, 59, 100, 103, 115, 116, 155, 174, 178, 183, 219
Doane Peak, 115
Dodge, John L., 224
Dornan, Jack, 168
Dornans, 175

Dry Hollow, 149
Dubois, 81
Dunn, Wm., 122

E

Eagles Rest Pk, 112, 115
Early People, 17, 51, 59, 80, 105, 230, 232, 246, 255
earthquakes, 74, 129, 142, 195, 255, 260
East Gros Ventre Butte, 68, 74, 75, 76, 194, 202
elk, 22, 26, 30, 43, 94, 103, 162, 170, 177, 197, 228, 240, 249, 254; feeding, 30, 42, 59, 201, 221, 244; migration, 90, 91, 197, 201; sleigh rides, 202; tuskers. See hunters
Elk Refuge. See National Elk Refuge
Elks (BPOE), 200, 201
Ellingwood, Albert, 156, 158
emergencies, Dial 911; Highway Patrol, 733-3126; Ambulance, 733-3636; First Aid: contact nearest ranger station
Emerson, Gov., 244, 250
Emma Matilda Lake, 118, 119, 129, 132, 188
equipment, mtn. climbing, 27
Erpenback, Chas., 117
expeditions: Doane winter. See Doane; Hayden Survey. See Hayden; Jones, Capt. W.A., 81; Raynolds, 51, 62, 80; Washburn (1870), 115
Exum, Glenn, 154, 158
Exum Mountaineering School. See schools
Exum Route, 154, 158
Eynon, J.L., 170

F

Fabian, Harold, 163, 169, 244
Fabian, Josephine, 163
Fall Creek Road, 58, 70, 219-221
Fall Creek Falls, 60
faults, 74, 78, 167, 193, 244, 263; Blacktail Butte, 254; Botcher Hill, 197; Cache Creek, 74, 203, 218; Hoback, 41, 42; Jackson, 74; Spread Creek, 129, 182; Teton. See Teton Fault; Warm Spring, 195, 196
fees, 25
ferries: Conrad, 188, 190; Menors, 58, 72, 73, 128, 130, 167, 168-9; Snake River, 73, 168
Ferrin, Josiah D. (Si), 185, 212, 232
Ferris, W.A., 38, 40, 62, 114

Ferry Pk, 56
Fesler, Chas., 127, 240
fires, 102, 105, 131, 132, 166, 246, 247
firsts: auto, 62, 122; bank, 230; binder, 43; brick kiln, 44; cemetery, 46; child, 49; church, 46; climbing guide, 134; dude ranch, 43; movie location, 127; gas launch, 127; moving picture, 43; post office, 45, 195; sawmill, 43, 46; settler, 229; school, 46, 48; teacher, 46, 48; townsite, 210; trial, 233; wagon, 233; white men, 18; woman mayor, 214, 229
fish, 21, 197; cutthroat, 21, 114, 142, 203; mackinaw, 21, 114, 115, 142
Fish Creek, 70, 219, 268
Fish Hatchery. See National Fish Hatchery
fishing, 211, 34, 37, 40, 54, 78, 108, 114, 123, 127, 142, 148, 153, 165, 166, 174, 185, 187, 195, 204, 234, 235, 254, 257, 262, 265, 267
Flagg Ranch. See ranches
Flat Creek, 21, 41, 42, 43, 44, 45, 196, 201, 203, 204, 208, 230, 235
Flat Creek Road, 227
Fonda, John, 104
fords, 37, 102, 128, 263, 266; Snake River, 45, 48, 50, 219
Forellen Pk, 123
forts: Fort Ellis, 100, 115, 185; Fort Hall, 53, 56, 65, 121, 138; Fort Washakie, 80, 81, 185, 256; Fort Yellowstone, 200
fossils, 88, 118, 254
Fox Creek, 63, 148
Foy (trapper), 40
Fryxell, F.M., 135, 137, 142, 143, 144, 145, 152, 155, 168

G

gambling, 205
Game Creek, 38, 40, 42, 229
Gannett Pk, 158
Garnet Canyon, 156, 160
gas seep, 92
geology, 13, 34, 57, 68, 92, 130, 141, 152, 182, 194, 195, 202, 255, 257, 265. Also see faults, fossils, glaciers, Ice Age, landslides
Germans, 179
Giltner, Mose, 181, 203
Gizycka, Countess. See Eleanor Patterson
Gizycka, Felicia, 67, 164, 237
Glacier Gulch, 153, 154, 155, 165

Glacier Gulch Turnout, 155, 159, 162, 177

glaciers, 16, 140, 142, 146, 149; Falling Ice, 133, 135; Middle Teton, 158; Schoolroom, 148, ; Skillet, 133, 134; Teepe's, 155, 159, 160; Teton, 153, 159, 165; Triple, 106

Glade Creek, 123

Glory, Mt., 44, 67

gneisses, 17, 146

Godin, Antoine, ;63

Goe, Ben, 59, 208

Goe, Jim, 208

gold, 19, 57, 59, 92, 118, 179, 188, 248, 265, 266

golf, 78, 226

Goodwin Lake, 218, 234, 239

Goosewing Ranger Sta., 268

Goss, C.A., 165

Grand Teton, 17, 27, 43, 65, 105, 112, 136, 141, 155, 158, 162, 174, 185

Grand Teton (newspaper), 50

Grand Teton City, 77

Grand Teton Lodge Co., 31, 173

Grand Teton National Park, 30, 50, 66, 73, 93, 101, 103, 166, 170, 171, 173, 196, 213, 253, 257; National Park Service H.Q., 28, 31, 167, 174

Grand Teton View Point, 118

granite, 17

Granite Canyon, 218

Granite Creek, 37, 217

Granite Creek Canyon, 218

Granite Creek Recreation Area, 217

Granite Creek Road, 217

Granite Falls, 218

Granite Hot Springs. *See* hot springs

Grassy Lake Road, 25, 102, 121-125

Grassy Lake Reservoir, 123

Graul, Johnny, 105

Gravel Mtn, 188

Gray, John, 55

Green River, 33, 176, 255, 256, 268

Greys River, 55

Grisamer, Fannie, 41

grizzly. *See* bear

Grizzly Lake, 263

Gros Ventre, name, 104

Gros Ventre Butte. *See* East & West Gros Ventre Buttes

Gros Ventre flood. *See* Kelly flood

Gros Ventre Indians. *See* Indians

Gros Ventre Range, 15, 17, 34, 37, 197, 204, 217, 229, 233, 268

Gros Ventre River, 72, 76, 78, 194, 195, 243, 255, 257, 265, 268

Gros Ventre Road, 255

Gros Ventre Slide, 129, 178, 250, 255, 258; Gros Ventre Geological Area, 258

Gros Ventre Wilderness. *See* wilderness

Grovont, 243, 252

guides: fishing, 22, 87, 113; hunting, 22, 87, 134; mountain, 27, 134; pack, 25, 87

Gunsight Pass, 267, 268

H

Hamilton, R.R., 110, 132

handicapped, 131

Hansen, P. C., 76

Hansen, Cliff, 76, 263

Hansen, Sylvia Wood, 76

Hardeman Mdws, 73

Harris, Mike,

Harris, Captain, 187, 188

Harrison, Pres., 88

Hayden, F.V., 12, 18, 55, 62, 133

Hayden, Mt.. *See* Grand Teton

Hayden Surveys, 18, 40, 54, 65, 92, 99, 100, 103, 115, 120, 121, 132, 138, 143, 144, 146, 158, 166, 185, 188, 190, 193, 223, 248

Hedrick, Chas., 66, 81, 90, 210

Hedrick Lake, 180

Hedrick Point, 180

helicopters, 144

Henderson, Ken, 159

Henry, Andrew, 32

Hermann, John, 54

Hidden Falls, 146

highways: ID 31, 33; ID 33, 63; US 26-89, 53, 54; US 187-191, 33; US 187-26-191, 40, 41, 42, 192; US 287, 25, 81, 84, 94, 101; WY 22, 51, 66, 67, 75, 226; Yellowstone, 25, 100

hiking, 20, 42. *Also see* Trails

Hoback Basin, 33, 36, 37

Hoback Canyon, 32, 35, 37

Hoback Entrance, 32

Hoback, John, 32, 33

Hoback Range, 36, 37, 42; Hoback Peak, 33, 34

Hoback Rim, 12, 33

Hoback River, 33, 37, 39, 217

Hoback Shield, 37

Hodges Pk,

Hoffer, Ivan, 54, 59

Holcomb Terrace,

Holland, John, 43, 85, 181, 231, 233, 234, 238, 256

Holly Lake, 139
Holmes Cave, 85
homesteading, 48, 91, 154, 241
Horse Creek, 38, 40, 41
horses, 22, 25, 119
Horsetail Creek & Ranger Sta., 250, 261, 263
horse thieves, 19, 94, 116, 121, 231, 237, 238
Horsethief Canyon, 42
Hosford, W.F., 231
Hosman, Slim,
Hospital, St. John's, 219, 227
hot springs, 106; Astoria, 59; Granite, 37, 218; Polecat, 122; Snake River, 101
Housetop Mtn, 193
Hoyt, Gov. J.W., 81
Huckleberry Mtn 102,
Huckleberry Mtn L.O., 102, 106
Huckleberry Ridge Tuff, 103, 131, 191, 257
Hudson's Bay Co., 12, 63
Huidekoper, Jim, 54, 215
Huidekoper, Virginia, 215
Huff, Dr. C.W., 98, 227
Huff, Guil, 260
Hunt, Mt., 194, 226
Hunt, Wilson Price, 18, 32, 39, 43, 61, 194
hunters; tusk, 103, 106, 121, 123, 200. *Also see* Indians, mountain men, rendezvous, trails, trappers
hunting, 30, 102, 188, 199, 240, 253
hunting seasons, 30
Hurricane Pass, 148

I

Ice Age signs, 16, 69, 105, 109, 113, 128, 132, 149, 179, 180, 197, 202, 203, 217, 219, 221, 254, 256, 266
Ice Cream Cone Pk, 156
Ice Point, 144
Idaho Falls, 54, 63
Imeson, James, 39, 46, 72
Imeson, Paul A., 163
Imeson, Susannah, 46
Indian: arrowheads & chippings, 51, 63, 80, 105, 262; camp sites, 105, 108, 123, 193, 219, 220, 24, 255, 266, 268; hunting, 35, 105, 182; Scare of 1895, 35, 50, 81, 182, 235
Indian tribes, 49: Bannock, 35; Blackfoot, 41; Crow, 55; Flathead, 63, 65; Gros Ventre, 40, 41, 62, 63, 194; Nez Perce, 65, 155; Piegan, 63;

Sheepeaters, 81, 196; Shoshone, 35, 196; Snake, 53
Inspiration Point, 146
Irving, Washington, 65
Isabel, Chas., 200
Izaac Walton League, 201

J

Jackass Pass, 123
Jackson, 203, 205-216
Jackson, David E., 18, 33, 84, 115
Jackson Peak, 194, 218, 234, 235, 249
Jackson Town Square, 207, 209, 210, 213
Jackson State Bank, 230
Jackson, Swede,
Jackson, Teton, 229, 231, 232
Jackson, Wm. H., 19, 132, 185
Jackson Hole, 11, 18, 230
Jackson Hole Chamber of Commerce, 31, 206, 208
Jackson Hole Courier, 49, 212, 235
Jackson Hole Historical Center, 207
Jackson Hole Mountain Guides & Climbing School. *See* schools
Jackson Hole Museum. *See* museums
Jackson Hole National Monument, 173
Jackson Hole Plan, 170, 212
Jackson Hole Ski Area, 73, 196, 216, 224
Jackson Hole Ski Club, 215
Jackson Lake, 105, 113, 120, 128, 130, 132
Jackson Lake Dam, 92, 102, 121, 127, 168, 188, 190
Jackson Lake Lodge, 119, 173
Jackson's Hole, 19; naming, 18
Jackson's Little Hole, 33
jeep roads. *See* roads
Jeffers, LeRoy, 134
Jenny Leigh. *See* Leigh
Jenny Lake, 129, 140, 141, 154
Jenny Lake boat dock, 152
Jenny Lake Lodge, 140
Jenny Lake Ranger Sta., 28, 151
Jenny Lake Road, 25, 140, 151
Jenny Lake Trails. *See* trails
Jenny Lake Visitor Center & Museum, 151
Jones, Capt. W.A., 81
Jones, Joe, 170
Judge, Frances, 91
Jump, Ethel Carlson, 251
junctions: Alpine, 55; Daniel, 33; Gros Ventre, 79, 195, 249, 254; Hoback, 39, 60; Jackson Lake, 120, 126; Moose, 175, 176, 192; Moran, 81, 93,

185, 186; The "Y", 44, 74

K

kayaking, 20, 37, 56, 217, 256, 258, 267
Kelly, 227, 253
Kelly Flood, 227, 243, 249, 250-252
Kelly Kill Line, 253
Kelly, W.J., 250, 252
Kelly Warm Springs, 256
Kent, Anna, 250, 252
Kent, Donald, 251, 253
Kent, Gladys May, 244, 247, 253
Kent, Raymond, 251, 252
Kieffer, Capt. Chas. H., 158
Kisinger Lakes, 82
Kneedy family, 243, 250, 252
Koven, Theodore & Gustav, 135, 249

L

Lander, 81
landslides, 41, 57, 60, 74, 85, 88, 106, 127, 197, 255, 260, 263, 265, 267
Langford, N.P., 12, 65, 158
Laramide Revolution, 14
Latterday Saints (LDS). See Mormons
Laubins, 241
Lava Creek, 92
Lava Mtn., 83, 268
Lavender Slide, 263, 265
Lawrence, W.C., 83, 105, 106, 112, 113, 116, 123
Leek Canyon, 43
Leek, Lester, 95
Leek Marina, 109
Leek, Stephen (S.N.), 43, 69, 109, 181, 188, 196, 220
Leidy Highlands, 90, 92, 118, 182, 263, 265
Leidy, Mt., 89, 90, 92, 118, 265
Leidy, Prof. J., 92
Leigh Canyon, 139
Leigh, Jenny, 138, 141
Leigh Lake, 129, 154
Leigh, Richard, (Beaver Dick), 65, 137, 141, 188, 219
Leigh, Sue Tadpole, 138
Leonard, Zenas, 62
Lewis & Clark, 17
license, fishing, 22, 30
hunting, 22, 30, 35
Lily Lake, 89
Little Horse Creek, 40
Little Granite Creek, 217
Lizard Creek, 104, 108
Long Hollow Road, 227, 253
Love, J. David, 51, 87, 88, 127, 182

Love, Charlie, 106, 266
Lovell, Frank, 127, 128
Lower Slide Lake, 251, 262, 263
Lozier Hill, 188
Lucas, Geraldine, 162
Lucas, Lee, 75
Lucas, Lt. Russell, 163
Lucas, Mary Jane Wilson, 48
Lunch Counter, 56
Lupine Meadows, 152, 153

M

Mad River. See Snake River
Major, Ted, 215
Manning, Wm., 36
Marion Lake, 148, 194, 226
Markham, Joe, 122
Marymere. See Sargent
Mauger, Olga Schultz, 87
May, Henrie, 243
May, James, 241, 243, 244, 252
May, Joe & Chloe, 178, 244, 250
May, Lester, 215
McBride, Roy, 235, 243, 266
McCain, A.C., 195
McCoy Creek, 55, 56
Meek, Joe, 35, 114, 115
Meldrum, Judge, 200
Menor, H.H., 168-9, 200
Menor, W.D., 168-9
Menor's Ferry. See ferries
Middle Teton, 12, 155, 156, 163
Miller Butte, 203, 227, 230, 232
Miller, Gov. L., 172
Miller, Grace, 210, 214, 229
Miller Home, 227, 228, 229
Miller, Robert E., 36, 62, 171, 181, 229, 234, 238
mining, 105, 123, 187
Mitchell, J.K., 138
Moccasin Creek area, 83
Molar Tooth, 159
monuments: Colter, John, 213; First Protestant Sermon, 34; Mormon, 44; Trapper, 109; Turpin, Dick, 95
Moody, E.N., 239
moose, 22, 126, 145, 164, 166, 177, 223, 225
Moose Village, 167, 222
Moose Creek. See trails
Moose-Wilson Road, 73, 173
Moran, 93
Moran Canyon, 116
Moran, Mt, 27, 106, 132, 133, 139; View Point, 133
Moran (old town), 103, 120, 127, 191

Moran, Thomas, 131, 133
More (trapper), 40
Mormons, 19, 44, 45, 62, 70, 214, 241
Mormon Row, 241, 254
Morse, E.B., 39
Moser, Mrs. Henry, 90
Mosquito Creek, 40, 48, 73, 220
Mosquito Creek Pass, 42, 48, 66, 219, 220
Moulton, Charles, 242
Moulton, Clark, 242
Moulton, John & Bartha, 241
Moulton, T. Alma, 241, 242
mountain climbing. *See* climbing, equipment, peaks by name
mountains. *See* peaks by name
movie locations, 60, 83, 127, 133, 178, 180, 191, 192, 218, 240, 241, 242, 247, 250, 254, 256
mudflows. *See* landslides
Munger Mtn., 40, 221
Murie, Adolph & Louise, 222
Murie, Marty, 222
Murie, Olaus, 222
museums: Colter Bay, 113; Jackson Hole, 34, 39, 41, 103, 112, 122, 187, 205, 207; Jenny Lake, 151, 241; National Wildlife Art, 201

N
National Elk Refuge, 21, 30, 173, 195, 197, 201, 227, 228, 244, 253
National Fish Hatchery, 30, 197
national forests: Bridger-Teton, 23, 30, 31, 33, 84, 85, 101, 102, 229, 241, 247, 257, 265; Shoshone, 82, 84; Targhee, 65, 123
National Park Service, 30, 101, 105, 109, 120, 130, 166, 172, 222, 244, 253, 263
Neil, Chas. (Beaver Tooth), 97
Neil, Mrs., 98
Neilson, Wilford W. and Adeline, 49
Nelson, Cora. *See* Barber
Nelson, Martin (Sloughgrass), 36, 201
Nez Perce Pk, 155
Noble Cabin. *See* cabins
Noble, Maude, 168, 169
North Park, 208
Nowlin Creek, 232
Nowlin, D.C., 111, 199, 232

O
Ogden, Peter Skene, 12
oil drilling sites, 57, 90, 268
O'Mahoney, Sen., 173

O'Neil, Breck, 60, 218
Open Door Pk, 218
Otter Body Snowfield, 159, 160
outfitters, 22, 25, 94
outlaws, 123, 127, 230, 231
overthrust ranges, 36, 42, 55, 57, 68, 203
Owen, Emma Matilda, 132
Owen, Mt, 27, 136, 141
Owen Route (Grand Teton). *See* Spalding-Owen Route
Owen, Wm. O., 132, 136, 158, 167, 188, 203, 248, 250
Owl Creek, 104, 105
Owl Creek Range, 87
Oxbow Bend, 186, 190, 191

P
Pacific Creek, 94, 187
Pacific Fur Co., 18, 55
pack trips. *See* outfitters, trails
Paintbrush Divide, 140, 147
Paleolithic Man, 17, 34. *Also see* Early People, Indians
Palisades Rsvr., 53, 54
Palmer, Dr., 211
Park Loop, 126-192
Parker, Rev. Samuel, 35, 38, 62
Patterson, Eleanor "Cissy" (Countess Gizycka), 67, 164, 237
peaks. *See* by name
permits, 20, 22, 25, 27, 28, 89, 174
Perry, Walter, 50
Petersen, Frank, 90, 181
Petersen, Charlie, 238
Petzoldt, Paul, 135, 137, 159, 162, 249
Pfeifer, Joe, 243, 244, 246
Phelps Lake, 148, 223, 226
Phillips Canyon Rd, 70
Phillips Pass, 66, 70, 148
photography, 20, 141
Pierce, John, 219
Pierre's Hole, 33, 40, 55, 61, 63, 115, 194
Pilgrim Creek, 118, 120
Pilgrim Peak, 118
Pilot Knobs, 12
Pinedale, 176
Pinedale Ice Age, 17, 34, 133, 135, 140
Pinnacle Butte, 82, 83, 87
Pitchstone Plateau, 101, 104
Platt, Doris, 182
Polecat Creek, 122
Porter, Bruce, 59
post offices: Antler, 109; Cheney, 42, 45; Colter Bay, 113; Elk, 93; first, 45;

Grovont, 240, 243; Jackson, 196, 209; Jenny Lake, 154; Kelly, 250, 252; Moose, 174, 220; Marysvale, 196; Old Moran, 127; Teton Village, 224; Wilson, 73

potholes, 133, 180, 266

Powder Peak, 42

practice rocks, 37, 59, 145, 176, 234

Pritchard Pass, 221

Prospector Mtn, 194

prospectors, 19, 39, 53, 190, 248

Purdy, Chas., 125, 200

R

Race Horse, Chief, 36

Rafferty, Neil, 213, 214

Ramshorn Pk, 34, 87

ranches: AMK/Berol, 110, 112, 113, 126; Bar BC, 133, 164, 171, 187, 237; Barber, 78; Buffalo River, 97; Climbers, 28, 163, 167; Crescent H, 219; Danny, 140; Darwin, 268; Diamond G, 83; Edwards, 104, 108, 122; Elbo, 165, 249; Elk Ranch, 185; Ferry, 170; Flagg, 102, 122; Flat Creek, 237, 238; Flying V, 257; Granite Creek, 218; Hatchet, 90, 91; Heart Six, 97; Hunter Hereford, 247; JY, 167, 171, 223, 224; Lakeview, 108; Lost Creek, 178; Lucas, 76, 77, 162; Marymere, 110-112, 132; Melody, 45; Moosehead, 182; Murie (STS), 222, 223; R Lazy S, 223; Red Rock, 265; Spur, 175; Square G, 137; Teton Valley, 200, 250; Three Rivers, 187; Trail Creek, 70; Triangle X, 180, 248; Turpin Meadows, 95; Warm Springs, 76, 197; Waterman, 78; White Grass, 223, 237; Woodward, 251, 257

Randolph Pk, 97

Ranger Pk, 115

Raynolds, Capt. W.F., 51, 62, 80

Reclamation Service. See U.S.

recreation areas: Brooks Lake, 81; Granite Creek, 218; Hatchet Campground, 89; String Lake, 137

Red Hills anticline, 263

Red Ledges, 37

Redmond, Bill, 75

Red Mud Hole, 67

Red Slide (near Redmond Creek), 263

Red Top Meadows, 221

Reed Hotel. See Crabtree Hotel

rendezvous, 33, 61, 63

Rendezvous Pk, 66, 196, 216, 224

rental: boats, 20, 113; boots, 29. Also see equipment

rescues, 143, 159-162

Research Center, 109, 126, 190, 191, 192

Resor, Stanley, 224

Reznor, Jacob, 32

Riniker, George, 243, 244

rifle pits, 50

roads (back country & jeep), 178; Ashton-Moran Freight Line, 103, 108, 111, 121, 122, 125, 128; Boyles Hill, 50, 52; Brooks Lake, 81; Cache Creek, 25, 218; Cliff Creek, 35; Curtis Canyon, 234; Dell Creek, 34; Dry Cottonwood Creek, 267, 268; Fall Creek, 70, 219; Fish Creek, 72; Flagstaff, 85, 89; Flat Creek, 227; Granite Creek, 217; Greys River, 54; Henry, 41; Jackass, 125; Mosquito Creek, 220; Old Marysville, 103, 121, 123, 125; Old Military, 81, 101, 102, 105, 108, 109, 111, 113, 183, 186; Old Swamp, 119, 120; Old Teton Pass. See Trails.; Old U.S. 287, 81, 82; Pacific Creek, 187, 188; Phillips Canyon, 70; Pilgrim Creek, 118; RKO, 25, 133, 164; Signal Mtn., 25; Slate Creek, 266; South Park Loop, 42, 45; Spread Creek, 89; Upper Hoback, 34

Robbins, Royal, 153

Robinson, Butch, 214, 265

Robinson, Edward, 32

Rockchuck Pk, 27, 145

Rockefeller, J.D., Jr., 50, 101, 119, 120, 163, 165, 171, 172, 173, 213, 224, 230, 244

Rockefeller, Laurence, 169

Rockefeller Memorial Parkway, 101, 122, 125

Rock Springs, 32, 33

Rocky Mtn. Fur Co., 84

rodeo, 208

Rodeo Wall, 59

Roosevelt, Franklin D., 173

Roosevelt, Theodore, 77, 138, 188, 241

Rosencrans, Rudolph, 59, 88, 97

Roseys Ridge, 88, 95, 97

Ross, Alexander, 12

Russell, Osborne, 38, 53, 121, 129, 142, 187, 220, 255;

S

St. John, Mt, 144

Salt River, 54, 55

Salt River Range, 36, 54, 55

Sargent, John D., 109, 132, 209, 225
Sargent Bay, 109
Sawmill Ponds, 223
schists, 17
schools: climbing, 27, 28, 151, 154; first, 48, 212; Great American Ski, 216; Grovont, 243; Teton Science, 248; Zenith, 78
Schwabacher Landing, 178
Scott, Wild Bill, 134
Seebohm, Wm., 199
Shadow Mtn., 178, 247
Shane movie, 178
sheep, 41, 62, 70, 74, 89, 125, 220, 244
sheep, mountain, 22, 53, 194, 197, 218, 233, 263
Sheep Mtn, 178, 194, 197, 232, 235, 258, 260
Sheep Gulch Takeout, 56
Sheffield, Ben, 102, 120, 127, 130, 133, 134
Sheffield, Ed, 102
Sheridan, General, 183
Shoshone National Forest. See national forests
Shive, John, 90, 91, 115
Signal Mtn., 127, 128, 131, 132, 183, 191
Signal Mtn. Lodge, 126, 131
Signal Mtn. Road, 126, 131
Simpson, John, 208
Simpson, Maggie, 196, 208
Simpson, Wm., 50
skiing, 67, 213, 224
Ski Lake, 70
Skull Creek Mdws, 90
Sleeping Indian. See Sheep Mtn.
Slide Mtn., 267
Smith, Jedediah, 18, 84, 115
Smith, Phil, 137, 142, 144, 155, 163, 256
Snake River, 19, 20, 33, 39, 40, 70, 94, 100, 115, 128, 149, 168, 178, 219; access, 57, 59, 127, 174, 178, 180, 187, 226; float trip, 20, 57, 119; fords, 45, 48, 50, 73, 101, 103, 104, 105, 129, 186, 196, 220; levees, 41, 50, 52, 73; Narrows, 56; rapids, 56; Upper, 18, 101
Snake River Canyon, 42, 53, 54, 55, 57
Snake River Entrance, 53
Snake River Institute, 72
Snake River Land Co., 127, 163, 169, 171, 180, 185, 213, 244
Snake River Military Station, 123
Snake River Overlook, 178, 179

Snake River Range, 36, 42, 56, 57, 66, 67, 68, 219, 220
Snake River Station, 102
Snow King Mtn., 194, 203, 207, 229
snowmobiling, 25, 122, 126, 131, 133
Soldier Mdws, 103, 122
Solitude, Lake, 140
Sorelle, Millie, 43, 234
South Buffalo Fork. See Trails
South Park, 40, 42, 45
South Teton, 12,
Spalding Bay, 135
Spalding, Bishop F., 158
Spalding-Owen Route, 158
Spalding Peak, 156
speed limits, 136
Spread Creek, 90, 182
Spring Creek Resort, 75
Spring Gulch Road, 74, 75
springs, 38, 69, 76, 101, 230, 246, 254, 256
Squaw Creek, 41
Squirrel Mdws., 122, 125
Static Peak, 148
Steck, Al, 153
Stegner, W., 128
Stephens, Capt. A.K., 40
Stevenson, James, 54, 65, 158
Stewart, Henry, 167, 224
Stewart Ranger Sta., 166
Storm Point, 27, 143
String Lake, 136, 137, 188, 241
Stuart, Robert, 38, 42, 55, 61
Sublette brothers, 55
Sublette Pk, 83, 84
Sublette, Wm., 18, 33, 61, 63, 83, 115
Sunset Lake, 148
Surprise Lake, 153
Surprise Pinnacle, 153
Survey Peak, 123
swan, trumpeter. See birds
swimming, 59, 137, 256; Astoria Hot Springs, 59; Colter Bay, 113; Granite Hot Springs, 37, 218; Jackson Hole Golf & Tennis Club, 78; Jackson Lake Lodge, 119; Kelly Warm Springs (muddy bottom), 256; Leigh Lake, 138; String Lake, 137
Symmetry Spire, 144

T
Table Mtn., 185
Taggart Lake, 166, 223
Targhee National Forest. See national forests
Targhee ski resort, 216

Teepe's Glacier. *See* glaciers

Teepe Pillar, 155

Teepe, Theodore, 153, 155

Teewinot, Mt., 136, 141, 142, 145, 155

Teewinot Lake, 15, 254

tennis, 78

Teton Basin, 33, 63, 116, 131, 137

Teton County, 29, 173

Teton County Historical Center, 112, 207

Teton Fault, 106, 129, 130, 136, 142, 145, 146, 194

Teton Glacier. *See* glaciers

Teton Jackson. *See* Jackson

Teton Lodge, 127

Teton, name, 12

Teton National Forest. *See* national forests

Teton Pass, 12, 15, 43, 44, 45, 53, 61-67, 68

Teton Range, 13, 15, 17, 67, 68, 99, 104, 131, 155, 174, 177

Teton Science School. *See* schools

Teton Village, 73, 216, 224, 226

Teton Wilderness. *See* wilderness areas

Tetons, Three, 12, 136, 155

Thompson, Edith, 87

Thor Pk, 135

Timbered Island, 162, 168, 242

Titanic, 120

Togwotee Lodge, 87

Togwotee Pass, 12, 25, 81, 84, 87, 268

Togwotee Pass Entrance, 80

Tonnar, John. *See* Germans

Torrey, Cap. R.A., 81

Tracy Lake, 97

Trafton, Edwin H., 116

Trail Creek, 65, 66, 67, 68

trails, 13; Arizona Creek, 106; Arizona Lake, 109; Astorians, 115; Avalanche Canyon, 166; Bear Cub Pass, 82; Berry Creek, 109, 123; Beulah Lake, 125; Blacktail Butte, 193; Blue Miner Lake, 264; Boone Creek, 125; Bottle, 183, 256; Box Creek, 95; Bradley Lake, 153, 166; Cache Creek, 229; Cascade Canyon, 140, 146; Cliff Creek, 35; Coal Creek, 65, 66, 148; Conant, 110; Continental Divide Snow, 25, 81, 101; Death Canyon, 148, 223, 226; DuNoir-Pinnacle Buttes, 82; Emma Matilda Lake, 190; Enos Lake, 95; Garnet Canyon, 153; Glacier, 152, 153; Goodwin Lake, 234; Grand View Point, 118, 119; Granite Canyon, 224, 226; Grizzly Lake, 264; Hidden Falls, 146; Highline, 217; Holly Lake, 139, 147; Holmes Cave, 85; Hominy, 123; horsethief, 94, 97, 121; Huckleberry Mtn., 102, 106; Indian-trapper, 37, 38, 40, 42, 45, 50, 2, 65, 66, 88, 104, 105, 108, 109, 111, 112, 121, 220, 255, 257, 262, 268; Jackson-Granite Creek, 218; Jenny Lake, 141, 145, 151; Lava Creek, 97; Lakes, 153, 166; Leigh Lake, 137, 138, 139; Lunch Tree Hill, 119; Mail Cabin, 68; Marion Lake, 148, 193, 226; Moose Creek, 63, 65; North Buffalo Fork, 95; Old Pass Road, 25, 68, 69; Old U.S. 287, 83, 84; Oliver Pk, 66; Open-Granite, 226; Oregon, 33; Pacific Creek, 188; Paintbrush Canyon, 17, 139, 140, 147; Phelps Lake, 148, 226; Pilgrim Creek, 118; Rendezvous Mtn., 226; Sheep Creek, 234; Sheep Mtn., 264; Sheffield Creek, 102, 106; Sheridan, 256; Signal Mtn., 131, 190; Skyline, 147, 164; Solitude Lake, 140, 146-7; South Buffalo Fork, 87, 95; String Lake, 138, 139, 146; Swift Creek, 218; Taylor Mtn., 65, 66; Taggart Lake, 153, 166; Teton Crest, 65, 66, 123, 148, 226; Teton Death March, 148; Togwotee Pass (Blue Diamond), 84; Two Ocean Lake, 118, 119; Valley, 153, 223, 226

Trois Buttes, 12

Trois Tetons. *See* Tetons, Three.

Turner, John S., 180

Turpin Creek, 251, 257, 262, 264

Turpin, Dick, 95, 234, 238, 264, 267

Turpin Meadows, 94, 264

Turpin Meadows Road, 88, 94, 264

Turquoise Lake, 218

Two Ocean Lake, 118, 119, 129, 132, 188

Two Ocean Road, 188

Two Ocean Pass, 81, 94, 187, 188

U

Union Pass, 12, 80, 81, 255

Upper Gros Ventre Slide, 255

— Slide Lake, 267

U.S. 8th Infantry, 36

U.S. Biological Survey, 171, 201, 222

U.S. Bureau of Land Management (BLM), 30

U.S. Bureau of Reclamation, 30, 57, 92,

121, 127, 129, 130, 172, 173
U.S. Fish & Wildlife, 30, 173, 180, 203
U.S. Forest Service, 28, 30, 58, 82, 88, 92, 166, 172, 173, 267
U.S. Highway Dept., 57, 70

U

Van Vleck, Roy, 205
Victor, 61, 63, 68
Victor, George, 63
Virginian, The, 116, 121, 163, 223, 230
visitor centers: Chamber of Commerce, 208; Colter Bay, 113; Jenny Lake, 151; Moose, 174
volcano, 77, 118, 202
vulgarians, 153

W

Wagner, Harry, 213, 267
Wall, The, 148, 164
wapiti. See elk
Ward, Abraham, 73
Ward Hotel, 73
Washakie, Chief, 87
Washakie Range, 87, 94, 95
waterfalls, 35, 60, 83, 105, 146, 218
Waterfalls Canyon, 115, 116
weather, 28, 29
Webb Canyon, 104, 105
West Gros Ventre Butte, 68, 74, 75, 77, 193, 201
West, John, 234
Whetstone Creek, 188
Whetstone Mine Co., 43, 62, 188
Whetstone Peak, 185
White, Fred E., 195
Whiteman, Herb, 109, 120, 192
wilderness areas: Gros Ventre, 34, 193, 218, 234, 237, 249, 265, 268; Jedediah Smith, 63, 65, 66, 125; Teton, 82, 84, 85, 87, 94, 101, 102, 103, 106, 118, 132, 185, 187, 188, 200; Winegar, 125
Wilderness Falls, 115
Wilderness Society, 222
wildlife, 26, 120, 223, 253
Williams, Frank, 167
Willie Handcart Co., 242
Williams, Otho, 62
Willow Flats, 120, 126, 127
Wilson, 68, 70, 219
Wilson, Effie Jane, 49

Wilson, Elijah (Uncle Nick), 42, 44, 46, 70
Wilson, Ervin, 36, 43, 46, 48
Wilson, John, 42, 46,
Wilson, Matilda R., 73
Wilson, Sylvester, 42, 43, 45, 46, 68
Wind River Lake, 83
Wind River Range, 37, 84, 158, 257, 268
Wind River Valley, 80
windsurfing, 131, 262
Winegar, W.L., 121, 125, 202
Winegar Wilderness. See wilderness areas
Winger, Dick, 170, 212, 244
winter sports, 25, 214-216
Wister family, 70, 223, 224
Wister, Mt., 163
Wister, Owen, 66, 110, 116, 128, 163, 230
Wolff, Emil, 120, 179, 183, 192
Wolff, Marie, 120, 183
wolves, 235, 266
Woodring, Mt., 27, 135
Woodring, Sam T., 135
Woodward, Mrs. Geo., 167
Woolsey, Betty, 70, 214
Wort boys, 207
Wort Hotel, 207
Wort, Chas., 131, 207
Wyeth, Nathaniel, 38, 41, 66
Wyoming Game & Fish Dept., 22, 23, 30, 172, 173, 235, 253
Wyoming Peak, 33
Wyoming Range, 33, 34, 36, 54, 57
Wyoming Tourism (Wyoming Travel Commission), 31

Y

Yellowstone Entrance, 101
Yellowstone, Fort, 158, 200
Yellowstone Lake, 87, 101
Yellowstone National Park, 15, 18, 65, 81, 115, 116, 122, 158, 170, 183, 191
Yellowstone Park Timber Reserve, 41, 88
Yellowstone River, 94
Yurtville, 253

Z

Zenith, 76, 78
zones, life, 23, 153

Other Grand Teton & Yellowstone Books Published by Homestead Publishing